The Contradictions of Love

The Contradictions of Love: Towards a feminist-realist ontology of sociosexuality offers a robust and multifaceted theoretical account of why and how, in contemporary western societies, women continue to be subordinated to men in and through sexual love. The book defends and elaborates Anna G. Jónasdóttir's thesis that men tend to exploit women of their 'love power', by means of an innovative application of critical realism, dialectical critical realism and the philosophy of metaReality. Gunnarsson also offers a critique of the state of affairs of contemporary feminist theory, demonstrating that the meta-theoretical framework of critical realism offers the tools that can counter the poststructuralist hegemony still prevailing in feminist theory. On a general level, *The Contradictions of Love* attempts at reconciling theoretical positions which tend to appear in opposition to one another. In particular, it offers a way of bridging the gap between the notion of love as a locus of exploitation and that of love as a force which can conquer oppression.

This book is a unique and timely contribution in the field of feminist theory, in that it offers the first elaborate assessment and development of Jónasdóttir's important but relatively neglected work, and in that it counters poststructuralist trends from the point of view of a robust critical realist framework that has hitherto been spectacularly absent in feminist theory, although it offers solutions to meta-theoretical problems at the forefront of feminist debates; in the field of critical realism broadly defined, in that it elaborates on crucial ontological themes of (dialectical) critical realism and the philosophy of metaReality via a discussion of the issues of love, sexuality, gender and power; and finally, in the field of love studies, in that it offers a sophisticated account of how gender asymmetries prevail in love despite norms of gender equality and reciprocity, and in that it reconciles feminist, conflict-oriented perspectives on love with notions of love as transcending conflict.

Lena Gunnarsson is a Researcher at Örebro University, Sweden.

Ontological Explorations

Other titles in this series:

From One 'Empire' to the Next
Radha D'Souza

Science for Humanism
The recovery of human agency
Charles R. Varela

Philosophical Problems of Sustainability
Taking sustainability forward
with a critical realist approach
Jenneth Parker

Dialectic and Difference
Dialectical critical realism
and the grounds of justice
Alan Norrie

Interdisciplinarity and Climate Change
Transforming knowledge and practice for our global future
*Edited by Roy Bhaskar, Cheryl Frank, Karl Georg Høyer,
Petter Naess and Jenneth Parker*

Conversations about Reflexivity
Edited by Margaret S. Archer

Relational Sociology
A new paradigm for the social sciences
Pierpaolo Donati

Sociological Realism
*Edited by Andrea M. Maccarini, Emmanuele Morandi and
Riccardo Prandini*

The Economics of Science: A Critical Realist Overview
Volume 1: Illustrations and philosophical preliminaries
David Tyfield

The Economics of Science: A Critical Realist Overview
Volume 2: Towards a synthesis of political economy and science and technology studies
David Tyfield

Ontology Revisited
Metaphysics in social and political philosophy
Ruth Groff

Childhoods, Real and Imagined
Volume 1: An introduction to critical realism and childhood studies
Priscilla Alderson

Naturalizing Critical Realist Social Ontology
Tuukka Kaidesoja

What's Critical about Critical Realism? Essays in Reconstructive Social Theory
Frederic Vandenberghe

Integrating Knowledge through Interdisciplinary Research
Problems of theory and practice
Dominic Holland

The Contradictions of Love
Towards a feminist-realist ontology of sociosexuality
Lena Gunnarsson

The Contradictions of Love

Towards a feminist-realist ontology
of sociosexuality

Lena Gunnarsson

LONDON AND NEW YORK

First published 2014
by Routledge
2 Park Square, Milton Park, Abingdon, Oxfordshire OX14 4RN

and by Routledge
711 Third Avenue, New York, NY 10017

First issued in paperback 2014

Routledge is an imprint of the Taylor and Francis Group, an informa business

© 2014 Lena Gunnarsson

The right of Lena Gunnarsson to be identified as author of this work has
been asserted in accordance with sections 77 and 78 of the Copyright,
Designs and Patents Act 1988.

All rights reserved. No part of this book may be reprinted, reproduced or utilised in
any form or by any electronic, mechanical, or other means, now known or hereafter
invented, including photocopying and recording, or in any information storage or
retrieval system, without permission in writing from the publishers.

Trademark notice: Product or corporate names may be trademarks or registered
trademarks, and are used only for identification and explanation without intent to
infringe.

British Library Cataloguing in Publication Data
A catalogue record for this book is available from the British Library

Library of Congress Cataloging-in-Publication Data
A catalog record has been requested for this book

ISBN 978-0-415-82411-8 (hbk)
ISBN 978-1-138-90462-0 (pbk)
ISBN 978-1-315-85146-4 (ebk)

Typeset in Times New Roman by
Cenveo Publisher Services

For Vide and Ask

Contents

Acknowledgements	xiii

1 Introduction

1

Feminist theory and sexuality 2
What's love got to do with it? 4
The tenacity of gender inequality 7
Feminism, ontology and the rejection of realism 9
Critical realism: an excursus 11
The structure of reality: necessity and complexity 12
The dialectical core of reality 15
Outline of the book: from sexuality to love 17

PART I
Feminist modes of theorizing sexuality and gendered power

23

2 Judith Butler and the deconstruction of reality

25

Sex and gender: performative effects of discourse 26
The subject: reversing the causal arrows 29
Sexuality: nature abjected 32
Power: inevitable and unacceptable 35
Fighting with power's own tools 37
Ad hoc realism 39
Conclusion 40

3 Anna Jónasdóttir and the organic roots of power

43

Sex/gender: a generative process 45
Sexuality: a historical-materialist ontology 47
Love power and the production of human life 49
The nature of love 50

x   *Contents*

Power: structural compulsion and human neediness 52
Male authority and female sociosexual poverty 54
Ecstasy versus care 56
Conclusion 58

PART II
Meta-theoretical interlude: Challenging
poststructuralist feminism   61

4   Feminist theory and nature   63

Feminist nature-phobia 63
Restoring the status of nature 65
The glorification of indeterminacy 67
Nature's constraining force 70
Transcending dualisms – the dialectical-emergentist solution 73
Dialectical antagonists and 'pomo flips' 76
Conclusion 78

5   Women and men as theoretical categories   79

The intersectional challenge: women are not only women 80
Anticategorical intersectionality 82
Discriminatory anticategoricalism: 'women'
  as particular minefield 84
The rejection of biological sex 85
Constructed, hence unreal? 88
The concrete and the abstract 90
Structures, positions and people 92
Conclusion 94

PART III
The reality of love and power: A feminist-realist depth approach   97

6   Loving him for who he is: The microsociology of power   99

Asymmetrical role-taking: or 'loving him for who he is' 101
'I am very demanding' 102
Women as technical problems 104
The gendered mediation of love: expectations and gratitude 105
The costs and benefits of conforming 107
The risks and promises of resisting 108
Conclusion 109

Contents xi

7 Love: Exploitable resource or 'no-lose situation'? 112

MetaReality – realism's self-transcendence 114
The causally efficacious illusion of 'demi-reality' 117
Love as the fundament of existence 119
The illusoriness of patriarchal reality 122
The necessity of conflict in the present world 125
Conclusion 128

8 Men in love: The work of repressing reality 131

Dialectical contradictions 131
The exploiter's burden 133
Men's dependence on women's freedom 135
The double-edged sword of control 136
Reality biting back 138
Men's ambivalent interest in women's pleasure 140
Male emancipation 143
Conclusion 145

9 Reality and change 147

The real and the 'really real' 148
Female withdrawal: laying bare men's dependency 150
Getting to the root of causality: a depth mode of
  feminist transformation 152
Women's anger 154
Diseffectuating the illusion of female powerlessness 156
Irigaray, Bhaskar and the ethics of letting go 158
Breaking the circle of unworthiness 160
Conclusion 162

10 Conclusion: Necessity and the power of love 166

A feminist dialectical-realist depth ontology
  of love and power 167
A project of reconciliation 169

References 171
Index 181

Acknowledgements

I want to thank the following people for invaluable support in the process of completing this book, which is a slightly revised version of my doctoral thesis in Gender Studies, defended at Örebro University, Sweden.

First, thank you Anna Jónasdóttir for breaking so many intellectual taboos, paving the way for my own courage to challenge poststructuralist 'truths' that I once felt were unchallengeable. Thank you also for guiding me with your passion, stubbornness and rigour through the process of writing the thesis. Thank you also Liisa Husu, my main supervisor during the last years of writing. Your professionalism and practical efficiency have been especially rewarding.

Many thanks to Andrew Sayer, faculty examiner at my doctoral defence, for so warmly yet mercilessly challenging some elements of the thesis in a way that impelled me to solidify my argumentation. Thank you also for taking the time to detail your advice on how to improve the manuscript for publication. Thank you also Valerie Bryson, for offering me your stringent and responsible critique of an earlier draft of this book. Your ability to rigorously assess my text on its own terms was invaluable.

Warm thanks to the whole Gender Studies team at Örebro University – Tobias Axelsson, Ida Maria Börjesson, Jeff Hearn, Liisa Husu, Anna Jónasdóttir, Gunnel Karlsson, Helena Magnusson, Ingrid Pincus, Moa Roshanfar, Sofia Strid and Berit Åberg. It is no exaggeration to say that you are one of the anchors in my life. Thank you for offering a milieu that knows the true meaning of the term 'constructive critique' and, above all, for being such great friends. Thank you also Anna-Lisa Fransson for enlightening many a coffee break with your always enlivening presence.

Thank you Anders Hylmö, for comments on an earlier draft of Chapter 5 and for your fervent intellectual curiosity, which I am grateful to have been accompanied by through the years. Thank you Stina Widell, for endless discussions about love, Zen meditation and politics. Your intellectual autonomy constructively helps me detach from academic dos and don'ts. Thank you Ann Ferguson, for the stubborn interest you have put into critiquing my work. Thank you Roy Bhaskar and Mervyn Hartwig, for being so supportive and enthusiastic about my intellectual project.

Thank you Alan Jarvis, editor at Routledge, and Damian Mitchell, editorial assistant, for your abundant niceness and for so smoothly carrying me through process of publication.

xiv *Acknowledgements*

Thank you Mamma and Pappa, Gunilla and Göte Gunnarsson, for being proud of me although you do not have much of a clue about what I am doing.

Thank you Per Molin, my life companion, for helping me think through some of the fundamental issues in this book by letting me look at the world through your eyes. And thank you, finally, Per and my sons Vide and Ask, for teaching me about love and life by just being you.

1 Introduction

> Love, perhaps even more than child-bearing, is the pivot of women's oppression today. I realize this has frightening implications: do we want to get rid of love? The panic felt at any threat to love is a good clue to its political significance. ... [Love] is portrayed in novels, even metaphysics, but in them it is described, or better, re-created, not analysed. Love has never really been fully understood, though it may have been fully experienced, and that experience communicated. There is a reason for this absence of analysis: *women and love are underpinnings. Examine them and you threaten the very structure of culture.*
>
> Shulamith Firestone (1970/1979: 121)

This book offers a theoretical account of why and how, in contemporary western societies characterized by formal equality and women's relative economic independence from men, women continue to be subordinated to men through sexuality and love. Setting off with an assessment of two important feminist theorizations of how gendered power is constituted through sexuality – those of Judith Butler and Anna G. Jónasdóttir – throughout the course of the book I shift focus to love, analysing how it forms a fundamental basis of men's power in these societies. By means of an innovative application of Roy Bhaskar's critical realism, dialectical critical realism and philosophy of metaReality, I investigate and elaborate Anna G. Jónasdóttir's claim that, in societies relatively freed from formal-legal and economic constraints on gender equality, a decisive part of men's power as men is based in their exploitation of women's 'love power', the term Jónasdóttir uses to designate the dialectic of our caring and erotic-ecstatic capacities. The book also provides a critique of the state of affairs of contemporary feminist theory. I demonstrate that the meta-theoretical framework of critical realism, broadly defined,[1] offers the tools that can counter the poststructuralist hegemony in feminist theory. On a general level, the dialectical approach endorsed in this work sustains a reconciliatory transcendence of theoretical positions that tend to appear in opposition to one another. In particular, it offers a way of bridging the gap between the notion of love as a locus of exploitation and that of love as a force that can conquer oppression.

In this introductory chapter I begin with an overview of how feminist theorists have dealt with sexuality and its relation to gendered power. I then address the

2 Introduction

issue of love's place in these frameworks and, highlighting the relative love deficit in feminist theory, I underline the particular importance for feminists to address the topic now. Next, I offer an overview of empirical research that bears witness to the tenacity of women's subordination to men as sexual beings in contemporary western societies. This is followed by an outline of the structure and content of the book. I then offer a meta-theoretical context to the project of the book, which has a strong philosophical undercurrent. I first address the ontological deficit in feminist theory, which is only now being challenged, and the widespread feminist scepticism against realism. I go on with a presentation of the basic tenets of critical realism and its more recent extensions, dialectical critical realism and the philosophy of metaReality, and clarify their role in the book.

The applicability of the theoretical framework advanced in this work is restricted to contemporary western societies where women are formally legally equal with men and relatively economically dependent from individual men, due to welfare state arrangements and women's large-scale employment. Most of the theoretical and empirical studies on which I draw are from the Nordic and Anglophone countries. The question of applicability is complex in that societies and gender orders are neither homogenic wholes nor neatly separated from one another. Even in a country like Sweden, with its relatively high level of economic gender equality, some women are economically dependent on individual men. The claims made in the book may be even more applicable to a certain section of Asian or African women's experiences than to the lives of some women living in the west. In this sense, the theoretical framework developed in this work is likely to have some relevance, although limited, for gendered relations worldwide, while being only generally applicable to the western welfare societies that are its strict object of analysis. This impossibility of neatly singling out an object of applicability is explained by the fact that, although different gender orders and societies have their own distinct dynamics, they are also part of one differentiated, yet internally related, whole.[2] The object of analysis in this book, then, should properly be understood as a *tendency* in the relations between women and men, which is concentrated to the west but partly stretching its reach globally.

Feminist theory and sexuality

The foundational concern of feminist theory is how our lives as sexed/sexual beings are organized by historically varying regimes of power. It was very much thanks to feminists that sexuality lost its status as being altogether given and 'natural' and was instead recognized as a field of practices, desires, norms and ideas determined at least partly by human-made, and thus transformable, institutions. With the famous slogan 'The personal is political', feminists of the so-called second wave highlighted that the problems we experience in our sexual relationships are not private, but expressions of the broader organization of society. Not only did feminists bring attention to the fact that the sexual desires, possibilities and vulnerabilities of women and men are shaped by historically evolved power structures; they also emphasized that the organization of sexuality is crucial for what is going on in the rest of society, such as the economy and the state. Sexuality, hitherto often claimed to be a remaining reserve of naturalness and privacy, was denaturalized and politicized.

To a large extent the differences between the diverse strands of second wave feminism that emerged from the 1960s to the 1980s can be grasped from the point of view of how they addressed sexuality. The question of exactly how crucial sexuality was as a basis of male power became a watershed between different groupings of feminist theorists. The characteristic radical feminist position was that sexuality is the pivot of men's patriarchal power. Lesbian radical feminists in particular, but also scholars non-aligned with the lesbian feminist movement, argued that sexual interaction between women and men is directed more by male power than mutual pleasure. Lesbian radical feminists also problematized the naturalness of heterosexuality and pointed out that the institution of 'compulsory heterosexuality' (Rich, 1980/1983), regulated by the state through marriage, was a central political device binding women to men and, consequently, to subordination.

While radical feminists were concerned with how male power is constituted through the sexual relation *as such*, for socialist and Marxist feminists the political importance of sexuality was less immediate and fundamental. They primarily called attention to the ways that the heterosexual bond is tied up with inequalities in the field of paid and unpaid labour, highlighting that, for a woman, sexual partnership with a man, mostly materialized in marriage, also meant that she had the main responsibility for unpaid household work and childcare and lesser possibilities to advance in the area of paid labour. As a popular saying had it, 'You start by sinking into his arms and end up with your arms in his sink'. From the point of view of these insights, the Marxist analyses of capitalism prevalent at the time were criticized for their neglect of the economic importance of women's domestic work. The whole capitalist apparatus, socialist and Marxist feminists argued, depends upon a sexual division of labour outside of it; most obviously, there would be no workers to exploit in the labour market if it were not for all the unpaid work performed by women in the home. Whereas Marxist feminists generally saw sexual relations as determined in the last instance by the forces of capital and focused on women's subordination as workers, socialist feminists distinguished themselves from Marxist feminists by their acknowledgement of sexuality's relatively autonomous political significance, and struggled with how to reconcile this stance with their Marxian focus on economic exploitation.

Most second wave feminists theorized the power structure of sexuality in terms of male domination or exploitation. When some radical feminists promoted lesbianism, they saw it mainly as a way out of the grip of the male dominance understood to be inherent in current heterosexuality. With the advent of poststructuralist queer theory in the late 1980s and its celebration of non-heterosexual practices, the focus on male dominance was downplayed and attention shifted to the ways that power constitutes the gendered subject as such. Sexuality kept its role as a pivot of feminist theorizing, but rather than being studied as concrete practice or relation, what was now the centre of attention was how the discursive hetero/homosexual binary structures the production of social reality. Most influentially, Judith Butler

4 *Introduction*

(1990/1999) argued that the discursive 'heterosexual matrix' makes intelligible only certain kinds of desires and identities, and reconceptualized political struggle as the general attempt to subvert such orders of intelligibility and the identities they produce.

The only 'great' male theorist who had put sexuality at the centre of his theoretical system was Sigmund Freud, and second wave feminists like Juliet Mitchell (1974/2000) drew creatively and critically on his work in order to grasp the specific dynamic of sexuality and gender constitution. In the poststructuralist approaches to sexuality dominating feminist theory today the dialogue with psychoanalytical theory is also pivotal. Postmodernist psychoanalytical theory is one of the key resources drawn on both in queer feminist ventures to deconstruct sexual identities and in the work of so-called French difference feminists, who challenge phallogocentrism by putting the specific female sexual identity and experience at the centre of philosophical discussions.

What's love got to do with it?

Inasmuch as it is as sexed beings that women and men come to occupy their different positions in the social order, it is no surprise that sexuality has been at the centre of feminist analyses of gendered power. What about love, then? In practice, sexuality is intimately connected to love. Any discussion of heterosexuality, for instance, implicitly or explicitly involves not only the issue of desire but of love too. Nonetheless, love is often ignored in feminist approaches to sexuality. While this is the case especially for the later poststructuralist theories of sexuality, perhaps largely due to their relative disconnection from concrete practices, the legacy of Simone de Beauvoir's essay on love in her famous *The second sex* (1949/1989) did reverberate in some of the second wave feminist thinking, notably in radical feminist work. When Beauvoir's existentialist take on love under patriarchy was that women's love of men constituted an instance of *mauvais fois*, locking women in immanence, the recurrent theme of second wave discourses on heterosexual love was that it was a kind of delusion or false consciousness, ensuring that women keep submitting themselves to their masters (see Douglas, 1990, for an overview).

The feminist tendency to reduce love to 'an ideological delusion; an idealized image of (inhibited) sexual desire; or a symbolic or discursive element performing disciplinary power' (Jónasdóttir, 2014: 19) precluded analyses of love itself, of what it is about *love* that makes it a vehicle of oppression. It also forestalled a theoretical acknowledgment of love's liberating potential. Diagnosing the history of feminist perspectives on love, bell hooks argues that it was a mistake that second wave feminists tended to see love itself as the problem. 'We were to do away with love and put in its place a concern with gaining rights and power', she remembers. This inhibited the development of a more complex feminist theorization of love, inasmuch as '[r]ather than rethinking love and insisting on its importance and value, feminist discourse on love simply stopped' (2000b: 102). One influential contemporary feminist theorist who does engage theoretically with

Introduction 5

love is the French philosopher Luce Irigaray (1992/1996, 2002b), but, while taken up in fields like philosophy and literature, her work has not had much impact on feminist social theory (Jónasdóttir, 2014).

Insofar as the search for love is a central motivation in most people's lives, in particular in the western world, and inasmuch as women continue to attach themselves to men in the name of love, this theoretical deficit is highly problematic. Despite women's particular ideological enmeshment in the realm of love, the absence of love seems even more marked in feminist than non-feminist works (Jónasdóttir, 2014). Indeed, as Margaret Toye suggests, it is probably precisely *because* of love's association with 'the realm of women, the home, the private, the apolitical, the "not serious"' that, struggling to be taken seriously, feminist theorists feel such a 'nervousness around the topic' (2010: 4). Meanwhile – and perhaps ironically – from the 1990s onwards, malestream sociologists interested in the general structural transformations of modern societies have begun to recognize love's sociological significance. In his influential *The transformation of intimacy* (1992) Anthony Giddens argues that the increasing disconnection of intimacy from tradition and judicial and economic regulation has given rise to a 'pure relationship', that he holds to imply a more democratic and equal bond between women and men. Ulrich Beck and Elisabeth Beck-Gernsheim (1990/1995) similarly pinpoint how wider societal changes transform our most intimate endeavours, yet arrive at less optimistic conclusions. Apart from acknowledging that gender inequalities seem to survive the rearranging of intimacy, they highlight that the new setting of love is the condition not only of more democratic ways of relating but also of confusion and power struggles. Even more pessimistically, Eva Illouz (2012) has lately argued that the institutional changes of modernity, whereby processes of commodification increasingly structure intimate encounters and partnership, have made it more difficult to form intense bonds. Although the feminist body of thought is not her point of entry into the theme of love, Illouz also argues that, far from eroding, male dominance has taken on a new emotional form.

Jónasdóttir, who is unique among feminist theorists in that she puts love at the structural centre of her theoretical system (1991/1994, 2009, 2011), notes that the topic of love is becoming increasingly present in academic works, addressed in its own terms rather than as 'an epiphenomenon, or a reflection of something more basic' such as labour, care, commitment or desire (2013: 19). Still, feminist theorists seem to have caught onto this trend to a lesser degree than non-feminist scholars. Insofar as I agree with other feminist scholars (de Beauvoir, 1949/1989; Firestone, 1970/1979; Haavind, 1984; Jónasdóttir, 1991/1994, 2009, 2011; Langford, 1994, 1999) that heterosexual love is a linchpin of the system that subordinates women to men, it is crucial that this love deficit in feminist theory be remedied. This is even more important since love, while arguably being a universal human phenomenon, seems to be more socially decisive than ever (Beck and Beck-Gernsheim, 1990/1995; Illouz, 2012; Jónasdóttir, 2011). Having earlier been subordinated to other rationales, love enjoys an increasingly *independent* social significance. For example, it is an unprecedented fact that the experience of

6 Introduction

love is the factor which determines how households and reproduction are organized. Also, as Illouz highlights, whereas in pre-modernity a person's social worth was largely based on the esteem received from fulfilling roles and duties, it is now increasingly based on personalized modes of recognition. While conceding that it seems to be a universal fact that love is a source of self-enhancement, she argues that:

> the sense of self-worth provided by love in modern relationships is of particular and acute importance, precisely because at stake in contemporary individualism is the difficulty to establish one's self-worth and because the pressure for self-differentiation and developing a sense of uniqueness has considerably increased with modernity.
>
> (2012: 112)

Along similar lines, Jónasdóttir states that '[i]n our time …, when individuals are forced/free to make and remake themselves under continuously changing circumstances, love as a source of creative/re-creative human power seems to be needed more and more strongly' (2011: 50). Hence, it seems plausible to suggest that the growing academic attention to the subject of love is a reflection of its de facto increasing social importance. Paradoxically though, the increased significance of love is combined with a destabilization of bonds of intimacy, due above all to the changes brought about by women's increased autonomy and the general individualization of social organization (cf. Bauman, 2003; Beck and Beck-Gernsheim, 1990/1995; Illouz, 2012). Hence, there is a sense in which contemporary western societies might be said to find themselves in a *love crisis*, opening up possibilities for a radical reorganization of love that feminists should be interested in seizing.

From a feminist perspective what is perhaps most interesting about love and sexuality today is that, for an increasing number of socio-economically non-dependent and formal-legally equal women in the world, it is the only thing that binds them to men as sexual beings. Indeed, many women also in the most gender equal societies are bound to men by economic dependencies. Still, the general trend of female economic independence and formal gender equality offers an unprecedented analytical opportunity to lay bare the specifically sexual-erotic mechanisms binding women and men to one another. In this sense too, then, if we are interested in understanding the mechanisms subordinating women to men and the conditions for challenging such subordination, the arena of sexuality and love should be even more crucial as a site of investigation than it has been before.

Although this book investigates the basis of men's power in sexuality and love, it should be emphasized that I do not see the dynamics inherent in these practices as the only ones accounting for gender inequality, nor do I believe sexuality and love can be understood in complete separation from other social forces. Doubtless, economic factors crucially affect the organization of gender relations and also shape the ways that sexuality and love are practised. For instance, the current structure of these practices cannot be fully comprehended in isolation from the intensified commodification of our sexual, loving and caring capacities (Bryson, 2011;

Introduction   7

Hochschild, 2003a; Illouz, 2007, 2012). Yet, I work from the assumption that the structural core of the power relation between women and men must be sought in their *immediate* existence as sexed/sexual beings (cf. Jónasdóttir, 1991/1994), where, as I clarify below, the sexual is understood in a broad sense so as to include caring and loving practices.

While the systematic power imbalance between women and men stretches through all sectors of society, it is as sexed beings that women and men, as well as those identifying themselves as neither, come to occupy their respective positions in the gendered hierarchy. Also, if only in order to explore the intersections between the sexual and other social relations, I see it as crucial to first deepen our understanding of sexuality's *own* distinct dynamic. As we shall see, sexuality as such is remarkably under-theorized among theorists of sexuality and power; hence, there is a particular need for ontological explorations of sexuality's inherent structure and mechanisms and of how these relate to power.

The tenacity of gender inequality

As should now be clear, it is a point of departure of this book that in the western world women are still sexually subordinated to men, across localities, classes and races. The objective of the book is thus not to argue the existence of such a gender hierarchy but to explain it (although explaining something is also in a sense a way of invoking its realness). Inasmuch as the obscuring of this power imbalance is an integral aspect of patriarchy, an initial defence of this empirical premise might be needed though.

Doubtless, there are trends that give testimony to women's growing power and independence vis-à-vis men in the area of sexuality and love. While the taboo on self-directed female desire has been a central pivot of the patriarchal order, for a growing section of women, especially in the western world, the position as sexual subject is opened up. Earlier the feminist stance was tightly connected to an attitude – if not practice – of sexual abstinence from men, a circumstance revealed by Barbara Sichtermann's observation in 1983 that '[i]f a woman stood up in a feminist meeting today and said that she thought men were seductive and desirable, she would be declared out of her mind' (1983/1986: 15). Today, by contrast, the feminist position seems to be more compatible with heterosexuality; most conspicuously, the role as female heterosexual predator has been culturally opened up and integrated in third wave feminist consciousness, as reflected in, for instance, the influential television series *Sex and the City*.

Yet, while it is likely that true sexual subjecthood *is* available to women to an unprecedented degree, the dominant pattern is still that women's sexual freedom is circumscribed by strongly gendered standards of respectability and the threat of male violence (Jackson and Scott, 2004). Moreover, as several commentators highlight (Jackson and Scott, 2004; Milnes, 2004; Stainton Rogers and Stainton Rogers, 2001), by lack of being underpinned by real power, women's greater sexual 'freedom' sometimes works to the detriment of women, who feel pressured to be sexually active while lacking the power to set the terms for sexual interactions.

8 *Introduction*

As Kate Milnes (2004) suggests, for many women the freedom to say no to sex is likely to have been reduced as a result of the so-called sexual revolution. This is complicated by the fact that the sexual double standard has by no means eroded, meaning that women may be blamed both for being 'frigid' and 'slutty'. As Stevi Jackson and Sue Scott highlight:

> Ideals of sexual self-expression have reshaped the old slag/drag dichotomy but have also narrowed the margins between excess and deficiency, between being too sexual and not sexual enough, thus producing an even more slippery tightrope for women to walk.
>
> (2004: 240)

Although increasingly challenged, the traditional script of male subject/female object retains a strong hold over heterosexual encounters. In her study of young women and sexuality Louisa Allen highlights the resistance that some women make against traditional heterosexual scripts, but at the end of the day a woman still 'appeared as the subordinate partner in (hetero)sexual relationships who was "acted upon", rather than "acting"' (2003: 218). This reflects the resistant sexual norm of female passivity and male activity, according to which '[t]he man is expected to initiate sexual activity and the woman to demur for as long as possible until she swoons in response', as Laurie Rudman and Peter Glick put it (2008/2010: 233). Similarly, Janet Holland *et al.* conclude from their study of young people and heterosexuality that, while to an increasing extent women are able to demand sexual pleasure, their behaviour is still very much monitored and directed by a hegemonic masculinity internalized as 'the-male-in-the-head' (1998/2004: 156). Perhaps the most obvious evidence for the fact that history does not simply unfold towards ever greater sexual equality is the intensified objectification of the female body brought about by an expanding pornographic industry and its imprints upon mainstream media and advertising.

When it comes to the broader setting of heterosexuality, including love and care as well as the division of unpaid labour, there is even more unambiguous empirical evidence that gender inequality prevails. That injustices based on gender are no longer seen as legitimate in the western world is in itself a crucial historical momentum (Weeks, 2007) and a growing minority of heterosexual couples, most notably in the Nordic countries, are approximating a real balance of responsibility for household chores and childcare (Aarseth, 2007). Yet, while the mere existence of fathers who share the parental leave equally with the mother tends to incite bursts of optimism by virtue of the contrast with earlier times, the dominant pattern is still that women have the main responsibility for care and household work. This imbalance is massively substantiated in research (Craig and Mullan, 2011), but can also be registered in the circumstance that, while most would find it absurd to talk about a woman 'helping out' in the home, this is not the case when it comes to men (Marecek, 2003: 263).

Furthermore, as Bekkengen (2006) highlights in the face of a widespread assumption, even if a couple is equal with regard to childcare and household chores, this does not necessarily imply that the *love relation* is equal. Compared to the organization of household work and child-care the heterosexual bond of love *per se* is under scrutinized, but the studies that do exist demonstrate that in heterosexual partnerships women are also the primary carers in the adult relationship, while often feeling that their needs for love are not met by their partner (Dempsey, 2001; Dryden, 1999; Duncombe and Marsden, 1993; Haavind, 1984; Holmberg, 1993/1995; Langford, 1994, 1999; Rubin, 1983; Strazdins and Broom, 2004; Wilton, 2004). The general pattern is that men set the terms of the loving interactions, such that the woman's needs are neglected unless they qualify as important in the eyes of the man (Haavind, 1984; Holmberg, 1993/1995), while men are often not even aware of their needs for love and recognition, since 'there's usually a woman quickly and easily available to obscure them' (Rubin, 1983: 127; cf. Benjamin, 1998; Duncombe and Marsden, 1993; Firestone, 1970/1979; Holmberg, 1993/1995; Jack, 1991; Medina-Doménech *et al.*, 2014).

Research shows that, globally, men gain more satisfaction from marriage than women (Bericat, 2013). This is also supported by the fact that women decide to divorce more often than men and tend to feel empowered by a divorce, while men are more likely to become depressed (Klose and Jacobi, 2004). Referring to Tamsin Wilton's (2004) study of female sexuality, in which the heterosexual women she interviewed appeared to be chronically disappointed with their men, Jeffrey Weeks highlights that the feelings expressed by these women 'echo those of married women in the 1940s' (2007: 142). While women have advanced their position in the realm of sexuality and love – due above all to increased economic independence, the Pill, the possibility of divorce as well as a general loosening of the grip of marriage, and the dissemination of feminist consciousness – the most striking feature of contemporary heterosexual relations is perhaps that, despite all this, gender inequality continues its monotonous beat.

Feminism, ontology and the rejection of realism

This book is concerned with ontology, more specifically the ontology of sexuality, love, power, sex, gender and their interrelation. Insofar as ontology represents the study of the nature of being, of what is, this simply means that I will examine what sexuality, love, power, sex and gender *are*. Although I will address the issue of the basic or necessary as opposed to the contingent features of being, following Bhaskar I do not use the term 'ontology' to denote only conceptualizations of the basic structure of being; inasmuch as it represents the study of being, it concerns everything that exists, including thoughts and concepts as well as contingent and transient phenomena and, even, absences and illusions (Bhaskar, 1993/2008b, 2002b).[3]

While feminist theorists have long been at the forefront of epistemological debates, critiquing simplistic notions of knowledge and objectivity and pointing out the gendered bias of supposedly neutral and objective science (see Longino, 2010, for an overview), self-conscious discussions about ontology – about the nature of the reality that our knowledge is about – have long been relatively absent in feminist theory, although, as we shall see below, the ontological taboo

10   *Introduction*

seems to in be demise. Insofar as 'all philosophy, explicitly or tacitly, honestly or surreptitiously … deposits, projects or presupposes a reality' (Bachelard, cited in Bhaskar, 1986/2009: 7), this is of course only half true. Even the anti-ontological poststructuralist declaration, which retains a strong hold over the collective feminist consciousness, that there is no reality independent from our concepts of it, is indeed a claim about the basic structure of reality (cf. Stone, 2004). As stated by Elizabeth Grosz, one influential feminist theorist who does engage with ontology, 'you buy into ontological commitments whenever you make certain political commitments' (in Butler *et al.*, 1998: 32). What is unfortunate is that the 'taboo on ontology' (Bhaskar, 2002a: 214) – even, the 'taboo on reality' (Bhaskar, 2002c: 81) – dominating the western philosophical tradition has precluded more systematic feminist interrogations of the dominant unreflected ontologies of malestream science and philosophy, most notably the one-dimensional worldview presupposed by positivist science and often tacitly accepted even by the most anti-positivist of theorists.[4] This has weakened the critical purchase of feminist theory, since it is premised on a radical challenge of received ontological categories. The unacknowledged necessity of such ontological interrogations is revealed by the fact that feminist theorists already engage in them, for instance when emphasizing the relational and historical nature of subject constitution in the face of biological reductionism and atomism. Yet, the ontological taboo has stopped feminists from engaging in a more elaborate and in-depth reconstruction of our understanding of the structure of social being.

It is therefore welcome that, lately, feminist theorists like Grosz (2005, 2011) and Susan Hekman (2010) have argued for a shift in focus from epistemology to ontology and that we see emerging a 'material turn' (Alaimo and Hekman, 2008a: 7) that displays no ontological inhibitions (e.g. Barad, 2003, 2007; Tuana, 2010). In Clare Hemmings' (2005a) view, we even witness an 'ontological turn' in cultural theory and feminist theory. Inasmuch as Bhaskar has long put ontology at the forefront of his critical realist philosophy (1979/1998, 1975/2008a, 1993/2008b), which, moreover, is explicitly emancipatory in intent, one might have expected that this new feminist plethora of explicit ontological accounts would draw on the insights generated by him and other critical realists. Yet, while Karen Barad (2003, 2007) revitalizes Niels Bohr's notion of 'agential realism', critical realism is remarkably absent in this ontological turn, despite the fact that an increasing number of critically oriented scholars in the social sciences have come to see it as a much-needed and robust alternative to both positivism and poststructuralism. The 'new materialists' in feminist theory willingly invoke the thoughts of modernist scientists like Bohr and Charles Darwin (Grosz, 2011) and are often portrayed as a challenge to earlier poststructuralist trends, since they deal with ontology, matter and nature. Nevertheless, this new field of theorizing takes place very much within the confines of the basic philosophical notions of poststructuralism (see Chapter 4), whereas realism is either ignored or somewhat carelessly rejected as untenable (e.g. Tuana, 2008).

In this moment of increasing dissatisfaction with poststructuralism combined with what seems to be an experience that there are no tenable alternatives, critical realism should prove attractive for feminists. That even sophisticated versions of realism

Introduction 11

suffer from a 'resounding unpopularity among feminist theorists' (New, 1998: 366) seems to be largely due to a lack of knowledge. As Tony Lawson (1999) highlights, feminists tend to reject realism since they identify it with what is commonly referred to as naïve 'realism', whose simplistic notions of reality and knowledge underpin positivist science. Critical realist contributions to feminist debates are not non-existent (see Assiter, 1996; Hull, 2006; Jónasdóttir and Jones, 2009; Lawson, 1999; Lovell, 2007; New, 1998, 2003, 2005; Sayer, 1997, 2000a, 2000b; Soper, 1995; Walby *et al.*, 2012). Yet, although these interventions deal with themes central to the meta-theoretical debates going on in the dominant forums of feminist theory and gender studies, their challenges rarely reach into the institutional centre of the field. Against the backdrop of this realist deficit in feminist theory, this book should constitute a much-needed meta-theoretical intervention in the field, in that it offers a comprehensive example of how critical realism can be applied to feminist concerns in a way, I hope to show, that deepens our understanding of gendered power.

Critical realism: an excursus

Critical realism is a meta-theoretical system originally developed by Roy Bhaskar (1975/2008a, 1979/1998), but elaborated by a range of different scholars active in the social sciences in particular (e.g. Archer *et al.*, 1998; Archer, 2000; Collier, 1994; Danermark *et al.*, 1997/2002; Sayer, 1984/1992, 2000a). With *Dialectic: the pulse of freedom* (Bhaskar, 1993/2008b) the original framework is developed into *dialectical critical realism* (see also Bhaskar, 1994; Bhaskar with Hartwig, 2010), while Bhaskar's most recent extensions of his philosophy are the *transcendental dialectical critical realism* (2000) and *philosophy of metaReality* (2002a, 2002b, 2002c; Bhaskar with Hartwig, 2010) which mark his 'spiritual turn'.[5] Critical realism was developed to serve both as a tool for critique and as 'underlabourer and occasional midwife' of substantive social theories and research (Bhaskar, 1989: 82). In this book it underlabours my critical assessments of existing feminist theory as well as my constructive elaboration of Jónasdóttir's thesis that in contemporary western societies men exploit women's 'love power'. Throughout the course of the book I introduce different concepts and arguments of this massive body of thought and apply it in my analysis. Here I offer an introduction of its basic tenets.

Broadly defined, realism is the doctrine that reality exists independently of our knowledge about it. It seems to me that resistance to this realist conviction is largely rooted in a misconception of the use of the term 'independently'. Unlike what sceptics of realism tend to assume (Harding, 2003; Tuana, 2008), at least for the *critical* realist 'independently' should not be interpreted in an absolute sense, as if there were no link between reality and our knowledge of it – not the least since knowledge is itself part of reality. On the critical realist view, the object of our knowledge is independent of the knowledge process only in the sense that we cannot reduce the former to the latter. This basic realist worldview is in fact a precondition for any meaningful quest for knowledge, since without a notion of reality as exercising some kind of 'resistance' against our notions of it, there is no ground for claiming one piece of knowledge to be more adequate than another.

12   *Introduction*

The scepticism that it nevertheless tends to provoke can be explained by reference to what Bhaskar terms the 'epistemic fallacy' (1975/2008a: 242), the move of collapsing reality into the categories we use to conceive it. In the hermeneutic and poststructuralist tradition, but also in analytical philosophy, this fallacy tends to take on a linguistic form (Bhaskar, 1979/1998; 1993/2008b). As we shall see later on, Butler's (1990/1999) famous discursification of biological sex is implicated by this kind of move. Highlighting that our *conception* of sex is necessarily mediated by culturally relative discourses, Butler deduces that sex has no *existence* independently of these discourses. Critical realists counter this kind of argument, which Bhaskar holds to be endemic in western philosophy, by applying a 'causal criterion' for ascribing reality to something (Bhaskar, 1979/1998: 12). From the point of view of this criterion, the ontological status of sexual difference can be argued to be independent from – in the sense of irreducible to – our conception of it, since it has causal effects in the world no matter how we conceive of it, such as the differentiated ability to give birth. Importantly, this is not to say that our ways of conceptualizing sex does not mediate its effects in the world, only that its effects are not *reducible* to such conceptualizations. This is really just another way of saying that being does not operate according to linguistic laws only.

What about non-biological social realities, then? How can we uphold the claim that they are independent from our concepts when concepts are in fact partly constitutive of social reality? While critical realism challenges the antinaturalism of hermeneutics and poststructuralism, it also disputes biological reductionism and emphasizes the specific character of social relations and its consequences for the knowledge process in the social sciences. It is a pivotal claim of Bhaskar's that there is no absolute gulf between the natural and social sciences, that both should engage in an explanatory movement 'from knowledge of manifest phenomena to knowledge of the structures generating them' (1979/1998: 13). Yet, he emphasizes the particularity of social structures, constituted by the fact that, while they possess an existence independent from human concepts and activities at any particular point in time, they are also in their entirety a product of such human practices and ideas. Hence, as opposed to Nancy Tuana's contention, realism is *not* 'the belief that what exists is both *prior to* and *independent of* human interactions' (2008: 190). What critical realists stress is that, although social reality is a product of human practices (informed by culturally specific concepts and ideas), it is also independent from them in the sense that human practice always takes place in a social reality which, *as* a product of human practices, pre-exists it. Hence, in the case of social science too, we must retain the distinction between the practice of knowing and the object to be known, for although they are related and dialectically co-constitute each other over time, at any specific point in time, social reality is other to the concepts we apply to it (Bhaskar, 1979/1998; Sayer, 1984/1992).

The structure of reality: necessity and complexity

When theorists do not make a reflected effort to think through ontological issues, their writings will mostly tacitly secrete a one-dimensional, 'actualist' ontology.

Introduction 13

'Actualism' is the term Bhaskar uses for the widespread conviction that reality amounts to actual events (1975/2008a: 63; 1993/2008b: 4). He instead argues that reality has ontological depth, such that the actual is only part of a more encompassing reality. He distinguishes between the *empirical*, those actual events that are experienced, the *actual*, which includes those actualities that are not perceived, and the *real*, which embraces the actual and our experiences of it but also the unperceivable structures and powers that produce events (1975/2008a). Bhaskar holds that it is this deeper stratum of reality that should constitute the main focus of science, since this is where the causal roots of manifest phenomena are to be found. Differently put, the empirical and the actual should be understood 'in terms of the non-empirical, non-actual, real' (2002b: 43). My endorsement of a broad or non-fragmented view of sexuality and love is an expression of such a non-actualist approach to reality, in that it attributes ontological and analytical priority to the causal-structural foundations of these practices rather than to their diverse manifestations.

This depth ontology of critical realism builds on Karl Marx's suggestion, underpinning his ground-breaking analysis of capitalism, that 'to understand the essence of some particular phenomenon is to understand the social relations that make the phenomenon possible' (Bhaskar, 1979/1998: 51). Here, the compatibility between critical realism and feminism also clearly emerges, inasmuch as the constitutive claim of the latter is that there is a patriarchal power structure behind the surface of disparate phenomena and experiences, which is intangible but can be theoretically inferred from its effects. Unfortunately, partly due to the lack of a robust ontology that can counter the dominance of actualist ways of thinking, today feminists, too, question the existence of a power structure that systematically privileges men at the expense of women, on the grounds that no seamless regularity can be found on the level of the actual (see Chapter 5). The complex depth ontology of critical realism can help remedy this unfortunate obscuring of oppressive realities.

For critical realists causality is a pivotal notion. Yet, while the actualist ontology tends to lead to a linear view of causality as unmediated chains of cause–effect, critical realists conceive of causality in terms of the conditioning power of structures.[6] Powers are seen as potentials, which may or may not be actualized depending on conditions, meaning that while they cause events they do not predetermine them. Hence, their necessity or lawfulness must be understood as *tendencies* (Bhaskar, 1979/1998, 1975/2008a). For example, that water has the power to quench fire is true even when this power is not exercised. Similarly, a man may have power over a woman without exercising it, or the power that he has over women by virtue of his maleness may be counteracted by forces pertaining to other structures. What determines what actually happens is a matter of a complex interplay of the potentials and constraints generated by the multi-layered net of different structures constituting reality. Crucially, from the critical realist point of view the contingent and infinitely complex character of the actual does not mean there is no structure or necessity pertaining to reality. It is here that critical realism offers an important alternative to the poststructuralist tendency to

14   *Introduction*

see complexity and contingency as evidence that there are no systematic or necessary connections in reality.

The concept of necessity refers to the fact that not all elements in the world are externally or contingently related but internally or necessarily so, such that one element in the relation is what it is only by virtue of the other element. For instance, there is a necessary relation between human existence and eating. This does not mean that all human beings are pre-determined to eat, but it sets a condition (which indeed shapes quite a persistent conformity): if you want to exist, you must eat. Bhaskar revitalizes Freud's notion of the 'reality principle' to indicate the ways in which our ability to do different things is premised on our adaption to the invincible rules of reality (1993/2008b: 55). For instance, inasmuch as there is a relation of necessity between the power to communicate and shared rules of communication, if we want to communicate with other people we must subordinate ourselves to the rules of language.

Necessity *in the world* (as opposed to logical and conceptual necessity) is often referred to as 'natural necessity', but this normally does not refer to nature as opposed to the social or cultural. It captures the sense in which, for instance, *it is in the nature* of communication to follow rules of language (Danermark *et al.*, 1997/2002). We can nevertheless distinguish between transhistorical and historically produced necessities. However cultural and social the phenomenon of communication is, it is a transhistorical fact that it is premised on following rules of language. By contrast, it is a historically produced necessity that the capacity for communication is in certain contexts premised on following the rules of Swedish. Similarly, while it is a transhistorical necessity that humans need to labour in order to survive, it is a historically contingent necessity that the majority of the population must subordinate themselves to the rules of wage labour in order to survive. Importantly, though, these two levels of necessity are in turn necessarily or internally related to one another, such that the historically produced need to sell one's labour is based in the more basic necessary relations constituted by the fact that humans must eat in order to survive and labour in order to eat. Hence, while we are not pre-determined by nature, we cannot understand the socially constituted necessities structuring our lives in isolation from the necessities of nature.

The notion of necessity is clearly not in vogue among contemporary poststructuralist feminists, who tend to see radical contingency as a necessary (!) condition of radical change. In particular, any invocation of transhistorical or natural constraints on the possible ways of fashioning human societies tends to be rejected as 'essentialist', a term that has become so derogatory as to signal the end of rational argument (Sayer, 1997). At the same time, few would, I assume, argue against the notion that human beings need to eat in order to survive. Likewise, a necessity which is implicitly central in many feminist accounts, albeit not acknowledged as such, is that implied by the fact that humans depend psychologically on one another for their existence. As I hope to show through the course of this book, the lack of explicit acknowledgement and specification of these kinds of needs not only makes it impossible to explain the reproduction and transformation

Introduction   15

of historically produced power structures, but also rids theories of their normative purchase.

The dialectical core of reality

The idea that reality is constituted by a complex meshwork of necessary/internal relations (whose elements are unified in that at least one presupposes the other) and contingent/external connections[7] forms the basis of Bhaskar's conception of being as a dialectical totality. While the dialectical character of the critical realist philosophy was affirmed and elaborated first in dialectical critical realism, it is implicit already in original critical realism. At its most basic, dialectics is 'the art of thinking the coincidence of distinctions and connections' (Bhaskar, 1993/2008b: 180) and as such it challenges the static either/or thinking characteristic of analytical reason. While dialectics was a matter wholly of logic or thought in the idealistic system of Friedrich Hegel, for Bhaskar – as for Marx – the reason why *thinking* dialectically is necessary is that *being* is structured dialectically.

In original critical realism the dialectical theme is expressed in the notion that reality is differentiated while interconnected and, more specifically, that it is constituted by different levels or strata which despite their existential unity are also distinct by virtue of the process of emergence (Bhaskar, 1979/1998; Collier, 1994; Sayer, 1984/1992). For example, humanity is not only dependent on nature but constituted by it, so that it must be conceived of *as* nature. Nothing that goes on in human relations could continue without the physiological and biological processes that constitute people and the artefacts on which they depend. At the same time, the reason why we have a specific concept of the social is that this human-social stratum of reality is *emergent* from nature, such that it has its own irreducible powers and properties impossible to derive or predict from natural ones. While ideas and thoughts, for instance, are based in the neurophysiological processes of the brain, no matter how well we understand these neurophysiological processes this knowledge will not help us understand the ideas and thoughts that they sustain. Here, then, difference coexists with unity in the sense that things can be indistinguishable from one another on the level of constituents, but distinguishable on the level of properties and powers (see Chapter 5).

The themes of dialectical critical realism as well as of the ensuing philosophy of metaReality depend on these notions of differentiation, stratification and emergence. Yet, whereas original critical realism focused on establishing important distinctions in the face of reductionist and one-dimensional philosophical accounts, in Bhaskar's dialectical work equal focus is put on the forces that bind distinct levels and entities together, whereas, as we shall see, in the philosophy of metaReality unity is put at the forefront. For instance, when original critical realism stressed the importance of distinguishing between epistemology and ontology in the face of the epistemic fallacy, in dialectical critical realism the 'constellational unity' (1993/2008b: 114) of them is also emphasized. As Alan Norrie highlights in his work on dialectical critical realism, although ontology must be distinguished from epistemology, this distinction is not absolute, since 'knowing is at the same

16 *Introduction*

time a subset of being, and the study or theory of being (onto-*logy*) is already epistemically committed' (2010: 17). Hence, here dialectical critical realism accommodates the insight put forward by many feminist theorists that ontology and epistemology cannot be altogether separated (Barad, 2003, 2007; Hekman, 2010), yet avoids the unfruitful non-dialectical conclusion that they have therefore no independent existence from one another, a conclusion that inevitably leads to one of them being subsumed by the other.

Bhaskar uses the figure of *constellation(ality)* to denote the idea of a holistic totality that embraces while not subsuming its different components. The partial, open, complex and constantly evolving character of such constellational totalities is articulated by the fact that one totality can also be part of another totality, as in the example of human beings being both nature and other than nature, or of language being both part of the world and distinct from it in that we use it to refer to the world. This idea of a dialectical totality counters not only atomist ideas of entities as fixed and only externally related, but also convictions that, by lack of such static and neatly demarcated entities, reality cannot be said to have any structure to it. As against widespread ideas that making analytical distinctions, thereby establishing distinct entities, is something of an arbitrary move, from a realist perspective this is not so. Despite the fact that a 'perspectival switch' (Bhaskar, 1993/2008b: 115) can determine whether two things appear as unified or distinct, this cannot be reduced to a subjective matter but is rooted in the structure of the world (which includes the perspectives that humans take on it). Hence, if a particular analytical distinction between two totalities has explanatory force – if it helps make sense of something – this reflects a real, albeit relative, hiatus in being.

It is important to note that the depth ontology of critical realism means that relations of 'identity-in-difference' (Bhaskar, 1993/2008b: 319) are mostly not 'flat' and symmetrical, but themselves differentiated and stratified, as well as developing in time. For instance, nature and humanity are not on a par, since the former is more basic and encompassing than the latter insofar as humanity cannot exist without nature while nature does perfectly fine without humanity. In the most recent extension of his philosophical system, the philosophy of metaReality (2002a, 2002b, 2002c; Bhaskar with Hartwig, 2010),[8] Bhaskar draws on this theme of existential asymmetry, arguing that on an overall level unity or non-duality is more fundamental than difference or duality as well as the antagonistic dualisms which prevail in present society. As will be clear, this existential hierarchy imposed by the 'natural ontological order', to use Andrew Collier's term (2002: 166), is pivotal for the arguments about oppression and emancipation laid out in this work.

Challenging the either/or thinking of analytical reason by acknowledging the fundamentally dialectical nature of reality is one of the most crucial elements, I contend, in the project of developing sustainable social theories. Therefore, it is important to remedy the dialectical deficit in feminist theory. I will demonstrate that dialectics can resolve a range of disabling confusions about distinctions and relationality that are endemic in feminist theory. It also provides a means of reconciling different theoretical stances, which tend to appear in opposition to one another because they emphasize different aspects of a dual reality, but which are really complicit in their one-sidedness.

Outline of the book: from sexuality to love

This book starts off with an assessment of Judith Butler's and Anna G. Jónasdóttir's respective theorizations of how gendered power is based in *sexuality*, but then shifts focus to *love*. This analytical switch can be understood only in relation to the conceptual development pursued throughout the book, based on my positive appraisal of Jónasdóttir's conceptualization of sexuality. Whereas most scholars, including Butler, theorize sexuality as something separate from love and care, more or less explicitly focusing on the desirous and ecstatic elements of sexuality (see Stoller, 2010), Jónasdóttir sees our erotic-ecstatic and caring capacities as dialectically conjoined. Articulating a broad materialist conception of sexuality, with concrete human practices as its point of departure, she contends that our capacity for love, our 'love power' – whose power is generated by the dialectical interplay of care and erotic ecstasy – should be seen as the basic motor in our existence as sexual beings, since sexuality has the power to empower us as persons only if it is to some degree loaded with loving care (1991/1994, 2011). Following this broad conception of (socio)sexuality and love, in the theoretical elaborations that follow I use the terms relatively interchangeably, thus breaking with the common-sense use of the terms. I use the notions of '(socio)sexual capacity' and 'love power' as synonyms, where both include the duality of our erotic-ecstatic and caring capacities. Consequently, when I refer to '(socio)sexuality' I do not have only erotic-desirous aspects in view, but practices of loving care, or lack of it, are included here too. Conversely, breaking with the dominant tendency in current society to compartmentalize the erotic, I see it as an integral part – to a greater or lesser extent – of all relations of loving care, also those that are not straightforwardly sexual in kind.[9]

Rosemary Hennessy notes that '[o]ne of the most remarkable features of the history of sexual identities is the lack of any consensus over how to understand precisely what sexuality is' (2000: 37). It will be a recurrent theme of this book that, peculiarly, theorists of sexuality generally have little to say about sexuality as such. The meaning of sexuality – and of love – is often implicitly taken for granted, so that critical discussions of their ontology are precluded. Instead of setting off with a more elaborate clarification of what definitions of sexuality and love I work with, these definitions will evolve with the general unfolding of the book. When I say that the task of the book is to offer a theorization of women's subordination to men in sexuality and love, a crucial part of this endeavour is precisely to elucidate the ontology of sexuality and love. What is sexuality? And what is love? As I hope to show, the answers offered to these questions have important implications for our understanding of the mechanisms of female subordination.

In the first part of the book, *Feminist modes of theorizing sexuality and gendered power*, I examine two different ways of conceptualizing how gendered

18   *Introduction*

power is constituted through sexuality, which means that along with the concept of *sexuality* I also investigate implicit or explicit understandings of *power* and *sex/gender*.[10] I make a comparative assessment of how sex/gender, sexuality and power and their interrelation are addressed in Butler's queer feminist theory of sex and gender and Jónasdóttir's materialist-realist theory of sociosexual exploitation. A comparison of these two accounts is analytically fruitful since they represent widely different approaches, while having in common that they both deal in a systematic, abstract and comprehensive way with sex/gender, sexuality and power as constituting a societal structure or system.[11] Another feature uniting them is that they treat sexuality, gender and power as intrinsically interrelated and constitutive of one other; power is not taken to work only externally on gender and sexuality, but also seen as constitutive of them. These commonalities aside, Butler and Jónasdóttir represent two radically different paradigms of feminist theory: poststructuralist queer feminism and what I refer to as materialist-realist feminism, of which the former has a dominant position in contemporary gender studies and feminist theory, whereas the latter is marginalized. A thorough comparison of the works of these authors will thus indirectly serve as a comparative evaluation of these paradigms. Since the distinctive features of the paradigms can be derived very much from the meta-theoretical assumptions underpinning them, my critique will also engage both indirectly and directly with a range of meta-theoretical issues that concern not only feminist theorists but social theorists generally.[12]

In the second part of the book, *Meta-theoretical interlude: challenging poststructuralist feminism*, I address more directly some meta-theoretical issues that are actualized in Part I and which are at the forefront of contemporary debates in feminist theory. Here I introduce and draw upon some important critical realist categories and arguments in an attempt to challenge the 'academic orthodoxy' of poststructuralist[13] feminist theory (Assiter, 1996: i). I discuss the place of nature in feminist theory and the question of how to understand the disputed category of 'women' (and, concomitantly, 'men'), and analyse the ways in which poststructuralist interventions on these topics tend to replicate the modernist assumptions that they set out to challenge. The poststructuralist trend in the humanities and social sciences has been particularly strong in feminist theory and it is no exaggeration to state that in this field poststructuralism has a hegemonic position. Although today it is habitually challenged and many feminist theorists and gender scholars are looking for post-poststructuralist alternatives, the basic tenets of poststructuralism have, I contend, become institutionalized in feminist theory and gender studies in a way that lends them a taken-for-granted and imperative status. This has created a range of disabling taboos that I challenge, not only in order to support the claims about gendered power, love and sexuality advanced in this work, but also as a means of contributing to the general meta-theoretical discussions in the field of feminist theory.

My positive appraisal of Jónasdóttir's work in Part I serves as the point of departure of the third part of the book, *The reality of love and power – a feminist-realist depth approach*. Here I elaborate some crucial but underdeveloped themes

Introduction   19

in Jónasdóttir's framework, which advances the claim that men exploit women's 'love power', so as to further develop my conceptualization of women's subordination to men in sexuality and love. Drawing on empirical studies, I first offer a theorization of the micro-sociology of power in heterosexual coupledom.[14] In the rest of Part III I introduce and draw on some central ontological categories formulated by Bhaskar in dialectical critical realism and the philosophy of metaReality. I address Jónasdóttir's claim that men are empowered by their exploitation of women's love power and, while defending and elucidating this claim, I also offer a partial recasting and relativization of it. Setting out with a detailed effort to claim the realness of male power, through the course of the book I elucidate the 'ontological fragility' of this power and expound on the crucial consequences this has for how to conceive of emancipatory transformation. I pursue, one might say, a *dialectical deepening* of Jónasdóttir's theses about the nature of sociosexual exploitation, anchored in a comprehension of the basic necessities structuring love and the human empowerment of which it is the source. Invoking in particular the notion of necessity, Bhaskar's dialectical idea of unity-in-difference and his differentiated conception of the real, I develop a feminist dialectical-realist depth ontology of sexuality and love, which should prove appealing to feminist theorists searching for alternatives to the dominant discursive approaches to sexuality and which attributes to love its proper place in our existence as sexual human creatures. Despite the fact that I make a strong case for the tenacity of the exploitative sociosexual structure, I end on a more optimistic note by elucidating a possible way of breaking the shackles of love.

Notes

1 I.e. including dialectical critical realism and the philosophy of metaReality.
2 See Bhaskar's dialectical conceptualization of totalities and parts on p. 16.
3 'For unless an illusion … actually existed', Bhaskar asks, 'what would be the point of unmasking the illusion … ?' (2002b: 44-5). As for the idea of absences as real, this is the crucial new element in dialectical critical realism (1993/2008b). The notion of absence is not at the forefront of this book, but Bhaskar's conceptualization of change as the *absenting of absences* underpins for instance my argument that the need for/lack of love is a crucial driving force of people and, hence, history.
4 For instance, Bhaskar (1979/1998) highlights that, while the hermeneutic tradition may seem radically opposed to positivism, its denial of the fact that causality operates in the human realm actually depends on positivism's mechanical and linear view of causality. Grosz similarly argues that '[f]ar from providing an alternative to the positivist approaches of contemporary analytical philosophy, structuralism and poststructuralism have shared uncritically in its reduction of ontology to epistemology' (2005: 172). As we shall see, my critique of feminist poststructuralism will be largely based on highlighting ways in which, similarly, it tacitly depends on the presuppositions of its modernist antagonists.
5 My engagement with Bhaskar's spiritual turn is restricted to his philosophy of metaReality.
6 Here a structure is understood as a set of relations the specific organization of which endows it with certain powers and liabilities. Structures in this terminology do not refer only to overarching, 'big' structures, but also to the internal organization of any entity.

20 Introduction

7 Bhaskar distinguishes between internal and external relations on one hand and necessary and contingent ones on the other (1993/2008b: 271), but I use the terms interchangeably, following critical realists like Andrew Sayer (1984/1992: 89).

8 Many, if not most, adherents of original critical realism are critical of Bhaskar's spiritual turn (Callinicos in Bhaskar and Callinicos, 2003; Creaven, 2009; Morgan, 2003). Although a greater number of critical realists have followed him into his dialectical turn, for instance Alex Callinicos (in Bhaskar and Callinicos, 2003) sees dialectical critical realism and its identification of absence as a fundamental ontological category as a problematic development of critical realism, which opened up for the spiritual turn. It is not within the scope of this book to engage with this critique, though.

9 This decompartmentalized view of the sexual/erotic is endorsed by a significant number of theorists. Ann Ferguson, for instance, defines her concept of 'sex/affective energy' as the specific human energy that is based in the 'social yet bodily based desire to unite with others' (1989: 78). In the psychoanalytical tradition too Eros is understood as the 'tendency for organisms to maintain the cohesion of living matter and to create new unities' (Laplanche and Pontalis, 1988: 240; see also Marcuse, 1955/1962). Feminist scholars have also highlighted how homophobia obscures the fact that same-sex relations which are held to be non-erotic often have an erotic charge (Ferguson, 1989, 1991; Rich, 1983; Sedgwick, 1985).

10 As will be clear, both the authors examined downplay the significance of the distinction between sex and gender.

11 Butler is likely to disagree that she conceives of gendered power as a structure or system, since she attempts to transcend such notions. Yet, it will be clear that there is indeed a systematicity or structuredness to the interrelations between gender, power and sexuality in her account, in the sense that these terms are systematically and intrinsically linked to the others. I agree with Mervyn Hartwig that 'if philosophers do not develop [a system] explicitly, their work will implicitly or tacitly secrete one' (1993/2008: xiii).

12 The criteria applied in my assessment of the theories are internal, logical coherence and external relevance or explanatory force. In other words, apart from not contradicting themselves, the theories should not contradict empirical realities but acknowledge and, preferably, explain them. Here, empirical realities include the scientifically substantiated data reviewed above but also more non-disputed premises, such as the fact that women are human beings who, as such, have agency. Berth Danermark *et al.* highlight that the process of evaluating the explanatory force of a theory can be guided by this question: 'To what extent can we, starting in the theory, understand and explain connections and processes of which we earlier had a more imprecise conception?' (1997/2002: 148). Are there experiences which contradict the theory? What can the theory *not* explain? Crucially, as Bhaskar emphasizes, any theory about social relations must, in order to be adequate, be able to explain both their reproduction and transformation 'and preferably … it should be able to specify the conditions under which such reproduction (and transformation) occurs' (1979/1998: 76, note 65).The fact that I make my assessment from the point of view of a critical realist conviction whose fundamental premises are shared by Jónasdóttir but not Butler needs to be addressed. It should be no surprise that Jónasdóttir succeeds best in such an assessment. Yet, that I bring my critical realist premises with me does not mean I do not have to argue logically and consistently for my case; rather, by *using* critical realism in my critical practice, governed by the criteria of logical consistency and explanatory force, I simultaneously demonstrate its plausibility. If someone sees my assessment as 'biased', they need to show, by means of logical argument, what is inadequate about my critical realist perspective and the arguments it underpins.

13 I will use the terms 'poststructuralism' and 'postmodernism' as synonyms, referring to them as a philosophical stance influenced in particular by Gilles Deleuze, Jacques Derrida and Michel Foucault and characterized above all by scepticism towards truth

Introduction 21

claims, disbelief in the coherence of the human subject and resistance towards grounding theories in ontological presuppositions about the nature of the world (cf. Callinicos,
1989).

14 It should be stressed that this is not a book about heterosexual couple love. The
woman–man relation and the heterosexual institution are at the centre of my analysis,
since I see them as ontologically pivotal in the current structure of gendered power. Yet,
my non-actualist, structural approach to sexuality and love, seen as a web of relations
stretching across the social totality, means that non-heterosexual practices, non-sexualized
loving bonds, as well as normal interactions in work, politics and leisure time are also
structured by the specific organization of the hegemonically positioned woman–man
relation (cf. p. 47 and p. 146, note 1). Although my empirical examples are often taken
from heterosexual coupledom, similar patterns structure relations between women
and men in other arenas. It remains unclear, though, what import the arguments laid
out in this book have for the understanding of power mechanisms internal to same-
sex relations. This also leaves undecided to what extent individual women's turning
away from heterosexuality constitutes a way towards emancipation for those particular
women. It would be of great value to continue, and perhaps revise, the themes of this
book by incorporating an analysis of same-sex relations, based on existing studies of
power in romantic same-sex relations, of homo-sociality and same-sex friendship, of
parent–child dynamics etc.

Part I

Feminist modes of theorizing sexuality and gendered power

2 Judith Butler and the deconstruction of reality

> If the world is a certain way, then we must necessarily in our practice act in conformity with the way the world is, irrespective of the nature of our beliefs, at least if we are to be at all successful, that is to fulfil our intentionality (as agents), or if the system of beliefs we hold (collectively) is to survive. So what is necessary for a false theory or way of being to be sustained is in fact the tacit presupposition of the reality or truth which underpins it, yet which it denies and may even altogether occlude.
>
> Roy Bhaskar (2002b: 51)

Though strongly criticized (e.g. Benhabib, 1995; Boucher, 2008; Epstein, 1995; Fraser, 1998; Jónasdóttir and Jones, 2009; Hennessy, 2000; Hull, 2006; Moi, 1999; Nussbaum, 1999), Butler's work has had an enormous impact on the development of women's and gender studies and feminist theory. As Martha Nussbaum states in a 1999 article, 'Butler seems to many young scholars to define what feminism is now' (1999: 38). Her seminal work *Gender trouble: feminism and the subversion of identity* (1990/1999) shook the fundaments of feminist theory by its radical questioning not only of gender but of biological sex too. Ever since, her theory of sex and gender as discursively produced performative effects is widely represented as *the* alternative to essentialist accounts of gender. As Hennessy states, the attention that Butler's work has received 'indicates that her ideas have struck a chord in a certain sector of the public imagination of new ways of knowing sexual identity' (2000: 55).

In the wake of *Gender trouble* Butler has sought to qualify many of her standpoints in order to repudiate what she sees as misinterpretations. *Bodies that matter* (1993), in which she elaborates her concept of materiality, is largely framed as a disclaimer against charges that her discursive-performative understanding of sex and gender amounts to idealism. Similarly, the collection of essays in *Undoing gender* (2004) are very much formulated as a mostly implicit response to the criticism she has received. Still, I see Butler's work as consistent over the years. The *focus* of her theoretical enquiries has changed slightly and Butler makes several attempts to qualify the framework laid out in *Gender trouble*, but with few exceptions[1] she never openly disqualifies and reworks the latter. In the following

26 *Feminist modes of theorizing sexuality and gendered power*

chapter I present and evaluate Butler's conceptualization of, in turn, sex and gender, sexuality and power.

Sex and gender: performative effects of discourse

While traditionally feminist theory has dealt with the systematic ways in which men are empowered and women disempowered, Butler and the queer-theoretical paradigm she represents shifts focus to how men and women are themselves produced as intelligible identities. There are no biological sexual categories independent of our understanding of them as such, Butler argues; sex itself should be understood as a discursively produced performative effect. She thus refutes the sex/gender distinction that feminists invented to highlight the socially constructed character of the gender system (Rubin, 1975), maintaining that '[g]ender ought not to be conceived merely as the cultural inscription of meaning on a pregiven sex ...; gender must also designate the very apparatus of production whereby the sexes themselves are established' (1990/1999: 11). That most people think of sex as a biological given is itself a function of this discursive apparatus of production, according to her: 'this production of sex *as* the prediscursive ought to be understood as the effect of the apparatus of cultural construction designated by gender' (1990/1999: 11, emphasis added). This idea of discourse as formative of material reality, that 'there is no reference to a pure body which is not at the same time a further formation of that body' (1993: 10), is the essence of the idea of *performativity*, which is central in Butler's work.

As Barbara Epstein notes, Butler's idea that the reality of sexed bodies is discursively produced arguably 'strains belief' (1995: 101). How can she hold that biological sex is not pre-discursive, when it is in fact a foundation of life itself? Here it is important to elucidate the theoretical alternatives with which Butler operates. She repeatedly assures us that she does not refute the reality of bodies, of age, illness, death (1993: 10) and declares that she does not believe 'words alone [have] the power to craft bodies from their own linguistic substance' (1993: x). Yet, she refutes the idea that we can demarcate what realities are 'unconstructed' without engaging in violent normative exclusions, since such boundaries will necessarily include some aspects of reality and exclude others (1993: 11). Here, in faithful alliance with Foucault, Butler endorses a view of knowledge and discourse as political to their core. To her, there seems to be no way of singling out 'unconstructed' biological realities in a way that respects the real structure of the world, so that it can be judged valid, scientific, true. She appears to rule out the possibility that certain discursive exclusions may correspond to causally effective boundaries in *being*, so that they are hard to grasp as politically problematic. For instance, when I claim that men cannot give birth due to their male biological constitution, this indeed refers to men's exclusion from a certain realm of possibility. But it is bizarre to see it as a political *act* of exclusion, since it is just a reference to structures that are at work in the world whatever we think about it.

Butler states that when someone claims that some part of sexed/gendered reality is not discursively constructed, 'the very boundary that is meant to protect some part of sex from the taint of constructivism is now defined by the anti-constructivist's own construction', which is itself discursively produced (1993: 11). What is clearly at work in Butler's theoretical operations here is the *epistemic* or, more correctly, *linguistic fallacy*, the conflation of our representation of reality with reality itself (see p. 12). I would argue that this fallacy is the key to the inconsistencies in Butler's work. '[I]nsofar as the extra-discursive is delimited', she states in a key formulation, *'it is formed by the very discourse from which it seeks to free itself'* (1993: 11, emphasis added). Hence, is her conclusion, discourse permeates everything. Here it is crucial to note that Butler is right that when bodies are situated in social reality their reality is always mediated by culturally contingent concepts. She is also correct when highlighting that discursive categories do not simply represent reality, but also to a certain degree take part in shaping this very reality and the impact it has on us. Yet, *neither of this implies that biological and material strata are not ontologically distinct from the conceptual level*. Nor does it mean that we cannot strive to construct reasonable, yet necessarily fallible, knowledge about them, grounded in our more or less systematized practical exchange with these biological and material structures. The fact that the biological sexual division inevitably structures reproductive practices in certain ways, no matter what discursive categories we use to make sense of it, is what makes sex qualify as irreducibly real, as ontologically distinct from the significatory matrixes through which it becomes intelligible.

But does Butler really deny that biological sexual difference structures reproduction in specific ways regardless of what discursive regimes prevail? When challenged on this issue upfront, she says she does acknowledge that there are biological limitations (e.g. 1994). Yet, as Andrew Sayer notes, she displays 'an extraordinary reluctance to concede that anything follows from this' (1997: 485, note 32). All in all, her appeal to biology is more rhetorical and pragmatic than theoretical. As Geoff Boucher highlights, Butler's has a tendency to make 'formal assertions' that are then 'belied by the theoretical content' of her work (2008: 147). This is the case also with her notion of 'materiality'. Although *Bodies that matter* (1993) claims to be about the material, she mostly puts the word 'materiality' within quotes (1993: 17, 28, 67) and argues that:

> the regulatory norms of 'sex' work in a performative fashion to constitute the materiality of bodies and, more specifically, to materialize the body's sex, to materialize sexual difference in the service of the consolidation of the heterosexual imperative.
>
> (1993: 2)

Apart from the functionalist inclinations to which this passage bears witness (cf. Fraser, 1998; see p. 33), it makes clear that it is in the regulatory norms of sex that all causality and structure is located, whereas the bodily and material are understood mainly as effects. Having examined Butler's concept of materiality, Carrie Hull concludes that '[t]he most that Butler will explicitly say about materiality is that it is "a demand in and for language, a 'that which' which prompts and occasions, … [and] calls to be explained"' (Hull, 2006: 58; Butler, 1993: 67).

28   *Feminist modes of theorizing sexuality and gendered power*

While conceding that reality is not a matter of language only, Butler rejects the notion of materiality as ontologically distinct from language. Although this seems a paradoxical statement, this way of thinking about distinctions is constitutive of the Butlerian paradigm and, as shall I elaborate more upon, a fundamental cause of its many inconsistencies. In Butler's view, '[t]o posit a materiality outside of language, where that materiality is considered ontologically distinct from language, is to undermine the possibility that language might be able to indicate or correspond to that domain of radical alterity' (1993: 68). At work here is the notion that two things cannot be related if they are ontologically distinct. This idea is a product, I contend, of the dialectical deficit in Butler's philosophical framework, which rids her of the possibility of thinking unity-*in*-difference (see Chapter 4), probably largely due to her being so caught up in linguistic and logical structures, which are inherently dualistic in that their categories are defined in terms of what they are not rather than what they are. For her, things are either totally separate or indistinguishable, with the consequence that the acknowledgement of a relation between two levels of reality inevitably leads to one of them being subsumed by the other. As we shall see below, this fallacy is operative also in Butler's conceptualization of the relation between sexuality and gender and in her reduction of sexuality to its imbrication in discursive power. And, as I will elaborate in Chapter 5, the same non-dialectical mode of thinking structures her claim that it is 'impossible to separate out "gender"' from the other discursively constituted identities with which it intersects' (1990/1999: 6).

Despite her claims to the contrary, pointing to the demands and promptings of the extra-discursive, Butler clearly does conceive of the material as somehow ontologically beyond the significatory processes in which it is enmeshed. Seeking to distance herself from the constructionist paradigm, she emphasizes that her deconstructionist stance does not amount to the claim that 'everything is discursively constructed'. Deconstructionism, she reminds us, emphasizes that 'there is an "outside" to what is constructed by discourse', although 'this is not an absolute "outside", an ontological thereness that exceeds or counters the boundaries of discourse' (1993: 8). Indeed, her recurrent idea of things not 'fit[ting]' within the current order of intelligibility (e.g. 1990/1999: 142) is premised on an idea of the autonomy of the extra-discursive. Importantly though, in Butler's account these demands and promptings seem to have no inherent structure to them. As soon as she addresses the issue of what regulates and structures human life, she takes recourse to discourse, so that it is always the discursive level that organizes the material, never the reverse. As Alison Stone states in a critique of feminist accounts that attribute no causal autonomy to the biological and material:

> Having no determinate natural character, there is nothing in materiality that could work as an internal principle of activity, impelling it to respond to, react upon, or redirect the representations that engage it. There is nothing inherent in corporeal matter that could galvanize it to shape or inflect the process of its own acculturation.
>
> (2004: 14)

'I confess', Butler writes, 'that I am not a very good materialist. Every time I try to write about the body, the writing ends up being about language' (2004: 198). This is noteworthy insofar as she rejects the idea of matter as a passive thing or surface that we shape by inscribing meaning on it (1993: 4). Although she clearly does not conceive of matter as lifeless, she nevertheless seems stuck in this 'inscription paradigm' insofar as, in her account, it is still significatory processes that administrate and shape matter (cf. Barad, 2007: 151). This leaves us, if we follow logical criteria, with the highly untenable conclusion that we could somehow, by means of a resignification of matter, make the structure of biological sexual difference inoperative.

The subject: reversing the causal arrows

A main concern of Butler's is the intimate connection between the performative effects of sex/gender and the production of the subject as such. Her idea of discursive-performative production only ambiguously embraces the product of this process of construction as *real*. Hence, to her, the claim that women and men are discursive constructs down to the bone implies that they are, at least in some sense, fictive or phantasmic.[2] Sexed/gendered identities are discursive-performative *effects* and only so; there is no analytical space for understanding these effects as themselves the cause or origin of something, since they are understood to possess no internal coherence or relative independence from the process that produces them: 'There is no gender identity behind the expressions of gender; that identity is performatively constituted by the very "expressions" that are said to be its results' (1990/1999: 33). As Timothy Kaufman-Osborn (1997) highlights, in her effort to question essentialist and static notions of gendered identities Butler reverses the causal arrows, such that discourse unilaterally becomes the cause and gender the effect.

It is not only the sexed/gendered subject that is deconstructed by Butler, but the subject as such. No more than sex and gender, she contends, do subjects exist apart from the continuous repetition of exclusionary discursive subject positions. Both sex and subjecthood are mutually independent phantasms, produced by means of the suppression of potentialities that are unintelligible within current discursive regimes (1990/1999, 1993). When debating with theorists who charge her with claiming that the subject does not exist, Butler is careful to stress that this is not what her deconstructive move amounts to: 'The critique of the subject is not a negation or repudiation of the subject, but, rather, a way of interrogating its construction as a pre-given or foundationalist premise' (1995: 42; cf. 1993: 7). However, tying in with psychoanalytical thought – in particular its Lacanian variant – and its central concern with the link between sexual identity and subject-constitution, she argues that subject-constitution is necessarily bound up with a kind of deception based on heterosexist norms: 'The forming of a subject requires an identification with the normative phantasm of "sex", and this identification takes place through a repudiation which produces a domain of abjection, a repudiation without which the subject cannot emerge' (1993: 3). Although these remarks

30 *Feminist modes of theorizing sexuality and gendered power*

indicate that the subject indeed exists, they seem to logically imply that, if we did not live in a world structured by the phantasm of sex, subjects would not emerge. As we shall see below, though, other passages in her work seem to suggest that this process of subject-formation is *inevitable*, despite its phantasmic ideological grounds, paradoxically indicating that sex too, in spite of its fictive character, is inescapable. As I discuss below, this depiction of the process of subject-constitution as simultaneously necessary and deceptive – and damagingly so – is not only intellectually perplexing but also rids Butler's theory of political potential.

It is when Butler explicitly endorses Friedrich Nietzsche's claim that there is no '"doer" behind the deed' (1990/1999: 33) that it becomes most clear that her framework does not really allow for a notion of the subject as a relatively autonomous entity with causal powers of its own. She in fact dismisses the idea that we need an agent in order to make sense of agency (1990/1999). Invested as she is in a typical interrogative and evasive manner of writing, she does not explain how agency is possible without an agent, though. For her it is more interesting to ask:

> What kinds of agency are foreclosed through the position of an epistemological subject precisely because the rules and practices that govern the invocation of that subject and regulate its agency in advance are ruled out as sites of analysis and critical intervention?
>
> (1990/1999: 183)

Although this is an important question, it does not solve the problem of how agency is possible without an agent. This problematic way of shifting focus away from unresolved inconsistencies in her arguments, often by means of an interrogation, is recurrent in Butler's work. As Nussbaum (1999) highlights, instead of making definite claims Butler tends to use mystifying questions and ambiguous sentences in a way that protects her from criticism.

Butler's claims about the subject seem to be underpinned by the supposition that whoever invokes the subject as a real and relatively stable entity, with an interiority accounting for its agency and intentionality, has fallen prey to the Cartesian figure of a subject totally untouched by the social. As I highlight in Chapter 5, this implicit idea that only that which exists in a static and non-relational way can be judged as real in fact reproduces rather than challenges problematic positivist notions of the nature of reality. Here is a passage that depends on these presumptions:

> If identity is asserted through a process of signification, if identity is always already signified, and yet continues to signify as it circulates within various interlocking discourses, then the question of agency is not to be answered through a recourse to an '*I*' *that preexists signification*.
>
> (1990/1999: 185, emphasis added)

Here Butler not only dismisses the idea that the constitution of the subject is independent from the significatory relations in which it is immersed; she also implicitly assumes that the deconstruction of the subject which she herself advocates is the only alternative to such a notion of the human being. She engages in a treacherous but rhetorically effective slippage between the liberal 'unitary' (2004: 193) and self-sufficient 'master subject' (2004: 194) and the subject as such. In contrast to this, I contend that it is possible to see the gendered subject as a changing and multi-dimensional product of social and discursive processes, while nevertheless comprehending this social product as real, and as irreducible to the process of its production. The critical realist Margaret Archer confronts this kind of fruitless search for a substantial entity as the only legitimate ground for claiming that the self exists: 'There is', she argues, 'no *entity* or *substance* to find, but that only means [one] is looking for the wrong "thing"' (2000: 123).

The crucial point is that something that is a product of signification can still, *as product*, pre-exist – and act on – future significatory processes. Here, the critical realist concept of emergence helps make sense of how the human subject, though relationally constituted, *emerges* from the relations constituting her so as to acquire a relative autonomy from them and, hence, a capacity to act back upon them (Archer, 2000; Bhaskar, 1979/1998). The same applies to gender. Even if we see gender as in its entirety an effect of significatory processes, nothing precludes that it has a reality of its own, *as* effect (see Chapter 5). Again, it is the non-dialectical approach, precluding an analysis of entities as both existentially interdependent and distinct, which is at the root of this collapsing of one aspect of reality – the gendered subject – into another – its constitutive roots in social processes.

One consequence of Butler's deconstruction of the gendered subject is that she does not – and cannot, if she is to be consistent – develop any positive theoretical claims about men's power vis-à-vis women, since such claims depend on the notion that men and women, however constructed, are real and relatively stable existences. Instead, focus is shifted to the ways that any subject comes into being only as an effect of the violent discursive exclusions that make some identities, bodies and desires intelligible and others 'unthinkable, abject, unlivable' (1993: xi). Inasmuch as Butler is a *feminist* theorist and invokes categories such as hetero*sexism*, it is likely that she would endorse the view that women's reality it somehow made more unthinkable, abject and unliveable than men's. Yet, the main political problem with which she is concerned, at least theoretically, is the process whereby the normative subject comes into being only as a function of the suppression of the non-normative, and this makes any invocation of words like 'women' and 'men' itself oppressive. In this way, within the Butlerian framework claims about the existence of a structure that systematically subordinates women to men can only be depicted as a 'colonizing epistemological strategy' (1990/1999: 46), suppressing what does not fit into the categories 'man' and 'woman'. Thus, to Butler the essential problem of gender is clearly not men's power over women, but the power of gendered discourses over people, although this way of putting it would probably not suit her, since it depends on some notion of a subject separable from the process constituting it.

32 *Feminist modes of theorizing sexuality and gendered power*

Butler refutes this interpretation of her work. In a response to an article by Susan Bordo (1988/1992), she argues:

> There are at least two different discursive tasks for feminist practice. In one, it is necessary to wield the abstraction of 'women' in the service of descriptions, arguments, policies that work to overcome gender hierarchy. In the other, however, it is important that we have public contexts in which the very generalizations that we wield to make our arguments are subjected to internal scrutiny.
>
> (1992: 164)

She also makes the insightful point that generalizations do not necessarily work as a cohering force that may help collective struggle, but may themselves '*produce* … the very fragmentation that they lament and oppose' (1992: 164). In her later work, Butler is also more markedly concerned with collectivist kinds of political struggle and she reassures us that she has no qualms about using a term like 'women', or 'the subject', highlighting that '[i]f the notion of the subject, for instance, is no longer given, no longer presumed, that does not mean that it has no meaning for us, that it ought no longer to be uttered' (2004: 179). In Chapter 5 I highlight the problems of the 'strategic essentialism' used by Butler and others as a way of retaining universalizing categories for political purposes while rejecting their ontological basis. The important point here is that, despite her insistence on the importance of collectivist politics, Butler's *theoretical* categories neither encourage nor logically allow for generalizing statements about women and men, since the sexed/gendered subject is attributed no relative autonomy from its constituents.

Sexuality: nature abjected

In Butler's framework the construction of sex and gender is intrinsically tied up with the discursive production of sexuality, governed by the heterosexual imperative. Theorists of gender should stop *presuming* heterosexuality, she argues against both feminists like Catharine MacKinnon and male giants like Claude Lévi-Strauss and Jacques Lacan. Instead we should explore how the heterosexual imperative itself is discursively constructed so as to appear as the natural premise of gender construction. Doing this, Butler finds that the heterosexual premise is actually *constitutive* of the very sexed/gendered identities upon which heterosexuality is based. Hence, deconstructing heteronormativity means deconstructing sexed/gendered identity and vice versa. In this sense, the deconstruction of sex/gender depends upon revealing that heterosexuality and its abject homosexual 'constitutive "outside"' (1993: 8) do not constitute a natural sexual structure; instead, these categories exist only by means of the discursive 'heterosexual matrix' (1993: 127) which makes unintelligible and so suppresses desires and identities that do not fit into its categorizations.

Again, Butler's non-dialectical approach has reductionist implications, in that she posits unmediated links between sex/gender identity and sexuality. In a revealing formulation, she criticizes 'some queer theorists [who] have drawn an

Judith Butler and the deconstruction of reality   33

analytical distinction between gender and sexuality, refusing a causal or structural link between them' (1990/1999: xiii). This is a remarkable sentence, for the very positing of a *link* between gender and sexuality indeed presupposes their distinguishability (cf. Jónasdóttir and Jones, 2009); otherwise, sexuality and gender would simply be the same thing and it would be meaningless to call them by different names.

Butler's deconstructionist mode of theorizing is often seen to represent a radical challenge to determinist and reductionist versions of feminist and other social theories. Yet, as I elaborate upon elsewhere (Gunnarsson, 2013b), Butler's tendency to collapse the categories of gender, sexuality and power into one another makes her approach remarkably similar to that of MacKinnon (1989), the feminist queen of reductionist thinking. Butler in fact acknowledges her affinities with MacKinnon, but only to immediately emphasize more central divergences: 'In [MacKinnon's] view, sexual hierarchy produces and consolidates gender. It is not heterosexual normativity that produces and consolidates gender, but the gender hierarchy that is said to underwrite heterosexual relations' (1990/1999: xii). This theoretical construct in which, in her interpretation, *gender causes gender* is a tautology, Butler argues. Instead, here too she shifts focus by interrogative means, asking '[t]o what extent does gender hierarchy serve a more or less compulsory heterosexuality, and how often are gender norms policed precisely in the service of shoring up heterosexual hegemony?' (1990/1999: xii).

Ironically, here Butler is indeed quite dependent on the analytical distinctions between gender and sexuality that she refutes; otherwise she would not be able to interrogatively suggest that gender acts in the service of heterosexual hegemony, since what is served must logically be something else than what serves it. But if we leave the question of distinctions aside for a while, it is noteworthy that Butler displays clear functionalist tendencies (cf. Fraser, 1998) insofar as she repeatedly states that the materialization of sexed identity occurs '*in the service of* the consolidation of the heterosexual imperative' (1993: 2, emphasis added). MacKinnon differs only inasmuch as, for her, the construction of gender occurs in the service of male power, assumed to be heterosexually structured.

Despite the fact that Butler sees the production of sexed identity and heteronormativity as aspects of the same process, as highlighted by the formulations quoted above, she attributes a more pivotal status to the heterosexual imperative than to sex/gender. Although they are mutually constitutive, the focus is on the ways that heteronormativity is both underpinned and served by the phantasm of sexed identities, rather than the reverse. It thus seems that the heterosexual imperative is what explains sex and gender, not vice versa. What, then, explains heteronormativity? And what explains the societal inclination to regulate sexuality in the first place? Is this inclination itself discursively produced or are there extra-discursive matters in some way accounting for it?

Following Foucault and Lacan, Butler resolutely dismisses any notion of pre-discursive sexual structures that could help explain why sexuality has come to be such a battleground. It does not make sense to picture sexual desire as suppressed – in Lacanian terminology – by the Law; it is the very prohibitions and

34 *Feminist modes of theorizing sexuality and gendered power*

exclusions that produce desire in the first place, she maintains. Both 'sanctioned heterosexuality and transgressive homosexuality … are indeed effects, temporally and ontologically later than the law itself, and the illusion of a sexuality before the law is itself the creation of the law' (1990/1999: 94). Yet, although rejecting the notion of a pre-discursive (heterosexual) *structure* to desire, Butler does implicitly presume that humans are fundamentally sexual, desiring beings. Hence, she does not succeed in living up to her rejection of 'foundationalism' (1995, 1997b, 1990/1999) but, to use Bhaskar's words, 'secretes an untheorized implicit ontology' of sexuality, so that it is 'denegated, i.e. expressed while being denied' (1997: 142). This reveals the impossibility of being fully 'anti-foundationalist', meaning that any theory claiming to be free from ontological premises will necessarily be caught up in a web of contradictions.

Although partly critical of his work, Butler's discussion of desire is largely informed by Lacan, who argues that desire is not biological but an effect of the human being's 'thrownness' into the symbolic order. However, although Lacan's emphasis is on the symbolic, he does acknowledge that there are pre-symbolic human needs. His central point is that desire cannot be *derived* from biological needs (Evans, 1996), which is a wholly different argument. The human being would not be the desirous being she is unless constituted, by nature, in such a way as to be unable to satisfy her needs by herself. This basic need for the Other is the root of the experience of lack, which constitutes desire and compels us to enter the symbolic realm that deprives us of our blissful unboundedness. We cannot understand why, in the first place, discourse gets a grip on people without some assumption of a biological constitution that precedes discourse (Sayer, 2011). Likewise, the fact that human sexuality is so malleable, though within certain confines, is itself a matter of human nature (Soper, 1995). Contrary to her intentions, Butler actually reinforces the nature/society dichotomy, in that she assumes, it seems, that any specified notion of the biological is *at odds* with a notion of radical sociality (see Chapter 4).

In the article 'Merely cultural' (1998), where Butler seeks to defend queer theory against charges of cultural reductionism, another side of her appears, though. Drawing on the classical Marxist- and socialist-feminist claims that 'the sphere of sexual reproduction [is] part of the material conditions of life, a proper and constitutive feature of the political economy' and that 'the sexual division of labour [cannot] be understood apart from the reproduction of gendered persons' (1998: 40), she insists that the discursive production of gendered, heterosexual persons must itself be understood as economic, hence material. Interestingly, the claims in this article are underpinned by blunt functionalist tendencies that make Nancy Fraser charge Butler with having resurrected 'one of the worst aspects of 1970s Marxism and socialist feminism: the over-totalized view of capitalist society as a monolithic "system" of interlocking structures of oppression that seamlessly reinforce one another' (1998: 147; cf. Boucher, 2008: 133). What I want to call attention to here, though, is the fact that Butler's invocation of classical Marxian theses depends on notions of extra-discursive structures that she elsewhere makes a strong point of rejecting.

The fundamental reason, after all, why the organization of sexuality is pivotal to the political economy is because the procreation of workers is a (hetero)sexual enterprise. Unless Butler acknowledges this, her recourse to Marxian claims is not credible. *If* she works with such a biological presumption, however, it begs the question of why she is not explicit about it and incorporates it in her theoretical framework. To me it seems plausible that the heterosexual imperative and the tendency of presuming a largely heterosexual organization of society have *something* to do with the natural fact that reproduction occurs heterosexually. If Butler acknowledged this, however, her whole theoretical framework would fall apart.

As remarked in the introductory chapter, Hennessy (2000) notes that there is a marked lack of agreement among theorists of sexual identities as to what sexuality *is*. It would hence be welcome if scholars of sexuality started thinking through the notion a bit more explicitly, before engaging in clever exercises about the infinite ways in which this enigmatic sexuality is imbricated in power regimes. As Jónasdóttir and Kathleen B. Jones state in their discussion of the kind of theory of sex and desire that Butler endorses:

> This theory stipulates discourse produces sex/desire but does not explain what constitutes sex/desire as a conceptually distinguishable element of social being. To account for sex/desire as such, we need both a set of ontological and epistemological assumptions and a specific theory with which to distinguish sex/desire from other aspects of social being.
>
> (2009: 29)

In Butler's work, sexuality is somehow everywhere and nowhere, thus continuing our civilization's peculiar theme of combining the suppression of sexuality with hyper-exposure. What *is* this sexuality? I wonder. Butler's account of sexuality is deeply non-substantial insofar as sexuality is defined and explained only in terms of its imbrication in power processes that do not themselves have sexual rationales. In my examination below of Butler's conceptualization of power, I elaborate on how this omission of any reference to natural necessity leads to irresolvable theoretical inconsistencies and lacunas.

Power: inevitable and unacceptable

It seems that a central purpose of Butler's theoretical project is to offer a radical challenge to the pervasive liberal paradigm that holds power to work only externally and constrainingly upon an essentially autonomous and self-directed subject. Following Foucault and Lacan, she emphasizes the productive character of power: the very subject that we assume to be constrained by power actually comes into being only by virtue of these 'constitutive constraints' (1993: 94), so that subjectivation is actually another name for subjection (1997b). Consequently, resistance cannot be formulated in terms of an opposition between oppressed and oppressor; resistance has no origin outside of that which it resists.

36 *Feminist modes of theorizing sexuality and gendered power*

I agree with Butler that power is productive, not only of subjects but of everything, if we think of power in the most general – and perhaps trivial – sense of the term. Still, on a less general level, it is not only possible but also crucial to discern different kinds of power structures and processes from each other. For instance, we can distinguish between the inevitable and enabling constraints implied in processes of subjectivation on one hand and the historically produced, institutionalized constraints based in the power of certain groups of people to shape other people's life conditions on the other (cf. Jónasdóttir and Jones, 2009).[3] In Butler's framework these different levels are collapsed into one another, leading to the paradox that whereas she conceives of the subject as *inevitably* produced by the regulating power of discourse, she nevertheless seems to see this as *politically* problematic. As Linda Martín Alcoff (2006) points out, this is an ambivalence permeating Butler's framework. Look at this passage, for instance:

> Called by an injurious name, I come into social being, and because I have a certain inevitable attachment to my existence,[4] I am led to embrace the terms that injure me because they constitute me socially.
>
> (1997b: 104)

We can emerge as subjects, as distinct persons with contours, only by means of the exclusion of some possibilities (cf. Carleheden, 1997: 63; Fracchia, 2005: 52). As relative, embodied beings we cannot exist and be absolutely free at the same time. Still, in Butler's account this most basic ontological fact is understood as *injurious*. I can perhaps agree with this idea in a very basic sense, but only so basic as to become trivial (cf. Lindberg, 2009: 184). In fact, although here Butler radically resists, and rightly so, liberal ideas of the subject as essentially untouched by its outside, she sides with liberalism in her more or less implicit depiction of constraints as normatively problematic. As Boucher highlights, in Butler's work 'the social norms that make sociality possible can only be conceptualised as a constraint upon the spontaneity of the self' (2008: 161). Despite her productive view of power, throughout her work she tends to view it as a threat to freedom rather than its condition. The general picture that emerges is one of a tragedy or, to borrow Terry Eagleton's description of the postmodernist condition, 'libertarian pessimism' (2003: 51), caused by the impossibility of being entirely self-made: 'The desire to persist in one's own being requires submitting to a world of others that is fundamentally not one's own' (Butler, 1997b: 28). Alcoff elegantly elaborates on this tendency in Butler's work, maintaining that it is premised upon 'a fear of the power of the Other' (2006: 81) and the notion that all identities are 'artificial and oppressive constraints on the natural indeterminacy of the self' (2006: 80). Sayer aptly captures the postmodernist oscillation between hopelessness and triviality, stating that 'in response to vaguely dystopic accounts of ubiquitous power and subjectification we may feel unsure whether to ask "is everything bad?" or "so what?"' (2006: 465).

This undercurrent in Butler's work is coupled with a peculiar tendency, inherited from Foucault, to depict power as *intentional*. If in Butler's account the human subject is if not dead then at least nothing's originator, there seems to be another

Judith Butler and the deconstruction of reality 37

diffusely defined subject behind everything: power itself. Butler refutes this reading of her work (1997b) but such a notion of power underpins many of her claims. For instance, when she describes how power produces agency, this is said to be '*unintended* by power' (1997b: 15, emphasis added). What does this mean? That power does not *want* subjects to be enabled but cannot help but do so? What, in that case, is this power, if not some kind of absolute spirit or god-like ultimate cause? As Toril Moi puts it, 'Butler makes "power" sound a little like the *élan vital*, or God, for that matter; power becomes a principle that works in mysterious ways behind the veil of appearances' (1999: 47). If Butler fiercely struggles against any notion of 'prior-ness' to materiality, sex and subjecthood, power and discourse appear to be before and behind everything else.

Fighting with power's own tools

Despite her seeming belief in an inevitable human destiny of subject(ivat)ion, Butler has offered a famous theory of how to dismantle the power of the heterosexual matrix. She reformulates the problem of resistance as one of *subversion*, assuming, it seems, that the more conventional concept of resistance draws too much on an idea of the resister as wholly external to the power she resists. Although we cannot become free from power, since we must subject ourselves to the symbolic order if we are to 'persist in [our] own being' (1997b: 28), Butler argues that we can engage in 'subversive resignification' (1990/1999: xxxi) by exploiting the internal gaps and inconsistencies in the regulating power of discourse. We cannot escape the exclusionary power of discourse, but in the possibility of combining discursive categories in new ways, by 'hyperbole, dissonance, internal confusion' and the like (1990/1999: 41-2), power can be deconstructed from within. Importantly, since we cannot step outside of oppressive discourses and undermine them from there, heterosexist categories like gender are not univocally oppressive:

> [T]hat 'gender' only exists in the service of heterosexism, does not entail that we ought never make use of such terms, as if such terms could only and always reconsolidate the oppressive regimes of power by which they are spawned. On the contrary, precisely because such terms have been produced and constrained within such regimes, they ought to be repeated in directions that reverse and displace their originating aims.
>
> (1993: 123)

Although she later downplays the political significance of drag (2004: 213-19), in *Gender* trouble it serves as Butler's primary example of how the imitation of that which is mistakenly held to be the 'original' gender identity can have a subversive potential, insofar as it 'reveals the distinctness of those aspects of gendered experience which are falsely naturalized as a unity through the regulatory fiction of heterosexual coherence' (1990/1999: 175).

Butler is indeed correct that, as Foucault put it, 'there is no single locus of great Refusal' outside of power (1978: 95), since we are always ourselves an intrinsic

38   *Feminist modes of theorizing sexuality and gendered power*

part of the society we resist. Yet, from a dialectical point of view, this does not necessarily imply that we cannot attribute any ontological stability and coherence to the subject, accounting for its distinguishability from society. In line with her general tendency, though, Butler refuses to make any such distinctions, and the collapsing of human agency that results from this refusal inevitably leads her into functionalism and determinism, despite her intentions to the contrary. For, as Boucher asks, '[o]nce we conceptualise the agent as a field of dispersed, multiple subject-positions, then who, or what, decides which position to adopt in a context?' (2008: 150; cf. Lindberg, 2009; Nussbaum, 1999). This crucial question, commonly raised by Butler's critics, still awaits its answer.

Similarly, Butler's unwillingness to invoke an ontological outside to discursive power and her failure to distinguish between agent, act and context preclude analyses of how the employment of certain significatory strategies, for example invoking the term gender, comes to be subversive or not. As Sayer highlights, the 'causal efficacy [of discourse] depends on how it relates to extra-discursive processes' (1997: 475). Hence, whether drawing on the concept 'gender' serves progressive or reactionary ends depends not on factors internal to discourse, but on the ways in which it hooks onto human realities and motivations that do not themselves operate discursively. Inasmuch as it is a central claim of Butler's that the discursive heterosexual matrix makes unintelligible that which does not fit its premises, so that, for instance, a homoerotic act is likely to be understood in heterosexual terms, it becomes even more difficult for her to make sense of what kind of act may possibly subvert this appropriatory power of discourse.

In her later work, she seeks to disarm this kind of criticism. In *Undoing gender* (2004) she raises the issue of how to single out resignifications that cause progressive change from those which only reproduce old dichotomies, by virtue of discourse's power to subsume the deviant under its own categorical matrix. She admits that '[t]he question remains … what departures from the norm constitute something other than an excuse or rationale for the continuing authority of the norm? What departures from the norm disrupt the regulatory process itself?' (2004: 53). Yet, although seemingly aware of the importance of this question, she does not offer any answer. In *Psychic life of power* she emphasizes that the context – understood as 'the effective historicity and spatiality of the sign' (1997b: 96) – conditions the effect that words and performances have (cf. 1997a). Yet, apart from the fact that this statement depends on an ontological distinction between performance and context which she rejects, she fails to specify how such conditioning operates.

Besides the fact that Butler cannot make theoretical sense of what it is that determines whether or not a subversive resignification will be intelligible as such, her argument also seems to depend on the unfounded premise that if it *is* received in a way that exposes the contingency and constructedness of sex, gender and identity, this will in itself have political effects. As Eve Kosofsky Sedgwick highlights, this assumption is rather naïve:

> What is the basis for assuming that it will surprise or disturb, never mind motivate, anyone to learn that a given social manifestation is artificial,

Judith Butler and the deconstruction of reality 39

self-contradictory, imitative, phantasmic, or even violent? ... [W]e must admit that the efficacy and directionality of such acts reside somewhere else than in their relation to knowledge per se.

(2003: 141)

The slave-owner, for instance, would hardly let go of his slave simply because someone reveals that his owning of the slave rests on phantasmic beliefs about racial hierarchies.

Also, no matter how subversive it might be to confuse the gender binary through parodic or hyperbolic performances, there are contextual constraints to the possibility of carrying out such performances in the first place. As R.W. Connell and James Messerschmidt point out, '[t]he costs of making certain [discursive] moves may be extremely high – as shown by the rate of suicide among people involved in transsexual moves' (2005: 842–3). This is because prevailing discourses are related to structural circumstances that cannot be reduced to a network of signs, and because there are certain basic human needs for recognition that tend to make people suffer if they do not fit at least roughly into hegemonic categories. However, Butler's theoretical categories do not allow for an acknowledgement of this.

Ad hoc realism

As already noted, Butler's rejection of any kind of 'foundationalism' also prevents her from making, in a logically consistent fashion, the normative claims upon which her project of subversion depends. In implicit response to critique which highlights that her framework seems to entail that all norms are undesirable, even the norms of equal human worth on which her work tacitly depends, Butler argues that this is not her standpoint:

We may argue theoretically about whether social categories, imposed from elsewhere, are always 'violations' in the sense that they are, at first and by necessity, unchosen. But that does not mean that we have lost the capacity to distinction between *enabling violations* and *disenabling ones*.

(2004: 213–14, emphasis added)

By what criteria, then, do 'we' make such distinctions? In drastic defiance of her anti-foundationalism, Butler asserts that norms are desirable if they 'sustain viable life' and undesirable if they do not (2004: 225). The norms needed to answer the question of what kind of resignifications and innovations should be pursued, she states, 'cannot themselves be derived from resignification. ... One must make substantive decisions about what will be a less violent future, what will be a more inclusive population' (2004: 224–5). It seems, then, that here Butler comes out of the closet as a full-blown realist, attributing to the extra-discursive a distinct and decisive ontological status denied by her overall framework. This is a welcome move indeed. Yet, this is a kind of *ad hoc* realism necessary in order

40 *Feminist modes of theorizing sexuality and gendered power*

to make sustainable political claims, but violently cut off from the rest of her theoretical discourse. As with her concept of biology and materiality, Butler occasionally makes recourse to ontological claims in order to stay coherent, but these isolated realist islands in her work are not allowed to inform a revision of her theoretical claims about sex/gender, sexuality and power, which rest a wholly discursive-internal matter. What constitutes a 'viable life' indeed cannot be decided without resorting to some idea of a human nature that makes us flourish under certain conditions and suffer under other (Sayer, 2011) and this human nature is partly constituted by sexual needs and capacities.

As for empirical and political relevance, the most central problem with Butler's account of gendered power is that she does not deal theoretically with men's systematic power over women, which cuts across sexual orientation and gender normativity. On a theoretical level, the feminist struggle is defined by Butler not as women's struggle against men, but as everyone's revelation of the performative character of sexed identities. Butler and the queer theory of which she is a central originator have done an important job in highlighting the violating character of the norms and conventions that tend to seem so natural. Although I would contend that other theoretical frameworks can underlabour this kind of theoretical-political project more consistently, it remains a fact that queer theory has shifted focus away from the somewhat one-sided focus of structuralist feminists on men's role as dominators of women. Ironically, the queer theoretical focus on the constraints that gendered orders of intelligibility impose on human life share interesting similarities with traditional sex role theory; it is only that the latter is more theoretically consistent in that it posits a subject *confronted* by gender norms. Sex role theory has rightly been criticized by feminist theorists for failing to acknowledge the power relations *between* women and men, though (Connell, 1987), and queer theory is vulnerable to the same critique.

It would be wrong to say that Butler does not acknowledge the importance of struggles on other levels; in her later work she declares her commitment to women's collective struggle (e.g. 2004). Yet, her theoretical tools cannot make sense, in a coherent fashion, of women's struggle against men as something irreducible to, albeit imbricated in, the discursive-performative production of gender. It does seem logical that if the significatory order of gender is destabilized, men's power over women will be destabilized as well, since it is premised on sex and gender being meaningful terms. Yet, reality works linguistically only to a certain extent and Butler goes wrong in assuming that the causal processes involved in this kind of destabilization inhere exclusively in discourse. Discourse, having no meaning for humans *in itself*, is rather the mediator of forces rooted in the embodied reality of humans. These relations, making the distinct realities of women and men a material fact to which discourse is external, must be directly targeted, no matter how mediated – even constructed – by discourse they are.

Conclusion

Much like her work is structured by an impulse to see any kind of constraint as a political ill, Butler seems to want be nowhere and everywhere as a theorist.

Rather than revising, in the face of cogent critique, her radical claims about sex, gender and subjects as discursive-performative effects, she refutes the critique by means of logical somersaults that relieve her from the burden of drawing out the consequences of her own claims. Perhaps in celebration of postmodernist indeterminacy, she seems to feel entitled to the freedom of being both explicit irrealist and pragmatical realist, warding off critique in a move that can only be labelled as scientifically dishonest. Although she is always ready to present reasonable realist arguments when put under pressure, these remain insulated from the rest of her framework, leaving her work fragmented and inconsistent.

Another problem with Butler's discursive strategy is its mode of obscuring important distinctions by a conflationary sliding between positions that are in fact different. This is perhaps most evident in her drifting between a mere critique of the liberal hyper-autonomous subject on one hand and, on the other, a fictionalizing of the subject as such. Failing to offer a way of retaining the notion of the subject as relatively autonomous and causally efficacious – as real – *while* acknowledging its essential relationality and dynamicness, she in fact reproduces static and atomist notions of the real (see Chapter 5 for an elaboration of this theme).

Butler's project is marked by a laudable aspiration to challenge distinctions and forge links between things commonly seen as separate. Yet, through lack of dialectical tools that allow her to retain distinctions between intrinsically related terms, this focus on co-constitution ends up in reductionism. Her claim that the gendered subject cannot be separated from the processes that subordinate it while constituting it makes it impossible for Butler to construct a notion of subversion that is theoretically coherent and normatively grounded.

This reductionist move is at work also in Butler's tendency to conceive of sex, gender, sexuality and power only in terms of discursive meaning. Butler does concede that there is something like biology and material forces, but this standpoint remains at the level of professing. Failing to recognize any structure and directionality inherent in biology and matter, it is in the discursive that she invests all analytical interest and locates all political significance. Not only does her framework preclude an acknowledgment of the constraints and possibilities that biological sexual difference poses no matter how it is made intelligible; also, it rules out a deeper understanding of sexuality as such. Butler does not manage to explain why sexuality is such a crucial site of a power struggle in the first place, since she offers no sense of what kind of human necessities are organized through the relations and practices we call 'sexuality'. This in turn leads to a univocally negative approach to constraint of any kind, such that it is impossible to single out oppressive and challengeable constraints on human freedom from those fundamental existential constraints that stem from our human condition as sexually needy.

Notes

1 Butler (2004) concedes that in *Gender trouble* she wrongly slipped between sexual difference as understood in the psychoanalytic tradition and the sociological concept of gender as a norm.

42 *Feminist modes of theorizing sexuality and gendered power*

2 Although Butler repeatedly invokes the word 'fiction' to describe the status of sex and gender (e.g. 1990/1999: 44, 1993: 6; see also Chapter 5), she does so only ambiguously, since the notion of fiction rests on realist views of reality and truth of which she is sceptical. In her suggestive manner she asks whether 'these very oppositions [between fiction and reality] need to be rethought such that if "sex" is a fiction, it is one in whose necessities we live, without which life itself would be unthinkable?' (1993: 6). This question points to an interesting complexification – and perhaps dialecticization – of the relation between the real and the fictive, which, as we shall see in Part III of the book, in fact resonates with Bhaskar's notions of demi-reality and ontological falsity as developed in his philosophy of metaReality and dialectical critical realism. Yet, Butler does not answer her suggestive question and, despite her invocation of an idea of fictive necessity, her invariable focus on how sex and gender are produced and her continuous oversight of the ways that they in turn produce outcomes, makes sex and gender appear much less real than, for example, discourse and power.

3 Bhaskar distinguishes between constraint[1], the basic existential constraints on human existence emerging from the fact that we are embodied, and constraint[2], which is limits caused by historically produced and unnecessary oppressive relations (cf. power[1] and power[2]) (1993/2008b:149).

4 It is interesting to note that here Butler postulates a pre-discursively existing attachment to one's own identity (Boucher, 2008).

3 Anna Jónasdóttir and the organic roots of power

> Probably the most significant type of event in the history of any science is that in which it comes to define – or rather redefine – its object of inquiry. … Typically this process will necessitate some scientists breaking free, perhaps under the stimulus of 'crisis', of the 'tissue of tenacious truisms' currently congealed in their field. Creatively exploiting the cognitive and technical legacy, they may succeed in identifying a hitherto unknown kind of generative mechanism, so for the first time elucidating a pattern of determination already efficacious in the world.
>
> Roy Bhaskar (1986/2009: 104–5)

In 1991, when poststructuralism was peaking in feminist theory, the Sweden-based political theorist Anna G. Jónasdóttir completed her seminal work *Love power and political interests* (subsequently published as *Why women are oppressed* (1994)), in which she lays out a theory of contemporary western patriarchy based on an innovative combination of the theoretical material so resolutely rejected by poststructuralists: historical materialism and radical feminism. Although developing her theory mainly in dialogue with earlier socialist feminist attempts to theorize patriarchy, 'through a method of exclusion' (1991/1994: 5) Jónasdóttir ends up identifying sexuality as the material base of patriarchy and produces what Kathleen B. Jones calls a 'much-needed radical feminist perspective with a socialist feminist twist' (1994: xiii).

Jónasdóttir develops her conceptualization of patriarchy in explicit parallel with Marx's analysis of capitalism, identifying sexuality as a field comparable to but distinct from labour. She argues that, in contemporary western societies characterized by formal-legal gender equality and women's relative economic independence from men, male power is largely constituted by men's exploitation of women's (socio)sexual powers, where this process is seen as qualitatively different from but comparable to the exploitation of labour underpinning the capitalist system. Jónasdóttir takes seriously the challenge of approaching sexuality in materialist terms, by grounding her framework in an ontology of specific sociosexual needs, powers and practices the organization of which makes up the fundamental material base of men's power, as men. As we shall see, Jónasdóttir's materialist sociosexual ontology differs from common ways of approaching sexuality. Perhaps most significantly, her notion of sexuality – or *socio*sexuality,

44   *Feminist modes of theorizing sexuality and gendered power*

as she prefers to call it – is radically decompartmentalized in that it is conceived of as a *current* in the totality of social life and involves both erotic ecstasy and loving care.

The question guiding Jónasdóttir's theoretical investigation is:

> Why, or how, do men's social and political power positions with respect to women persist even in contemporary Western societies, where women and men are seen as formally/legally equal individuals, where almost all adult women are fully or partly employed, where there is a high proportion of well-educated women, and where welfare state arrangements, which obviously benefit women, are relatively well developed?
>
> (1991/1994: 1)

I think Jónasdóttir exaggerates somewhat the extent of women's economic independence from men, since for a large number of women also in the western world their sexual bonds with men are still very much regulated by economic constraints. Yet, the fact that an increasing amount of women do enjoy a hitherto non-existent kind of formal and economic independence indeed serves as grounds for analytically isolating the specifically sexual mechanisms subordinating women to men. There is a general societal *tendency* of decoupling the sexual from the economic bond (Giddens, 1992) and it is to this extent that Jónasdóttir's question is valid.

While sticking to the historical-materialist tradition – 'seen as a realist *research tradition*' (2009: 59) – which rules out explanations in terms of culture or discourse, Jónasdóttir argues that men's power as men cannot be explained primarily in economic, in the sense of work-related, terms. Instead, her central feminist thesis is that, on its most *basic* gender-specific level, the material base of contemporary western patriarchy is constituted by *men's exploitation of women's love power*. 'Love power' is the concept she constructs, in parallel to 'labour power', to designate the distinct productive power, comprised by the dialectically related elements of care and erotic ecstasy, that humans have as sexual beings. '[M]en', she states, 'tend to exploit women's capacities for love and transform these into individual and collective modes of power over which women lose control' (2011: 49).

As will become clear, the specific sociosexual ontology that Jónasdóttir develops is immediately linked to her view of power. In her framework, it is because sexuality encompasses a power in the elemental, creative sense of the term – 'a world-creating capacity', with Gregor McLennan (Jónasdóttir, 2009: 65) – that it is possible for it to become constitutive of oppressive power structures. It is the fact that love is a necessary 'good' that incites struggle and control over its realization and use. This distinctively historical-materialist or realist view of power differs radically from Butler's approach and, I shall argue, makes it possible to account in a more consistent manner not only for the perseverance *and* instability of gendered power, but also for why we should see the current gender order as a problem in the first place.

Sex/gender: a generative process

Jónasdóttir clearly departs from the discursive approach to gender categories. Acknowledging the natural basis of sex/gender categories, she states that '[w]omen and men are the two substantial sections humanity is built of' and that, *as sexes*, they are 'the generative source of the species'. At the same time, in line with the Marxist non-dualist approach to nature and society, she also emphasizes that the sexes 'are social by nature' (1991/1994: 41). Hence, the notion that women and men are natural kinds on which any society depends does not imply they are static, ahistorical entities: women and men are what they are only by virtue of the relations and processes through which they are produced, and these relations and processes are both natural and historically specific. Anchoring her account in Marx's realist view, which takes as its point of departure 'the *real individuals, their activity* and the *material conditions under which they live*' (Marx and Engels, cited in Jónasdóttir, 2009: 69), Jónasdóttir clarifies:

> To propose that women and men are the main parties in a feminist analysis of society does not mean – and this is extremely important – that I conceive of them simply as biological entities, and even less as universal, static categories. I view women and men in a historical, materialist and *realist* way. Women and men as 'enminded bodies' are always formed/form themselves under certain historical, sociosexual circumstances. The sociosexual circumstances, in turn, influence, and are influenced by, other social circumstances, such as those prevailing in the economy and state.
>
> (1991/1994: 219–20)

Although Jónasdóttir eschews distinctions between the biological and the social and, hence, sex and gender, due to her focus on the concrete, practical level at which they are inseparable, in relation to the Butlerian paradigm it is important to highlight that her framework rests on a notion of a biological level that constrains what we can do as social beings. First, as already pointed out, the very sexual division has a biological basis, which is causally efficacious no matter how we conceptualize it or technologically mediate it. Second, although inherently social, the basic material 'stuff' that Jónasdóttir sees as constitutive of our sociosexual or gendered existence is based in needs and powers stemming from our biological constitution.

In a short article published in Swedish, Jónasdóttir takes issue with the pervasive tendency in contemporary feminist theory to see categorizations as such as the basic problem of gender. She highlights that while the dominant way of thinking of gender is 'in terms of a logical-classificatory division, the parts being discrete from each other and blurred boundaries and mixed categories impossible', gender can also be thought of as 'an organic – including social – process ... where the parts are involved with each other through certain activities and flows of power' (1998: 9; cf. 1991/1994: 251, note 18).[1] While a focus on meaning and language tends to entail a preoccupation with what Jónasdóttir

46 *Feminist modes of theorizing sexuality and gendered power*

calls 'logical-classificatory divisions', her own materialist approach directs her attention to the processual relations through which we produce and reproduce, in historically shifting ways, ourselves as sexual beings and in the process society itself.

In my view, a crucial constituent of Jónasdóttir's approach is the positing of internal ontological links between gender *categories* on one hand and gendered *practices* and *relations* on the other. That these aspects cannot be disconnected accounts for the linguistic slippage operating in her work, where 'gender' refers both to categories and identities and to a specific kind of processes and activities. When she speaks of the 'sexes' or 'genders' the ultimate meaning is people *as sexual beings*, rather than discursively – and hence dualistically – constituted identity categories that have no connection to the substantial life processes of sexuality. She emphasizes that 'women and men are not two formally different aggregates of individuals who happen to be women and men' and opposes the view, articulated by Margrit Eichler, that the uneven power relations between women and men should be seen as 'social inequalities which *happen to coincide* with certain biological differences' (cited in Jónasdóttir, 1991/1994: 40–1, emphasis added by Jónasdóttir).

Although she does not spell this out, it is my estimation that this totalized or non-atomistic sex/gender ontology is one reason why Jónasdóttir does not want to let go of the term 'sex', although it is rarely used by feminists writing in English unless specifically biological aspects are addressed (throughout her work Jónasdóttir uses 'sex(es)' and 'gender(s)' interchangeably and she often writes 'sex/gender'). The term 'sex' is semantically superior to the extent that, more clearly than 'gender', it conveys the essential link between sexuality as structure, power, process and practice on one hand and sex as identity, category or property on the other.[2]

Despite her focus on practices and processes, sex/gender categories are pivotal for Jónasdóttir insofar as the sexual division is the basic organizing principle of these practices and processes, at least in the society that is the object of her analysis. Indeed, her theoretical project originated with the question of why *men* are more powerful than *women*. In contrast to the Butlerian deconstructionist paradigm, which relates to gender categories only negatively, Jónasdóttir attempts at constructing positive claims about what, on an abstract or basic level, it means to be a woman or a man in contemporary western patriarchy. Crucially, she emphasizes that her theory does not purport to explain and cover the totality of women's and men's lives (which would, indeed, be the totality of social life as such). Her theory is a 'basic theory of patriarchy', as distinguished from the kind of 'total theory' that she holds to be common among socialist feminists. 'The total theory', she writes, 'assumes that all main forms of contradictions and oppression in a society should be covered by one and the same theory, and – as it seems – at the same level of abstraction' (1991/1994: 35). By theoretically isolating 'the specific agents and activities of the sex/gender system', what she instead seeks to *single out* from the social totality is the relative composite totality of relationships that makes up our existence as sociosexual/sexed beings (1991/1994: 35–6). The specific

Anna Jónasdóttir and the organic roots of power   47

agents of this system, thus, are not women and men in their concrete totality, but women and men *qua* women and men (a theme I expand on in Chapter 5). This is similar to how a basic theory of class is concerned with the capacities and activities of workers and capitalists *as* workers and capitalists and nothing else. Sometimes Jónasdóttir marks this abstracted character of her gender categories by writing 'Woman' and 'Man' (e.g. 1991/1994: 224).

Although, as we shall see, Jónasdóttir makes claims about what men and women do and undergo as men and women, notably that men exploit women's love, these claims must, hence, be interpreted not in actualist terms but as a structural *tendency*. She states that:

> just as not all economic activity and work relationships in societies where capitalist market economies dominate … are necessarily capitalist and exploitative by definition (for example, cooperative firms do exist), so not all sexual activity and love relationships in otherwise patriarchal societies are necessarily exploitative. In both cases – the fields of economy and sexuality respectively – non-exploitative modes of production do exist, although on difficult conditions and as marginal phenomena.

> (2011: 53)

This means that it is possible, even within the confines of patriarchy, for an individual woman to sociosexually exploit an individual man, although structural conditions work against the materialization of such relations. Jónasdóttir also stresses that, while she sees women and men as the main parties in the sociosexual power structure, this does not mean she equates sociosexuality with heterosexuality or takes the heterosexual organization of society for granted. For her, in a 'substantive empirically oriented theory', the patriarchal organization of heterosexuality must be the pivotal axis, since it is the dominant form of sexual organization and as such 'functions oppressively both internally and with respect to people who engage in other forms of sexual encounters' (1991/1994: 219). Also, as already indicated and as I elaborate upon below, her concept of sociosexuality is not confined to 'straightforward' or 'pure' sexual acts. It refers to the 'interactive practices relating people actually and *potentially* as sexes', implying that 'the way sexual love is practiced influences significantly both the way other love relations are practiced, for instance those between parents and children, and also the way people tend to practice person-to-person relations in other social contexts' (1991/1994: 221, emphasis added). Hence, the focus on the sexual woman–man relations does not mean that non-heterosexual practices are seen as insignificant, only that they are not perceived as constituting the ontological core of the exploitative structure of current sociosexuality (cf. p. 21, note 14 and p. 146, note 1).

Sexuality: a historical-materialist ontology

In Chapter 2 I pointed out that although Butler puts a lot of effort into showing how sexuality is imbricated in heterogendered power, she has little to say about

48 *Feminist modes of theorizing sexuality and gendered power*

sexuality as such. What is this sexuality, one wonders, more than a vehicle of gendered power? And what is it that makes sexuality so liable to being immersed in such power relations? This deficit is widespread within contemporary critical scholarship on sexuality, due to the antinaturalist imperative produced by post-structuralist hegemony, and to this extent Jónasdóttir's most significant and ground-breaking contribution is her elaboration of a basic (socio)sexual ontology.[3] Seeking to 'move (dialectically) through – and beyond – the opposites of self-sufficient radical feminism and a rigid, omnipotent Marxism' (2011: 48) via 'a realist radical-feminist reading [of] Marx's method', Jónasdóttir theorizes socio-sexuality as the specific set of '*practical*, human-sensuous' relations between people as sexual beings (2009: 65). Her theoretical points are developed on two main levels of abstraction, where the sociosexual capacity that Jónasdóttir calls 'love power' is seen 'both as a general human capacity and as socio-culturally varying and historically shifting lived reality' (2011: 53). The statement that men tend to exploit women's love power is an empirically informed thesis belonging to the latter level, but at the same time its viability is rooted in the identification of a basic, transhistorical sociosexual structure.

From the historical-materialist-realist point of view, in contrast to poststructur-alist assumptions, the idea that societies are historical products is not at odds with the notion that natural necessities serve as their foundation. Taking seriously the Marxist premise that 'meeting human needs is the baseline of history' (Hennessy, 2000: 210), Jónasdóttir's historical-materialist conception of sexuality is tied up with her identification of a certain species of primary human needs, intrinsically connected to 'certain *human dispositions or potential capacities ... to act practically* to satisfy these needs' (2009: 70). Whereas historical-materialist analyses have traditionally been restricted to the economic production based on our need and capacity to produce our means of existence, that is, to work, '[w]hat is continually overlooked', Jónasdóttir notes, 'is the specific natural (socioculturally shaped, of course) compelling needs and power of sex-gender itself' (1991/1994: 101).

Most other feminists inspired by Marx have tended be loyal to the traditional Marxist notion that historically significant material transformation or production is a wholly work-related matter. Drawing on Marx's at times inclusive concept of labour, socialist feminists have theorized not only care but even sexuality in terms of work, as a means of analysing gender-specific interactions in terms of production and exploitation (e.g. Ferguson, 1989, 1991), thereby upgrading the political significance of the personal sphere while sticking to materialist principles. Jónasdóttir takes a different route, arguing that our activities as sexual/gendered beings should not be seen as a subspecies of labour, but as a distinct kind of productive practice.[4] She sticks to the historical-materialist paradigm of *production*, in which historical change is understood as a matter of the specific ways in which we collectively produce society in the course of using our human capacities and meeting our needs, thus breaking with the tenacious notion that sexuality is only *re*productive. This is a crucial element in her framework, since the widespread strategy of analysing sexuality only in terms of *re*production conveys that we do not produce anything qualitatively distinct and necessary in and of itself as sexual

Anna Jónasdóttir and the organic roots of power 49

beings, only as labourers.[5] In this paradigm, the production going on in the intimate sphere tends to be understood either as a mere procreational and biological matter, whose historical element is located outside of sexuality: in the capitalist demand for workers and consumers; or in asexual terms, so that emphasis is put on the productive character of unpaid household *work*. Jónasdóttir ground-breakingly transcends these unfortunate dichotomies, by conceiving of sexuality as rooted in natural human needs and capacities, while stressing that the mode of meeting these needs and realizing these capacities are historically contingent.

Love power and the production of human life

What, then, are the sex/gender-specific needs of humans and what do we produce when acting practically to meet these needs? I would argue that Jónasdóttir's historization of sexuality is premised on the unusually inclusive or broad notion of sexuality that she espouses. While as labouring beings we produce our means of life, she states, as sexual beings we produce human life itself.

> What, then, do I mean by the 'production of life'? Much more than bearing, nourishing, and raising children, even though these activities are extremely important in this context. Women and men, in their total intercourse in pairs and groups, also create each other. And the needs and capacities that generate this creative process have our bodies-and-minds as their intertwined living sources. These needs and capacities must be satisfied and developed for the human species to survive, and for us individuals to lead a good and dignified life. Our bodies and souls are both means of production and producers in this life process, and herein lies the core of the power struggle between the sexes.
>
> (1991/1994: 23)

In Jónasdóttir's conception, then, the power of human beings to 'make – and remake – "their" kind', our 'love power', is not only a matter of making children, but also of the continuous creative process going on all the time between people, empowering us as 'active, emotional, and reasoning people' (1991/1994: 18), as 'socio-sexual individuated and personified existences' (1991/1994: 221).

> Certain aspects of the total process of life and society have to do with the fact that we are sexual beings, driven by desire for and need of one another. These needs and desires enable us to empower each other as human beings, and to create others, as individuals and species.
>
> (1991/1994: 12)

In order to persist as biological creatures, food and shelter may be enough, at least for the adult person.[6] Yet, in order to develop into and stay *persons*, with worthiness and power to act in the social world, we need to be *loved*, Jónasdóttir states. We are dependent on one another not only because we need to cooperate in order to produce our means of subsistence; we are also existentially dependent on one another in a

50   *Feminist modes of theorizing sexuality and gendered power*

more immediate sense. Seen at its narrowest, the force that is generated by this socio-sexual neediness is manifested in 'erotic links between people and compelling erotic need for access to one another's body-and-mind' (Jónasdóttir, 1991/1994: 101).

While sexuality is traditionally conceived of in exclusive erotic-ecstatic terms, in Jónasdóttir's conception the generative power of sexuality is constituted also by an element of care. This explains why she chose to think of our capacities as sexual beings as 'love power': the notion of love embraces both the ecstatic and caring dimensions which together generate our power to produce personhood. Whereas the term love has more restricted connotations in common-sense use, analysing sociosexuality as a 'fundamental part or *current* in the social existence of individual persons' (1991/1994: 101), 'of the weaving together of society as a processual whole' (1991/1994: 12), Jónasdóttir's view of love transcends narrow notions of romantic, 'platonic' and parental love. It includes the broad continuum of practices and attitudes involved in the production of human life, ranging from an approving nod to intense erotic union.

The nature of love

Jónasdóttir develops the concept of love power in explicit parallel with labour power. Why, then, does she insist that what is exploited in sociosexuality is not a kind of labour? As we have seen, she distinguishes between sociosexual and economic production with respect to their different *products*: the means of human life as opposed to human life itself. When Marx singled out the specificity of human labour as distinct from the instinct-driven and thus ahistorical activity of other animals, he emphasized the consciousness of purpose characterizing human labour: 'what distinguishes the worst architect from the best of bees is this, that the architect raises his structure in imagination before he erects it in reality' (Marx, cited in Jónasdóttir, 2011: 54). Jónasdóttir notes, though, that the famous architect–bee paradigm cannot be used to capture what is distinctive of human sexual love as opposed to biologically determined sexuality. Indeed, the instrumentality of labour is *at odds* with love. 'If individuals practice love and trust in relation to other persons, primarily as a result-oriented activity, in order to create or shape the other person into some imagined "object"', Jónasdóttir states, 'these activities become something else; they become "impotent", as Marx put it' (2011: 54). She concludes:

> What should distinguish love as a typal concept is that its practitioner acts without aiming to shape the love object according to his or her own lights. On the contrary, it is essential that the object in receiving love win the capability of 'shaping' himself or herself and his or her goals.
>
> (1991/1994: 73)

However, as Ann Ferguson argues, when conceived of as an activity love might indeed be seen as something 'done as a means to an end, viz. to promote both the loved person's wellbeing, and also the relationship of loving and being loved, which is considered a good in itself (an end)' (email correspondence, 2012). I would

Anna Jónasdóttir and the organic roots of power 51

argue that Jónasdóttir's and Ferguson's different takes on the matter are both plausible, depending on to what level of reality we direct our attention. In my view, the specific nature of sociosexuality can better be singled out by reference to the fact that its 'object' is necessarily a subject.[7]

A way of elucidating the importance of the fact that the 'object' of love – both in terms of its recipient and its 'material' – has a subjective constitution is by drawing out the implications of Marx and Friedrich Engels's failure to acknowledge the 'enminded' (Jónasdóttir, 1991/1994: 220) aspect of sexual production. Although Marx's later focus was on labour in capitalist production, Marx and Engels did operate with a more inclusive concept of productive labour, which embraced sexual activities. In the introduction to *The origin of the family* Engels states that the production of immediate life is comprised by both 'the production of the means of existence' and 'the production of human beings themselves' (cited in Jónasdóttir, 2009: 65). And Marx and Engels's statement that 'the division of labour … was originally nothing but the division of labour in the sexual act' (1845/2011: 167) is well known. In Marx and Engels' conception, however, it seems that the material worked upon in sexual production is entirely bodily and instinctual in kind, rather than the 'human matter' (Jónasdóttir, 2009: 78) that Jónasdóttir sees as comprised by 'our bodies-*and-minds*' (1991/1994: 23, emphasis added).

In my view, the fact that the 'object' drawn on in sociosexual production has a constitutive subjective component comprises the main ground for its specificity (and as we shall see particularly in Chapter 8, this has important implications for the understanding of the exploitative process of sociosexuality). While Jónasdóttir does not elaborate on the importance of the partly subjective or 'enminded' constitution of love's productive power, she does point out further characteristics of love which stem from this fact. Most centrally, unlike labour, love cannot be forced from someone. While the bodily aspects of sociosexuality can be commanded, the ultimate source of the empowering effects of sexuality is 'loving care showed to the desiring individual as a particular person' (2011: 56), and this has to be offered spontaneously and voluntarily. Hence:

> [w]hat above all characterizes sexual goods/values 'proper'[8] – in contrast to economic ones – is that they cannot be bought, and still less extracted by force, without severe loss of effect or productivity. … [T]he essence of sexual goods is that they need to be *given* voluntarily, or rather that they are made available for use – without conditions. Hence their extreme vulnerability.
>
> (1991/1994: 107)

It should be noted that many activities qualifying as work in capitalist societies also have 'human matter' as their material, ranging from teaching and care work to sex work. Jónasdóttir emphasizes that the distinction between love and labour does not rule out the fact that '[w]ork can be loving and love laborious' (1991/1994: 73). Again, she sees love – as well as labour – as an *element* of material production as a whole, such that loving and labouring processes do not appear in pure form at

52 *Feminist modes of theorizing sexuality and gendered power*

the level of concrete practice. What qualifies as work within the parameters of capitalism may thus have a significant sociosexual component, however alienated. Jónasdóttir in fact notes that:

> [t]he competitive conditions under which capital itself lives today are such that it cannot really sustain itself by consuming ordinary (or even the most qualified) *labour power*. Capital seems to need *love power* too. ... As the production of value increasingly depends on people in social intercourse with other people, love will become more actualised as a factor of production *in* the economic work process, and not only as a precondition to be taken for granted and counted on (without counting the costs) within 'the family'.
>
> (2009: 77–8)

Hence, although the interaction between the economy and sexuality is not Jónasdóttir's primary object of analysis, she acknowledges the importance of this interplay and highlights that the struggle over love seems currently to be intensified partly due to factors internal to capitalism.

Power: structural compulsion and human neediness

In Butler's account 'power' takes on a reified form in that its living source is not explained. The consequence is that it seems that the gender structure somehow reproduces itself without the active – *and reasonable* – participation of people. As Sayer (2011) states, such approaches not only lack explanatory force but are also demeaning to the people they are about. This alienates lay people from academic practice and feeds 'the mutually-reinforcing poles of academic-élitism and anti-intellectualism' (Sayer, 1984/1992: 98). This has great relevance in the context of feminist accounts of heterosexual love, which too often fail to theoretically acknowledge and integrate the good reasons women have for loving men, even when it reproduces their subordination. In its tendency to reduce women's love of men to a matter of patriarchal ideology (Jónasdóttir, 2014), feminism has failed to make sense of women's lived reality, thereby, as hooks (2002) points out, alienating the majority of women from feminism.

Instead of understanding power only as an effect of discourse or ideology or in the radical feminist terms of dominance and violence, Jónasdóttir anchors her account of oppressive power in a notion of the basic, creative power we have as sexual beings. She aligns with the view of the agency/structure relation endorsed by Marx and later elaborated by critical and Marxist realists (see 1991/1994: 243–4, note 9). In this view, the reproduction of social structures has a pervasive regularity to it; yet, it is not understood as mechanically brought about but as an effect of the ways that, via natural necessity, structures materially constrain – while enabling – the possible ways that people can live their lives by meeting their needs and exercising their powers. Jónasdóttir states that she wants to go beyond the mere recognition of empirical regularities to an understanding of *what* it is about the gender relation that enables these patterns; in realist terms, what underlying generative or causal mechanisms explain them (1991/1994, 2011).

She analyses the power relation between people as sexes in terms of *exploitation*. This is as opposed to analysing the power relation in terms of 'oppression' or 'domination', which are hard to explain in other terms than some alleged will to dominate, which is itself left unexplained. Exploitation can be explained by reference to the basic needs, vulnerabilities, liabilities and capacities we have as human beings. Only the concept of 'exploitation', Jónasdóttir states, can make sense of the gendered power 'as a relationship of exchange ... where something substantial, something that *matters*, is taken and given, won and lost, used/ enjoyed' (2011: 52, emphasis added). And the reason why things matter – in the sense of being in a way a matter of life and death – is basically that we are needy beings (Sayer, 2011).

Although we are endowed with powers that enable us to meet our needs, we cannot do this in isolation but only by virtue of the productive life process generated in relation to other people's powers and needs. As I see it, it is this ultimate dependence on others that makes it interesting for people to control the ways that other people can exercise their powers, that is, to exploit them. Also, it is only with reference to this inexorable neediness that one can explain why people 'voluntarily' involve themselves in relations that subordinate them. As we shall see, in a context where men exercise a large amount of control over the possible ways that women can meet their needs for love, such that 'the power *of* love and the power *over* love are systematically divided' (Jónasdóttir, 1991/1994: 225), it is a rational choice for most women to submit to these conditions although this enables men to exploit them. Not having one's sociosexual needs met at all is no more empowering than having them met under exploitative conditions.

It is from this point of view that we can combine structural force with freedom of choice and make sense of Jónasdóttir's statement that women tend to be 'circumstantially *"forced"'* to *voluntarily* give their love to men, even 'if they dislike the conditions offered' (1991/1994: 224, emphasis added). Jónasdóttir states that the structural force inherent in patriarchal sociosexuality can be compared with the economic compulsion of capitalism.

> Even if wage-labor often is experienced as debasing and constraining, propertyless people continue to sell their labor power because realizable material alternatives do not exist. The laborer needs that which can be bought for his or her wage. ... Women continue to give/attach themselves to men because they need that which they get and are allowed to do in the intimate coupleship and in other relationships with men.
>
> (1991/1994: 45–6).

The structural injustice enabling capitalist exploitation is constituted by the fact that, although capitalists depend on the labour of workers, they control the means through which the latter can exercise their capacity for labour, thus enabling capitalists to control how and to what ends they use their labour power.

54 *Feminist modes of theorizing sexuality and gendered power*

Jónasdóttir argues that patriarchal sociosexuality has a similar structure. When 'Woman' meets 'Man', she states,

> she comes to this meeting and is, so to speak, the owner of her capacity to love, which she can give of her free will. No law or other formal rules can force her into a relationship with 'man'. And still there are forces in these circumstances. 'Woman' needs to love and to be loved in order to be socio-sexually empowered, in order to be a person. But she is without effective control over how or in what forms she can legitimately use her capacity; she lacks the authority to determine the conditions of love in society and what its products should be like.
>
> (1991/1994: 224)

Male authority and female sociosexual poverty

How, then, does Jónasdóttir make more exact sense of the forces at work in these interactions? Given that men need women's love too, what kinds of constraints and powers inherent in the sociosexual structure make women's neediness more actualized than men's?

As a parallel to capital, she coins the term *male authority* to articulate the specific structural property or generative mechanism emergent from men's collective exploitation and accumulation of women's alienated love.[9] Since 'men can continually appropriate significantly more of women's life force and capacity than they give back to women', she states, they 'can build themselves up as powerful social beings and continue to dominate women through their constant accumulation of the existential forces taken and received from women' (1991/1994: 26). Men's accumulation of women's sociosexual capacities creates a 'surplus worthiness' endowed in all men regardless of the specific strengths they have as individuals. Crucially, the nature of this male authority is that it conceals its very maleness; it 'has the appearance of being not male but generally human and generated from individually achieved merits exclusively' (1991/1994: 227). In a historical context where being loved is very much dependent on our alleged individual qualities, this personal appearance of male authority means that men are likely to meet more esteem – more love – only by being men.

This is but one expression of the fact that all meetings between women and men – from straightforwardly sexual encounters to interactions in work, politics etc. – are structured by a constellation of forces that structure women and men's socio-sexual vulnerabilities and possibilities in a way that enables and encourages further exploitation. While the privileged access to worthy personhood that men enjoy by virtue of male authority 'de-actualizes', as I would put it, their need for particular women, the situation is quite the opposite for women. For most women, Jónasdóttir asserts, the consequence of the exploitative sociosexual process is 'a continuous struggle on the boundaries of "poverty" in terms of their possibilities to operate in society as self-assured and self-evidently worthy people exerting their capacities effectively and legitimately' (1991/1994: 225).[10] Thus, from the perspective of women the accumulated product of men's exploitation of women's sociosexual forces is a 'relative powerlessness' (1991/1994: 227), constituted by their structurally brought about weakened capacity as persons, as worthy agents effectively affecting the world. Importantly, for Jónasdóttir this is not a matter primarily of the psychological make-up of individual women acquired through socialization. Women's powerlessness is material-structural in the sense that every situation in which a woman finds herself is constituted by a web of constraints – which are the accumulated product of a long history of particular ways of practising our basic sociosexual capacities so as to jointly fulfil our basic sociosexual needs – that tend to drain her of her sociosexual-existential power. These conditions 'leave women unable to build up emotional reserves and authoritative social forces that can be used freely and "invested" for women's self-defined interests and for the good of all – as defined by women' (1991/1994: 100) and make women's dependence on men more actualized than men's dependence on women.

Jónasdóttir argues that '[a]lready when coming to the meeting [with "Woman"], "Man" is entitled and authorized to make use of his entire range of existing and potential capacities as a person', but this is not the case for 'Woman'. When the sexes meet, she continues,

> [t]hose who meet are, in short, women as sexual beings and men as personal authorities. This means that men, in a different way than women, can act independently in particular sociosexual meetings. Men are not, in the way that women are, circumstantially 'forced' to award their sexual capacity to the other sex, if they dislike the conditions offered. Men can stand off temporarily; they are less dependent on a particular woman than women are on a particular man.
> (1991/1994: 224)[11]

It should be clear from this that men's power over women is not primarily a matter of discourses and norms, but grounded in a 'psycho-organic' – to borrow Sean Creaven's term (2000: 73) – compulsion. It should be noted, though, that this does not mean norms and ideology are insignificant. Just as the capitalist economy is legitimated by a bourgeois ideology and mediated by an elaborate system of meaning prescribing rules of exchange, the value of money etc., so sociosexuality is underpinned by norms and frames of interpretation that legitimize 'men's claims to access to women' (2011: 49).

> [P]revailing social norms, accompanying us from birth and constantly in effect around and in us, say that men not only have the right to women's love, care, and devotion but also the right to vent their need for women and the freedom to take for themselves. Women, on the other hand, have the right to give freely of themselves but have a very limited legitimate freedom to take for themselves.
> (1991/1994: 26)

The efficaciousness of men's power thus lies very much in the *legitimacy* it acquires through the dominant norm system, legally sanctioned by the marriage

56 *Feminist modes of theorizing sexuality and gendered power*

institution.[12] Hence, the term 'male *authority*'. Yet, from a materialist point of view, what ultimately lends such force to these institutional forms is their rootedness in 'human matter', in psycho-organic powers and needs. Jónasdóttir stresses that:

> [t]he creation of surplus worthiness and the reproduction of male authority is far from merely a question of subjective ideas dwelling more or less intensely in the heads of individual people. It must also be understood as an objective ongoing process whether or not individuals are conscious or not of what is going on.
>
> (1991/1994: 227)

That male authority and female sociosexual poverty are not only based in false ideas about women and men is crucial. An implication is that women will not be able to challenge male authority simply by means of an awareness of its true basis, since there are forces operating through women's – and men's – bodies-and-minds despite such awareness. This means that feminist change can never be a matter only of seeing through the gender ideologies that obscure the reality of male power. Women may be fully aware of the inequality structuring their relationships with men, yet continue to 'comply' by lack of a material force that could support attempts to change the situation. This is important to note not only for strict scholarly reasons, but also inasmuch as it prevents us from moralizing about women's choices.

Ecstasy versus care

Jónasdóttir states that 'what is peculiar about sexual love – when defined dialectically as care and erotic ecstasy – is that it is (potentially) both self-interested and other-oriented simultaneously' (2011: 56). The generative force of love, as defined by her, is constituted by the internal relation between care and ecstasy, meaning that one cannot exist without the other. The fact that women and men, despite the potential win-win character of sexual love, 'are stuck in a structure of opposing interests' (1991/1994: 227) can thus be understood only in relation to the fact that sociosexuality's current institutionalization means that 'love's two elements – care and erotic – ecstasy – find themselves in continuous opposition' (1991/1994: 102). This dialectical contradiction (see Chapter 8) is such constituted that women tend to practice sociosexuality through care – at the expense of their ecstasy – while men tend to live their sociosexuality ecstatically, while failing in their caring capacity.

> Women are 'forced' to commit themselves to loving care – so that men can be able to live/experience ecstasy. But it is not legitimate for women to practice ecstasy on their own terms, that is, as self-directed and self-assured sexual beings, who, in doing so, need men's caring. Men's systemic position, on the other hand, presses them to limitless desire for ecstasy (as a means of self-assuredness and personal expansion), while the practice of loving care in their relations to women is generally experienced as burdens and constraints, as a spending of time and energy that must be 'economized'.
>
> (1991/1994: 102)

Women do indeed experience ecstasy, but, as I interpret it, Jónasdóttir's claim is that its realization is mostly conditioned on being validated by male desire. Even if a woman has a confidence in herself as a desiring subject as opposed to a mere object of male desire, 'the probability that she will be able to live/realize this confidence is rather small' (1991/1994: 103). Men, by contrast, have a 'specific, legitimate power ... to give full expression to their sexuality and need of care, and to expect/demand of women that they provide the means for satisfying them' (1991/1994: 107). Again, then, it is far from the case that male erotic self-assuredness is independent of women; it is only that this dependency is 'de-actualized' by men's structural control over women's care.

It needs stressing that the thesis that men tend to exploit women of their love is not a moral one. In Jónasdóttir's account men too are structurally constrained by the intrinsic connection between male personhood, as currently constituted, and socio-sexual exploitation: 'As the capitalist must exploit the laborer in order to remain a capitalist, men today are dependent on an exploitative "traffic in women" if they are to remain the kind of men that historical circumstances force them to be'. She clarifies, though, that '[i]n neither case does this structural force exclude the possibility for other kinds of socioeconomic and sociosexual arrangements to exist as nondominating modes of economic and sex/gender production, respectively' (1991/1994: 225). Hence, again, the structural tendencies should be understood in the realist terms whereby any social system is always *open*, that is, in dialogue with other structures and mechanisms whose tendencies may work as counteracting forces.

Jónasdóttir does not specify, however, what kinds of conditions may work as a force potentially counteracting the male compulsion to exploit women's love. In Part III of the book I demonstrate that these conditions are inherent in socio-sexuality itself and highlight that this is obscured in Jónasdóttir's account since it embraces only one emergent level of current sociosexual reality, which, I shall argue, is in fact only half-real, or *demi-real* in Bhaskar's terms (2002a, 2002b, 2002c). The exploitative logic of this demi-real level of sociosexuality is premised on a more basic ontological stratum, whose structure is intrinsically at odds with exploitation. I shall argue that being empowered at the expense of others is therefore possible only if crucial dimensions of reality – on which we necessarily depend – are denied, entailing that male authority is inherently fragile and contradictory – and in a certain sense false or illusory.

Jónasdóttir's failure to highlight this complexity makes her side, to a certain degree, with Butler in her tendency to reduce men and women to their current social determination. While she posits that there are transhistorical properties to sexuality and human existence, she does not sufficiently draw out the implications of how these necessities constrain sociosexual exploitation in a way that creates disempowering contradictions for men too. Given, for instance, that at the basic level of sociosexuality there is an immutable dependency between care and ecstasy, how are men affected by the demi-real split between them? I do not agree with Jónasdóttir that men have a legitimate power to 'give full expression to their sexuality and need of care' and this is precisely because of the structural contradiction between care and ecstasy, which blocks the possibility, for both women and

58   *Feminist modes of theorizing sexuality and gendered power*

men, of realizing their *whole* sociosexual-existential being when practising love. In particular, while in the current sociosexual order men often have their needs for care met without having to ask for it, this very fact also constrains their possibilities of experiencing and expressing such needs. Thereby, they lose out on the experience of vulnerability which is crucial for full sociosexual realization (cf. Sichtermann, 1983/1986). This has important implications for how men's and women's sociosexual interests should be conceptualized, in that it opens up the notion that men have an emancipatory interest in ending exploitation.

The basic ontology of sociosexuality, which accounts for men's need for love, also has implications for the possibilities of women to bring about feminist change. Jónasdóttir does not elaborate on this, but the dynamic character of the historical-materialist approach lies precisely in the fact that, at the end of the day, if we take the example of capitalism, workers are in possession of powers without which the capitalist system would collapse. The same applies to patriarchal sociosexuality: the notion that 'Man' is less dependent on a particular woman than vice versa does not rule out the fact that 'in order to maintain this empowerment, he is dependent on having access to "Woman"'s particular creative powers' (Jónasdóttir, 1991/1994: 224), only that this access is generally secured by virtue of the asymmetrical structural features outlined above. The ultimate vulnerability of capital will be materialized if workers collectively withdraw their indispensible labour power. Similarly, as I elaborate on in Chapter 9, there is a possibility for women to organize their sociosexual powers in ways that counterweigh male authority, thereby actualizing men's underlying dependency on women so that women gain the power to co-determine the conditions of love.

Conclusion

By innovatively applying – and in the process reworking – Marxist categories to feminist concerns, Jónasdóttir has produced a ground-breaking feminist theory characterized by both internal consistency and external relevance and adequacy. It is resonant with empirical patterns that cut across class and ethnicity and, unlike Butler's theory, it provides the means of explaining both the perseverance of male power and the possibility of challenging it. The basis for this dual explanatory power is, most essentially, Jónasdóttir's anchoring of the historically contingent patriarchal structure in a basic sexual ontology, which gives us a sense of what the struggle between the sexes is all *about*. Without such a grounding in natural necessity we can explain neither from where social structures derive their force nor why any specific social order is worse than another. The fact that we have basic sociosexual needs explains why sociosexual exploitation is possible as well as appealing, but it also grounds our judgement that the current sociosexual deprivation of women is an ill that ought to be fought. The basic structure of sociosexual-human existence also serves as grounds for our estimations of what a non-patriarchal way of organizing sociosexuality could possibly look like. In contrast to Butler, who, against her intentions, tends to conceive of power and constraint in purely negative terms, Jónasdóttir's account allows for a distinction

Anna Jónasdóttir and the organic roots of power 59

between the exploitative constraints that are historically contingent and the existential constraints implied by our inescapable sociosexual neediness. This precludes utopian, in the sense of unrealizable, ideas of what a feminist future could look like (cf. Chapters 4 and 5).

Yet, I have argued that Jónasdóttir does not draw out the full implications of her elaboration of a basic sociosexual ontology, so that in some respects she tends towards reducing the sociosexual agents of women and men to their current social determination. This, I believe, reflects a more widespread ambivalence in Marxian scholarship between social reductionism on one hand and the acknowledgement of a natural stratum with its own irreducible structure on the other (Soper, 1979, 1995; Williams, 1978). Jónasdóttir sees the structure of sociosexuality as *'potentially'* (2011: 56, emphasis added) dissolving oppositions between self-interest and care for others, yet seems to conceive of this potential as on a par with the equal potential, currently actualized, for organizing sociosexuality as a win/lose relation. By contrast, in Part III I argue that this non-dualistic structure is not only a potential equal to that of antagonism but, unlike antagonism, *essentially constitutive* of sociosexual existence even in its exploitative form. This, I show, has crucial consequences for how we should conceive of the contradictions of exploitative sociosexuality and the conatus towards transformation to which they give rise.

Notes

1 My translation.
2 Sayer notes that necessities in reality are sometimes reflected in language (1992: 160). The dual meaning of sex is clearly an example of this, reflecting as it does the internal relation between sexual practices and sexed/sexual identity.
3 This is in line with Bhaskar's claim that scientific progress unfolds dialectically by virtue of the *absenting of absences* (1993/2008b).
4 Independently of Jónasdóttir, the feminist philosopher Ann Ferguson has developed a feminist theory of 'sex/affective work' or 'production' (1989, 1991), which has considerable similarities with Jónasdóttir's theory, despite the fact that, unlike Jónasdóttir, Ferguson sees the productive character of sexual-affective practices as a matter of their being a kind of work.
5 See Jónasdóttir's discussion about how feminist uses of the passage in Friedrich Engels's introduction to *The origin of the family*, where he specifies the twofold character of production and reproduction, 'suffer from chronic misinterpretation' (2009: 66).
6 As for children, René Spitz's (1946) famous studies of orphans showed that the long-standing absence of affection hinders not only children's emotional development but the physical too. There is now plenty of neuroscientific evidence that affection, including 'love, and the lack of it … shapes a baby's brain' (Lewis *et al.*, 2000/2001: 89).
7 Insofar as the nature worked upon in sociosexual production is not merely subjective and includes the human matter of the agent herself, there is also a sense in which Marx's concept of labour as a material transaction with nature controlled by the labourer is applicable to the concept of love too. I contend that in order to love efficaciously we need to exert a certain amount of control over our own sociosexual forces, since these may be conducive of non-loving practices if left undisciplined. Vice versa, there is a sense in which Marx's instrumental concept of labour overlooks the 'agency', inherent causality

60 *Feminist modes of theorizing sexuality and gendered power*

or independent conatus of non-human matter. The distinction between love and labour is thus not absolute, the reason being that the subject/object distinction is not absolute.

8 The term 'sexual goods/values "proper"' alludes to John Elster's idea of 'exploitation proper', which he sees as pertaining only to the unjust extraction of economic goods based on materially self-interested and voluntary transactions (Jónasdóttir, 1994: 104).

9 'If capital is accumulated alienated labor, male authority is accumulated alienated love' (1991/1994: 26).

10 Wendy Langford also uses the term 'poverty' to describe women's condition in 'the economy of love' (1994: 94).

11 Illouz (2012) similarly analyses the asymmetry between women and men as based in women's more urgent, structurally produced interests in creating a bond, while explaining it in terms different from Jónasdóttir's.

12 Jónasdóttir sees the role of marriage in sociosexuality as equivalent to that of private property in capitalism. She does not, however, restrict the meaning of marriage to its legal characteristics, but uses the term more broadly to depict 'a set of institutionalized norms concerning possessiveness in sexual goods and gendered persons. These norms operate in men–women relations throughout all of society, and not only between particular married couples' (1994: 228).

Part II

Meta-theoretical interlude: Challenging poststructuralist feminism

4 Feminist theory and nature

> Hegel was the first to state correctly the relation between freedom and necessity. To him, freedom is the appreciation of necessity. '*Necessity is blind only in so far as it is not understood*''. Freedom does not consist in the dream of independence of natural laws, but in the knowledge of these laws, and in the possibility this gives of systematically making them work towards definite ends.
>
> Friedrich Engels (1878/1939: 130)

In my assessment of Butler's and Jónasdóttir's works, nature emerged as a crucial theme, although I did not always use the term 'nature' but also invoked the notions of the 'transhistorical', of 'necessity' etc. to call attention to relations beyond historical intervention.[1] I argued that Butler's failure to theorize sexuality *as such*, an endeavour that is premised on notions about human nature, undermined the explanatory force and normative purchase of her framework. By contrast, I identified as one of the strongest features of Jónasdóttir's work its ground-breaking way of elucidating the nature of the needs and powers that humans have, naturally, as sexual beings. Although basic human needs and capacities may be organized and expressed in an immense variety of ways, I highlighted that the notion of a power structure rooted in sexuality does not make sense unless we have some conception of what sexuality is as apart from the power in which it is immersed. When we claim sexuality to be 'socially constructed', we should, as Sayer prompts, 'take the metaphor of construction seriously: attempts at construction are only successful if they take adequate account of the properties of the materials they use' (cited in New, 2005: 14). Hence, in order to reconstruct the structure of sexuality into a less oppressive one, we must be aware of what natural forces it depends upon, forces which, being natural, cannot themselves be dislocated. Also, such natural structures need to be acknowledged insofar as we cannot define what a non-oppressive structure of sexuality would look like unless we have a conception of what basic human needs are frustrated within the current one.

Feminist nature-phobia

It is not surprising, however, that feminist theory has a complicated relationship to nature. As Kate Soper highlights, '[t]he inaugural move of feminism … was

64 *Challenging poststructuralist feminism*

the challenge it delivered to the presumed "naturality" of male supremacy' (1995: 121) and ever since a crucial part of the feminist struggle has been to demonstrate that what is commonsensically seen as natural, and thus destined to be, is actually historically formed, hence open to change. When Gayle Rubin (1975) coined the concept of *sex/gender system*, it was an attempt to emphasize that the cultural sexual order (gender) is something else than biological sexuality (sex), where the former is in no way determined by the latter. Still, in the second wave feminist paradigm it was unusual to question that the basis of the historically evolved sexual order was to be found in the natural order, which prescribes that humans procreate sexually under conditions not of their own making. With the poststructuralist turn, however, assumptions that the social gender order is in any way linked to nature became something of a taboo. This seemed to involve an underlying presumption that the only way of avoiding biological determinism is to deny that the biological has *any* significance for social matters. Consequently, for a long time within feminist academia, the only way of safeguarding oneself against charges of biologism has been to align oneself with the paradigm of thought prescribing that nature, although it might be rhetorically acknowledged, has no influence on gender and sexuality whatsoever.

Not unexpectedly, the persistent nature-phobia of poststructuralist feminism has given rise to challenges. It is indeed justifiable to claim that a naturalistic turn is emerging within feminist theory. This naturalistic turn is part of what is commonly referred to as *new materialism(s)* (Coole and Frost, 2010; Grosz, 2011), *material feminism(s)* or *the material turn* (Alaimo and Hekman, 2008b), currents defining themselves as a much-needed answer to the failure of feminist theory to take matter and nature seriously. The authors of this naturalistic turn operate largely within a poststructuralist framework, with Gilles Deleuze as a major source of inspiration. Yet, following Deleuze's own intellectual legacy, it has also become something of a commonplace among the new feminist naturalists to draw on Nietzsche and vitalist thinkers like Henri Bergson. Perhaps most controversially, the Australian philosopher Elizabeth Grosz has lately sought to save the work of Charles Darwin from its sociobiologist interpreters and put it into the service of feminism. The dominant theme of this naturalistic turn is the insistence that, unlike what both positivists and social constructionists are held to assume, there is nothing fixed or static about nature. Nature is dynamic and historical and should, as such, be embraced rather than feared by feminists opting for change.

This chapter engages in the feminist debate about nature and its relation to the social from a Marxist-critical realist point of view. First, I address the naturephobic tendencies within feminist theory, disentangling the problematic premises underpinning them and demonstrating that these tend to affirm rather than challenge the idea of nature on which socio-biologistic arguments draw. Acknowledging that nature underpins the social, I argue, is not only compatible with theorizing social change but *necessary* for any tenable account of how social processes work. Second, focusing on the work of Grosz, I introduce the feminist naturalistic turn as a welcome effort to counter nature-phobic tendencies. Yet, I show that its poststructuralist inclinations, involving in particular a glorification of the indeterminate and unbounded, leads to a one-sided conceptualization of nature in which its constraining dimensions are overlooked. I seek to demonstrate that a theoretical acknowledgement of nature's limiting force is crucial for any coherent understanding of socially constructed, oppressive constraints. Finally, I point out that the commonplace feminist ambition to transcend the dualism between nature and culture is often underpinned by remarkably unclear notions of what such a transcendence might mean. Highlighting the difference between dualisms and distinctions, I show that the concept of emergence offers a solution to prevailing dilemmas.

Restoring the status of nature

Although it seems undisputable that human societies are rooted in organic and non-organic natural realities, the challenge of such claims by feminist theorists like Butler has had an enormous influence on feminist discourse. As already highlighted, in Butler's view the very appearance of sex *as* pre-discursive is in fact an effect of discourse (1990/1999), and this intellectual manoeuvre has acquired something of a hegemonic status within feminist theory. While Butler has sought to refute claims that she reduces biology to its enmeshment in discourse, her framework precludes an analysis of what effects biology might have on discourse and performative processes. Likewise, her appeal to 'materiality' (1993) is unconvincing to the extent that she insists on locating to discourse the force which structures, constitutes and governs the material.

It seems that denying biology any significance for social matters is aimed at putting a final nail in the coffin of biological determinism. Yet, the move actually depends on a deterministic notion of the biological. Seeking to avoid biological determinism by avoiding biology does not challenge the basic sociobiologist conviction that, if biology is admitted to be a basis of human functioning, then it must *determine* human behaviour. As Sayer points out, radical constructionism 'fails to challenge its enemy's mistaken belief that natural powers are deterministic rather than potentials and constraints' and thereby 'it can only defend a realm of social determination by excluding nature and positing a socially constructed realm in which biological constraints are either absent or inconsequential' (1997: 476). Toril Moi argues along similar lines:

> I get the impression that poststructuralists believe that if there *were* biological facts, then they would indeed give rise to social norms. In this way, they paradoxically share the fundamental belief of biological determinists. In the flight of such unpalatable company they go to the other extreme, placing biological facts under a kind of mental erasure.
>
> (1999: 42)

Wary of feminist theorists' 'flight from nature', Stacy Alaimo and Susan Hekman warn that 'the more feminist theories distance themselves from "nature", the more that very "nature" is implicitly or explicitly reconfirmed as the treacherous quicksand of misogyny' (2008a: 4). The radical constructionist stance may be

66 *Challenging poststructuralist feminism*

opposite to biological determinism on a superficial level, but it operates within the confines of the latter's categorical structures, only in inverted form. What characterizes both camps is reductionism, insofar as that which is really *both* biological and socially constructed is reduced to a matter of either biological or social determinations. It is only if we concede that there is a natural dimension to social existence, and seek to specify its conditioning role *while demonstrating that such conditioning is not the same as determinism*, that we have reached the core of the determinist argument and challenged the notion that if there is nature, nature overrides everything else.

The naturalistic turn emerging among feminist theorists during the last decade frames itself as a challenge to nature-phobic trends in feminist theory. Grosz, for instance, confronts 'the strong resistance on the part of feminists to any recourse to the question of nature' (2005: 13) and the way that '[w]ithin feminist scholarship and politics, nature has been regarded primarily as a kind of obstacle against which we need to struggle, as that which remains inert, given, unchanging, resistant to historical, social, and cultural transformations' (2005: 13; cf. Alaimo and Hekman, 2008a). The concern is primarily to challenge Cartesian notions of nature as a passive object that culture shapes, dynamizes and inscribes itself upon. Instead, the active force of nature as well as its essential indeterminacy and unpredictability are emphasized and explicitly or implicitly characterized as something feminists have reason to embrace. As a leading scholar within this current of thought, Grosz has recently made daring efforts to revitalize Darwin's work by combining it with readings of Deleuze, Nietzsche, Irigaray and Bergson. Since Grosz's work both offers one of the most elaborate new materialist theorizations of nature and is highly representative of the major philosophical tendencies of the naturalistic turn, it will be the focus of my assessment.

Directing her edge against social constructionism, similar to Sayer, Grosz highlights that if we are to make sense of the forces of social construction and inscription we need an account of 'what these bodies are such that inscription is possible, what it is in the *nature* of bodies, in biological evolution, that opens them up to cultural transcription, social immersion, and production' (2004: 2), and that 'without some reconfigured concept of the biological body, models of subject-inscription, production, or constitution lack material force' (2004: 4). This is a crucial insight of which most contemporary feminist theorists seem to have lost sight. For instance, the whole bulk of literature on the social construction – or performative production – of gender and sexuality depends upon the implicit notion that humans are, by their nature, desiring and needy and as such vulnerable to social influences. Yet, such assumptions are rarely made explicit or specified. Unfortunately, Grosz follows up this theme of how to make sense of the relation between bodily natures and social construction only in very general terms, where the prime concern is to challenge notions of nature as some kind of 'timeless, unchanging raw material, somehow dynamized and rendered historical only through the activities of the cultural and the psychical orders it generates' (2005: 45). Instead, she makes a case for a nature conceptualized not only as dynamic in and of itself, but also as unpredictable, constituted by nicks, cuts and ruptures. And to the extent, she argues, that feminism and other political movements are 'directed to bringing into existence futures that dislocate themselves from the dominant tendencies and forces of the present' (2004: 14), this quality of nature should be affirmed.

Another central theme in Grosz's work is her challenge to the notion of nature and biology as that which limits and constrains social being. Drawing on Darwin, she argues that '[b]iology does not limit social, political, and personal life: it not only makes them possible, it ensures that they endlessly transform themselves and thus stimulate biology into further self-transformation' (2004: 1). The two-way movement, in which the social is not only made possible by but also incites change in nature, is important; Grosz does not want to replace social reductionism with biological reductionism (2005). Her work, she argues, focuses on 'the space between the natural and the cultural, the space in which the biological blurs into and induces the cultural through its own self-variation, in which the biological leads into and is in turn opened up by the transformations the cultural enacts and requires' (2004: 1). Yet, she is clear about the primacy of nature, in the sense that it is the basis or ground of cultural life. And, importantly, the constraining force so often ascribed to nature tends in her account to be attributed to culture: while nature enables, the influence that culture exerts on nature is one that 'diminishes, selects, reduces ... the complexity and openness of the natural order' (2005: 48). Although there are no clear-cut boundaries between nature and culture in Grosz's theoretical account, there is thus no simple collapsing of the distinction such that one subsumes the other. The relation, for Grosz, is one of emergence: 'Nature is the ground, the condition or field in which culture erupts or emerges as a supervening quality not contained in nature but derived from it' (2005: 44). While theorists like Butler have sought to reveal the natural 'ground' of the social as itself a social construction, Grosz thus revitalizes the more common-sense notion that social phenomena should indeed be seen as ultimately based in organic and inorganic structures, relations and forces that pre-exist and transcend their cultural expressions. Yet, defining the relation between nature and culture in terms of emergence – a theme I will get back to below – this grounding status of nature in no way implies that it determines culture, since the latter takes its own unpredictable routes.

The glorification of indeterminacy

Radically challenging the taboo on nature dominating feminist theory, Grosz's work is a welcome and robust effort to counter the trends of cultural reductionism. Yet, I want to point at some of the problematic assumptions saturating Grosz's work, stemming very much from the fact that she, like most other new materialist thinkers, operates within the postmodernist tradition that she shares with her social constructionist adversaries.

A major problem is Grosz's emphasis on and glorification of *indeterminacy*. As mentioned, a major organizing thread in Grosz's work is her thesis that nature is not static, inert or predictable, coupled with an only rarely articulated assumption that it is this unpredictability and indeterminacy of nature that renders it a friend

68   *Challenging poststructuralist feminism*

of feminists and other radicals. Now, there are some crucial distinctions that Grosz fails to make. While first emphasizing the inherent *dynamism* of natural life, she quickly slides into highlighting nature's unpredictability, indeterminacy and defiance of 'precise causal analysis' (2005: 38). This conflation is analytically problematic since, first, change and dynamism can indeed follow determinations, even predictable ones: there is nothing about dynamism as such that is at odds with structuredness. Second, while change is indeed a central concern for feminists since they oppose status quo, it is far from self-evident that feminists would embrace change as such or that they would wish for unpredictable and indeterminate change. Contrary to Grosz's assumptions, I would say that the problem that nature is often seen to pose for feminists and other progressives is not that it does not undergo change, but that, if it changes, it does not necessarily do so in the direction we prefer. Put differently, it is hard to make sense of why change in itself should be glorified by social movements, for what these aspire for is *change of a certain emancipatory kind* and such aspirations fit badly with unpredictability and indeterminacy, since they require some amount of control. Moreover, a question that is raised is how Grosz's political glorification of indeterminate dynamism goes together with her insistence that indeterminate dynamism is the very heart of life. If life is inevitably constituted by the kind of innovative indeterminacy that she embraces as a political promise, what is the problem with things as they are? By universalizing and thus trivializing change and innovation (cf. Callinicos, 2006: 3), Grosz offers no way of distinguishing between the dynamism that is constitutive of life and the kind of change that would bring about a better world.

When she does apply her principle of indeterminacy to concrete matters, she salutes the fact that:

> [g]ayness (or straightness) is not produced from causes, whether physiological, genetic, neurological, or sociological; nor is it the consequence of a free choice among equally appealing given alternatives. It is the enactment of a freedom that can refuse to constrain sexuality and sexual partners to any given function, purpose, or activity.
>
> (2011: 73)

This is a good illustration of the fact that nature, including human nature, is not a neatly functioning machine but a complex vital process involving emergence and qualitative leaps, opening up 'a "fringe" of freedom, a zone of indetermination' that elevates all life 'above mere automated response to given stimuli' (Grosz, 2011: 69). This non-mechanical character of life is indeed a crucial ontological fundament of freedom in its most basic, 'cosmological' sense, the kind of non-confinement that lends life such beauty. Yet, pointing out the unruly character of sexual desire is not a solution to the problem of gendered and sexual oppression. *Human* freedom can hardly be a matter of being non-determined or 'uncaused', since it is only if we are enmeshed in determinate structures that we can exercise the control over ourselves and our world which any meaningful concept of freedom must involve.[2]

Feminist theory and nature   69

It is not that Grosz denies that qualitative change and unpredictable eruptions presuppose order. Firmly grounded as she is in Darwin's dialectic of evolution, she states that '[i]t is [the] relative stability and orderliness, predictability, that is the very foundation or condition for a life of invention and novelty' (2011: 30). Yet, when it comes to the normative underpinnings of her discourse, invention is always privileged, such that stability and predictability tend to be reduced to their role as foundation of novelty and change. Revelatory of Grosz's Nietzschean legacy, it is the unruly *as such* that is glorified here, while the politically more pertinent question of to what extent human beings can gain some *control* over their destinies is wholly left out. This is similar to the way that the theoretical logic of Butlerian poststructuralism entails an implicit celebration of transgression as such, although there is no reason to assume that all kinds of transgressions are liberatory and all kinds of stability oppressive.

The abstract and generalized privileging of indeterminacy and unruliness endorsed by Grosz and other new materialists makes them pay very little attention to the specificities of human freedom and political change. While the 'posthumanist' orientation of the new naturalist turn is promising inasmuch as it works against the dualistic juxtaposition of the human and the non-human (Barad, 2003; Hird and Roberts, 2011; Kirby and Wilson, 2011), it is unfortunate that it seems to imply a neglect of the specificities of *human* nature and what these mean for a feminist politics. Feminism, after all, is primarily a matter of the future of human beings, so a truly feminist concern with nature ought to focus not so much on nature as such but on how we might better understand the conditions for changing human life in light of its basis in nature.

If we accept that there is a human nature in the sense that humans 'are possessed of preordained features, and subject to their order of needs in the way that other creatures also are' (Soper, 1995: 27), then a crucial aspect of our freedom, which is an essential goal of feminist politics, is to have our needs met. And insofar as our needs are not particularly indeterminate but part of enduring natural structures, freedom involves *submitting* to forces that are both structured and beyond our control. As Andrew Collier argues, '[m]ore or less freedom … means more or less effective interaction in one's world – not disengagement from the causal processes operative in the "outside world"' (2003: 15). Such freedom, moreover, goes very well with stable social arrangements that predictably ensure that people's needs are met, while unpredictable ruptures of this pattern might prove destructive. In an explicit discussion of freedom, this passage by Grosz seems to endorse a similar view, stating that:

> the capacity to act and the effectivity of action is to a large extent structured by the ability to harness and utilize matter for one's own interests. Freedom is not a transcendent quality of subjects but is immanent in the relations that the living has with the material world.

> (2011: 68)

However, although here it seems that Grosz equals (human) freedom with effective action, she never reconciles this bypassing statement with her more insistent

70 Challenging poststructuralist feminism

endorsement of a Bergsonian concept of freedom that is linked 'not to choice but to innovation and invention' (2011: 72), nor with her conviction that it is that which disrupts – rather than harnesses – determination and causation that constitutes the promise of 'a future unlike the present' (2011: 73).

The theme of stability versus dynamism is closely connected to the dialectic between constraint and enablement and here I discern a second major problem in Grosz's account. As in the case of stability and dynamism, she seems to acknowledge that nature's constraining and enabling capacities are two sides of the same coin. Yet, when she characterizes nature's relation to the social realm, she repeatedly downplays its constraining role. There is an ambivalence in her work as to whether nature is limiting at all or just not *only* limiting. In one place she writes that '[n]atural selection does not *simply* limit life, cull it, remove its unsuccessful variations; it provokes life, inciting the living to transform them-selves' (2004: 64, emphasis added), indicating that she wants to complement the view that natural selection is a constraining force with an emphasis of its enabling role. More often, however, she delivers more closed statements, such as 'The natural does not limit the cultural; it provokes and incites the cultural' (2005: 51), thus altogether challenging the notion that nature has constraining effects on culture. In spite of this ambiguity, what is clear is that an implicit assumption is at work here: if the concept of nature is to be useful for feminist theorists, its association with limits and constraints must be omitted.

As a counterweight to perspectives that view nature and biology as only constraining, this is welcome. Yet, something important gets lost when nature's enabling dimension is overemphasized at the cost of its constraining role. It is quite obvious that nature, in both its organic and inorganic forms, is enabling for socie-ties, since without it societies would not exist. However, in a finite world enabling forces always also imply constraints, in the sense that not *anything* is possible. If we are to develop serious conceptions of in what feminist change might consist, we need to ground them in notions of what possibilities *and* limits nature offers human existence. Grosz is right to highlight the Darwinian insight that natural structures and forces also evolve – in interaction with culture – so that their enabling and constraining effects are not given once and for all. Yet, in relation to the desires and dispositions of humans and their institutions, feminist movements included, the make-up of biological relations nevertheless constitutes a relatively stable element that resists and undermines many of our attempts to change.

Nature's constraining force

The vindication of nature as dynamic is a central theme not only for Grosz but in the feminist naturalistic turn as a whole. For example, arguing that 'it is possible to imagine nature in such a way that it is unrecognizable as the ground for essential-ism', Stacy Alaimo invokes Lynda Birke's charge that the 'underlying assumption that some aspects of biology are "fixed"' is what feminists need to challenge, not biology as such (in Alaimo, 2008: 240). Although it is certainly true that nature in general and biology in particular are dynamic – and I doubt that many would contradict this claim when taken in its basic sense – I am concerned about this somewhat overhasty tendency to overlook the relatively stable elements of nature. I shall argue that without an acknowledgement of the relatively 'fixed' and limiting features of the natural world, including human nature, our conception not only of nature but also of the social dynamics that it underpins will prove incoherent.

When sociobiologists invoke biology as the cause of the current social order, they tend to focus on how hormones, chromosomes and other substances inherent in the individual determine behaviour. We can, however, shift focus to the more structural features of the natural order and conceptualize them as the broad conditions enabling us to act and create our social world within certain confines. At the level of human nature, the productive and constraining features of nature are expressed as human powers and needs. From a Marxist perspective, it is the dialectic interplay between them that gets history going. As Joseph Fracchia states,

> those corporeal factors that prevent us from making our history as we please – that which we lack and need, want or desire, that which constrains and even limits our capacities – should not be understood exclusively in negative terms as mere and passive limits. First of all, constraints and limits give definition and form to an organism that would otherwise be the living contradiction of a shapeless form. Constraints and limits force the organism to focus its energies, to direct them in relation to its predispositions or *Anlagen*, to exercise and develop the capacities and dexterities that it does have. Furthermore, ... they also present challenges that provoke the production of artefacts ranging from material goods to symbolic forms.
>
> (2005: 52)

Without a rough notion of what constitutes the natural limits and capacities of human beings, it is impossible, I contend, to make sense of any kind of social system or phenomenon. Even theorists who are extremely wary of invocations of human nature cannot but operate with some implicit notions of it. For instance, as already noted, the entire theoretical framework of Butler depends not only on the assumption that human beings are inescapably sexual, but also on the notion that we are constructed in such a way as to be affected by discursive meanings. In a critique of Butler, Pheng Cheah highlights that we need to ask what the nature of human bodies is, 'such that discourse can have a formative or even causal power over bodies that the ideational scenario of psychical identification implies' (1996: 120). Similarly, Sayer calls attention to the fact that norms and discourses 'don't seem to work on non-humans – on lumps of rock or plants – so there must be something about humans that makes them susceptible to such norms and discourses' (2011: 98).

We cannot make sense of from where socially constructed power structures derive their oppressively constraining effect on people without a notion of constraints that are not socially constructed, such as the need for love, care and recognition that underpins our vulnerability to other people's views. Also, the acknowledgement that the nature of human beings makes us needy in this way serves as one of the necessary normative bases for social theories. For how could we conceptualize a social order as problematic or oppressive, unless we operate with the notion that there is something about the nature of human beings that makes us thrive under certain conditions and suffer under others (cf. Sayer, 2011; Soper, 1995)? This takes us back to the issue of change and the preposterousness of celebrating change as such. It is only in relation to the relatively stable transhistorical structures, forces and needs that change – or status quo – becomes *meaningful* to people.

It is in a way paradoxical that the theorists of the naturalist turn do not break the postmodernist taboo on claims about human nature, although the very concept of 'human nature' so beautifully transcends the opposition between humanity and nature. It is also unfortunate, since the marked lack in feminist theory of explicit and specified accounts of the natural ontology of human existence has created a serious explanatory deficit. For example, as already highlighted, feminist theorizations of sexuality generally have little to say about sexuality as such, with Jónasdóttir's work as one radical exception. This leaves unclear both what it is about human sexuality that makes it so prone to become a central field of political struggle and what is it about the needs we have as sexual beings that makes us reproduce oppressive sexual orders. Also, the failure to acknowledge that being sexual is naturally associated with constraints and vulnerabilities that defy compromise obscures the distinction between unfreedoms that are a matter of unnecessary, oppressive social constructions and those stemming from the existential condition of being human. As we have seen, Butler provides no way of distinguishing between the existentially necessary powerlessness or vulnerability that stems from our relational nature and the powerlessness produced by historically specific oppressive systems. Such vagueness undermines any *serious* attempt to imagine what a feminist future may look like and instead locks us inside an unproductive wavering between pessimism and utopianism.

Alex Callinicos states that 'to be effective practically social critique has to develop an understanding of the limits of the possible' (2006: 181). Jónasdóttir's grounding of her framework in basic sociosexual necessities offers a basis for developing realistic strategies about what kind of change we can achieve, given our human capacities and the constraints imposed by our neediness. Also, it provides a basis for discerning what kind of social order is *desirable*, given the conditions for human thriving and suffering. For instance, with the acknowledgment that love is a basic human need that must be met if we are to thrive comes the conclusion that getting rid of love is neither a realistic or desirable way out of sociosexual exploitation. While this may seem self-evident, as hooks (2002) points out, by lack of an explicit feminist acknowledgement of our need for love, feminist discourse on love has long been either absent or dominated by the idea that love, at least in its heterosexual version, is something from which we had better keep away. Most feminist women continue to love men despite this, but the lack of a public discussion based on an acknowledgement of women's search for love compels them, I would contend, to pursue their struggle in relative isolation and in a state of incongruity between theory and practice. As Bhaskar

Feminist theory and nature   73

(1993/2008b) states, the resolution of such theory/practice inconsistencies is at the heart of any quest for truth and emancipation. Contemporary feminist theorists would indeed need to put more effort into resolving such incoherences.

Transcending dualisms – the dialectical-emergentist solution

If we accept that human existence is simultaneously natural and social(ly constructed), such that it makes no sense arguing that something is natural while something else is social, we are confronted by a dilemma: on what grounds do we distinguish between the natural and the social? Among feminist theorists the endeavour of transcending binaries or dualisms has become something of a given imperative. As Vicky Kirby states, 'it is somewhat routine within critical discourse to diagnose binary oppositions as if they are pathological symptoms' (2008: 215). The nature/culture divide is one of the principal targets, since it underpins so many other modern dualistic pairs, most notably the one that relegates the feminine to the realm of the natural, bodily, material, while reserving culture, mind and spirit for men (Ortner, 1974). The latest version of this traditional feminist concern is the posthumanist paradigm, which challenges the opposition between the human and the non-human. But what does it mean to transcend a dualism? I would argue that a remarkable confusion prevails about this question in feminist theory and that this confusion is at the heart of difficulties to deal with the nature–society relation.

For instance, in the introduction to *Feminist Theory's* special issue on the non-human, Myra Hird and Celia Roberts ask: 'Can and/or should a human/nonhuman delineation be made? … By identifying distinct categories, do we reify a dualism that we seek to dismantle?' (2011: 109). The question reveals a categorical mistake that is epidemic among feminist theorists and yet rarely challenged. What Hird and Roberts fail to do is to discriminate between *distinction* or *difference* on one hand and *dualism* on the other (see also Kirby and Wilson, 2011). In their conventional usage, however, dualisms or binaries refer to the kind of absolute separation which ignores any interconnection and mutual constitution between the two terms in question, while distinction simply means that two things are not the same, which does not necessarily mean they can be neatly separated from one another. If we see distinctions as such as the problem, we rid ourselves of the possibility of examining the *relation* between the two terms and one will inevitably subsume the other.

Noela Davis also gives testimony to the prevailing confusion about these distinctions, when arguing that:

> [new materialists] theorize an entanglement and non-separability of the biological with/in sociality, and what they criticize in much feminism is the conventional assumption that the biological and the social are two separate and discrete systems that then somehow interact.
>
> (2009: 67)

But what if, as Kirby suggests, it is 'the difference between separability and inseparability' (2008: 216) that needs to be destabilized? It indeed seems that a

74 *Challenging poststructuralist feminism*

lot of phenomena in this interconnected world are inseparable in the sense that they are mutually dependent and unified at the concrete level, yet separable in that they can be thought of as interacting with one another. As Sayer notes, it is 'strange to say that something like sexuality is *not* natural or unnatural *but* socially constructed' (1997: 480), since we can make no such distinction on the level of concrete human practices, which are always both natural and socially constructed. Yet, this inseparability does not make Sayer altogether dispense with the distinction between the natural and the social, on which his claim depends. It is when we reject any distinction that we fall prey to reductionism, such that human practices are inevitably conceived as a matter only of either the natural or the social. The ontological duality implied by this 'identity-in-difference' (Bhaskar, 1993/2008b: 319) between the natural and the social explains, I would argue, why deconstructionists struggling to altogether overcome the distinction are likely to reproduce it. I shall here seek to show how we might better address this 'binarity riddle' (Kirby, 2008: 216), with the aid of Marxist materialism, the critical realist conceptualization of emergence and the dialectics on which they are premised.

Kate Soper (1995), a Marxist and realist feminist philosopher whose excellent work on nature has had little impact to date on dominant feminist debates, highlights that the ambivalence concerning whether to distinguish nature from humanity or not resonates throughout all of the western history of philosophy. As I see it, this is no arbitrary historical fact; it is rooted in the ontological structures of the world in which the human *is* distinct from nature while being part of it. A theoretical framework that has taken this dialectic seriously is the materialism developed by Marx. Soper recapitulates its fundamental tenets:

> Humanity is ... belonging with the order of Nature, and sharing in a structure of dependencies on the environment that is common to other animals; but also ... differentiated from that order in its very capacity to create the conditions of its own alienation (and, so Marx would argue, of its eventual emancipation).
>
> (1995: 46–7)

As Sean Creaven highlights, Marx was concerned with challenging the nature/humanity divide that characterized the philosophical frameworks of his time. On one hand, he fought the idealist view of Hegel and his followers, which conceived of human beings as 'a semi-divine species, a race of rational beings, set apart from the rest of organic nature by the Creator's "ultimate purpose"' (Creaven, 2000: 72). Marx highlighted that humans are material beings like other animals and that this materiality has its ultimate base in organic and inorganic nature. On the other hand, the *historical* materialism of Marx differentiated itself from the mechanical materialism of the time, which saw human beings as determined by material laws. By virtue precisely of their specific nature, Marx argued, human beings are endowed with gifts that render them social and by virtue thereof they are not simply determined by the nature on which they depend, but can also manipulate it in line with their own purposes. As Soper puts it, 'we may speak of

Feminist theory and nature   75

[human beings] as endowed with a biology that enabled them to escape the "necessity" of nature in a way denied to other creatures: to live ways that by comparison are extremely underdetermined by biology' (1995: 139).

This Marxian approach, condensed in the popular statement that *man is by nature social*, elegantly transcends the dichotomy between nature and society, while still relying on a distinction between them. It specifies the ways that nature enables humans to transcend nature, while not denying that it is still nature that has this conditioning power or claiming that the independence of the human is absolute. Consequently, when human beings harness natural forces according to their own aims, this does not imply that nature is overcome in any absolute sense. Successful use – even 'control' – of nature always depends on an adaptation to its constraints and powers. Reproductive techniques such as artificial insemination, for instance, are in one sense a liberation from biological constraints, but they are successful only insofar as they submit to conditions determined by nature (Soper, 1995). As Collier (1994) stresses, our relative freedom from natural determinations does not mean we *break* the laws of nature.

How can we make more precise theoretical sense of this somewhat enigmatic identity-in-difference between nature and humanity? Often scholars in the human and social sciences handle the paradox by claiming to make only an 'analytical distinction' between things that are really undistinguishable, but from a realist perspective analytical distinctions make sense only to the extent that they reflect some kind of ontological hiatus. This theoretically thorny issue, which is pertinent not only to the relation between nature and humanity but to all of being, is solved by the concept of *emergence*.

One of the central strengths of Grosz's work is that she theorizes the relation between the natural and the social as one of emergence. In her Darwinian meditations she repeatedly highlights that increasingly complex forms of life emerge from earlier forms, thereby challenging both stark juxtapositions between human and non-human life and notions that human life is mechanistically determined by non-human laws of nature. Here, Darwin's essentially realist ontology seems to work as a healthy counterforce to the Deleuzean postmodernism that permeates Grosz's thinking. Grosz (2004: 91) rightly points out that the emergentist Darwinian notion of nature, according to which nature grounds and enables but does not contain or determine culture, provides a way of overcoming the dualism between nature and culture. While, in its everyday sense, emergence is mostly thought of in its temporal sense, whereby something qualitatively new emerges from the old, there is also emergence in the synchronic sense. This refers to the fact that something, here and now, is composed by the powers and properties of something else while still possessing its own unique powers and properties (Bhaskar, 1979/1998). Nature not only temporally precedes the humanity that emerged from it; it is also the causal foundation of humanity in any moment in time, this being revealed by the fact that nature can exist without humanity while humanity cannot exist without nature. Yet, humanity cannot be *equated* with the nature of which it is composed – it has its own distinct powers and capacities. As noted in the introductory chapter, this paradox is reflected in the fact that while

76   *Challenging poststructuralist feminism*

all human endeavours can be studied in terms of the physiological processes of which they are composed, this gives us very incomplete knowledge about what is actually going on. As Bhaskar (1979/1998) highlights, the neurophysiological organization of human beings provides the basis for our power of speech, but speech can nevertheless 'do' things which neurophysiological mechanisms are not capable of. Hence, we cannot understand the logic of speech, nor predict it, by understanding the neurophysiological processes constituting it.

From a critical realist perspective, emergence is not a phenomenon exclusive to the nature–society relation, but characterizes the relations between all different levels or strata of the world. Collier, for instance, describes the phenomenon of emergence by pinpointing the relation between the biological and the chemical:

> Biological organisms … are composed of chemical substances. It is because they are so composed that they are rooted in chemistry. But they are also emergent from it: they obey laws other than chemical laws, and can do things that could never have been predicted from chemical laws alone.
>
> (1994: 116)

To refer back to Davis's reluctance to see the biological and the social as two distinct systems, we see here that we may indeed think of the chemical and the biological as different systems in that they are constituted by different kinds of laws and mechanisms, while still retaining the notion that the biological is composed by and thereby inseparable from the chemical. The same goes for the relation between the social and the biological, and for any relation between strata of reality interconnected by a relation of emergence (e.g. the psychological and the social). Collier further clarifies this slightly enigmatic character of emergence, arguing that, although '[t]here is a sense in which a tree is "free" from mechanical determination … [i]t doesn't *break* mechanical laws (neither do we)'. Yet, 'it grows according to its own nature in ways impossible for something subject *only* to mechanical laws' (1994: 119). Similarly, as social beings, humans operate according to laws and enjoy capacities that cannot be derived from the natural laws and powers of which our sociality is composed.

Importantly, this leap of emergence between levels of reality implies that higher order levels can act back upon the lower order levels of which they are composed. As Grosz highlights, the causal influence is not one-way between nature and culture, but the specific powers we have as social creatures can to a degree change the course of nature, even human nature in the long run. We know this only too well when it comes to climate change, although this is also a phenomenon that aptly shows that we do not have total control over nature, that it will act back upon us unless we play by its rules.

Dialectical antagonists and 'pomo flips'

The reason why the concept of emergence helps us transcend dualisms between interconnected levels of reality is because it transcends the most fundamental dualism of all, that between identity and difference or unity and distinction. It clarifies how the cultural, social or human can be both part of nature and something else than nature. Collier emphasizes that the theory of emergence fights on two fronts, both against dualism and pluralism, which deny intrinsic connections between entities, and against reductionism and holism, which deny that things can be distinct and irreducible to one another although they are not absolutely separate. As exemplified in Butler's work, when feminist theorists challenge atomistic separations they only too often fall into the trap of reductionism, by overemphasizing relatedness at the expense of distinctness. This is perhaps most common when poststructuralists challenge the idea of the autonomous liberal subject, rightly pointing out that the subject is constituted by its relations, but wrongly concluding from this that the subject is nothing more than these relations, that its relative autonomy is a fiction. What characterizes both the atomist view of a self-contained subject and the view of the subject as exhausted by the social or discursive relations constituting it is the non-dialectical notion that existential interdependence rules out autonomy and vice versa. Much as the autonomy of the subject is here sacrificed at the altar of its relationality, it seems that the current posthumanist trend runs a similar risk of sacrificing the specificity of the human on the altar of its animality.

Sayer coins the term 'pomo flip' to denote this flipping tendency among poststructuralist theorists. 'Faced with theoretical or philosophical positions that seem untenable, it is tempting to counter them by reversing or inverting them', he states. The problem with this strategy, however, is that it 'retains the problematic structures that generated the problem in the first place' (2000: 67), 'perpetuating', to borrow Karen Barad's words, 'the endless recycling of untenable oppositions' (2007: 133). As long as the dialectical deficit in feminist theory is not remedied, efforts to subvert modernist dualisms will necessarily end up *in*verting them, locking us inside an oscillating movement between, for instance, biological reductionism and its social ditto.

For Bhaskar, the failure to acknowledge the dialectical ontology of unity-in-difference is a central problem in the history of western philosophy. He invokes the concept of *antinomy* to denote, in Alan Norrie's words, the 'one-sided appropriations of questions concerning thought or being', whereby '[p]hilosophy wrenches one side of what is in effect a dual out of its overall context and falsely hypostatises it with regard to the other side' (2010: 101; Bhaskar, 1993/2008b, 1994). Antinomial thinking results in false dichotomies or oppositions that repress the internal relation or intra-action between the different terms or aspects, such as structure/agency, nature/culture, body/mind and objective/subjective. As we have seen, this tendency is at work in the typical way that feminist theorists challenge the dualism between nature and culture. Through lack of a way of grasping the co-existence of unity and difference, nature is collapsed into culture or vice versa, a move which, against intentions, reproduces dualism inasmuch as it forces us to choose between one of the terms. Echoing the theme of 'pomo flips', Bhaskar highlights that this oscillating between poles tends to create tacitly complicit 'dialectical antagonists' (1993/2008b: 117), theorists who are superficially opposed

78 *Challenging poststructuralist feminism*

to one another in that they emphasize different sides of a duality at the expense of the other, but who share the fallacy of one-sidedness. This leaves theoretical antagonists, as Norrie puts it, 'tugging on one side of an antinomy [which is really] resoluble in terms of a duality' (2010: 103).

Conclusion

As I see it, the essential task of feminist theory is to explain what makes social phenomena such as patriarchy and heterosexism possible and what the conditions are for getting rid of them. Since nature has so often been invoked as an obstacle to gendered and sexual change, it is understandable that feminists have tended to deny that any gendered order is inevitably underpinned by natural forces beyond human control. Yet, I have sought to show that since all social phenomena, even feminism, are based in nature, it does not make sense to see nature as politically problematic. The struggle for political change would lose its meaning if we were not part of a natural world that constrains and partly directs our lives, by making us suffer under certain social conditions and thrive under others. This conditional force of nature means that we cannot create *any* kind of feminist future, for instance one in which we are liberated from sexuality or from needing other human beings. This should not, however, be that disheartening, since the freedom we seek would not make much sense if it were not in accord with our human natures. It is a pity, therefore, that the theorists of the emerging naturalist turn, who admirably break so many other ingrained taboos, seem anxious to face the limiting force that nature exerts on our feminist projects. This does no good to the feminist cause, since it paves the way for utopian notions of what a feminist society could look like. And utopias tend not to be realized.

I would hope that the naturalistic turn could direct its energies more towards examining more concretely how nature conditions the social. Although I sympathize with the posthumanist project of emphasizing the continuities between the non-human and the human, if we are to better understand the *political* it is crucial that we do not avoid the question of what is specific about human nature. Although I would not downplay the significance of the non-human world as such, for specifically *feminist* concerns the non-human and the natural is interesting only inasmuch as we cannot understand the human and social without it. What is needed is more theoretical accounts of nature that help make better sense of from what material sources gendered power structures derive their force, of how our nature constrains as well as enables our struggle against them, and of what a feminist future could and should look like given our specific needs and powers as human beings.

Notes

1 An earlier version of this chapter appeared in *Feminist Theory* 14(1) as 'The naturalistic turn in feminist theory: a Marxist-realist contribution' (Gunnarsson, 2013a).
2 The clumsiness of astronauts 'freed' from gravitation well illustrates the fact that constraints are not at odds with freedom but its precondition.

5 Women and men as theoretical categories

> It would be nice if 'feminist theory' could eventually come to mean a kind of thought that seeks to dispel confusions concerning bodies, sex, sexuality, sexual difference, and the power relations between and among women and men, heterosexuals and homosexuals. Such theory would aim to release us from the metaphysical pictures that hold us captive, and so return our words to the sphere of the ordinary.
>
> Toril Moi (2001: 120)

This book theorizes women's subordination to men in sexuality and love.[1] At the present moment, such a study is likely to evoke some criticism in circles of feminist theory only due to the fact that it takes the categories of women and men as its positive point of departure. The category 'women', and concomitantly 'men', has become something of a minefield among poststructuralist-minded feminist theorists and gender scholars, for reasons that I shall elucidate and critique in this chapter. As Butler has been immensely influential in this development of a feminist taboo on the category 'women', I will here continue my critical engagement with her work.

The taboo on 'women' as a category of analysis can be illustrated by an anecdote from the closing plenary session of a feminist conference that I attended, where the moderator asked what it is about feminist theory that makes it *feminist*. One of the conference participants offered an elaborate answer, without ever mentioning the words 'women' or 'men' or anything representing specifically gendered relations. Instead, the fabric of the answer was general assumptions about power and resistance. Slightly disturbed, yet not very surprised by this, I asked what made this answer apply specifically to *feminist* theory, when actually it could pertain to all theoretical frameworks somehow occupied with issues of power and resistance. Interestingly enough, my question seemed to take the individual by surprise, who then answered that he 'had not thought about that'.

How can this be? Is it not the very point of departure of feminist theorizing that women are oppressed/exploited/discriminated/excluded *by virtue of their being women*? And is it not the case, as Iris Marion Young states, that 'without some sense in which "woman" is the name of a social collective, there is nothing specific about feminist politics' (1994: 714), nor about feminist theory? For any

80 *Challenging poststructuralist feminism*

theorist before the deconstructionist turn, the answer to these questions would indisputably be in the affirmative. However, the anecdote above shows that within contemporary feminist academia there is no unanimity about this question; on the contrary, the stigmatization of the category 'women' has become such a taken-for-granted element in feminist discussions that the conference participant who excluded 'women' from his feminist vocabulary had never even been compelled to reflect upon the tensions such an exclusion implies, until confronted by my rather basic question. Another illustration of this taken-for-grantedness is the way Clare Hemmings defends feminists of the 1970s against the charge of essentialism, by invoking that they too 'challeng[ed] "woman" as the ground for feminist politics and knowledge production' (2005b: 116). This cognitive structure, wherein intrinsic links are held to exist between essentialism and appeals to the category 'woman'/'women', helps explain why I felt somewhat awkward about posing my unanticipated question in the conference plenary. 'Women', as Susan Gubar states, has become 'an invalid word' (1998: 886). Even, as Alison Assiter highlights, it has become a mainstream position that 'those who use the category "woman" collude in oppressive discursive practices' (1996: i).

Since I agree with Young that the category 'women' is absolutely indispensible to the feminist project – and, more specifically, to the arguments laid out in this book – in this chapter I lay bare some conceptual confusions underpinning the widespread tendency to write it off. I show that the category 'women' is vital since it relates to something real, and that this statement implies neither essentialism nor homogenization. First, I examine the characteristic ways that feminist theorists have influentially argued against the use of 'women' as a category of analysis, on the grounds that it implies ethnocentrism, essentialism etc. I scrutinize the meta-theoretical assumptions underpinning these arguments, which can be said to emerge from specific versions of what I call the *intersectional* and *constructionist* paradigms. The theorists I examine do not reject the category 'women' in any wholehearted way, but acknowledge the analytical and political problems implied by such a rejection. Prescribing parodic (Butler, 1990/1999) or strategic (Spivak, 1987/2006) uses of identity categories like 'women' are solutions that have been offered to the dilemma produced by this acknowledgement. Still, what remains throughout all these ambivalences is a deep scepticism against any positive (as opposed to deconstructive) theoretical validity, not to say *realness*, of the category 'women'. It is this scepticism that I confront by demonstrating that it rests on implicit meta-theoretical premises that are untenable. Second, informed by critical realism, I present an argument about how we can think about the category 'women' in more fruitful and consistent ways.

The intersectional challenge: women are not only women

Intersectionality is a theoretical perspective, method and concept that has recently gained an immense influence among feminist theorists (see Davis, 2008; Lykke, 2007; McCall, 2005; Zack, 2005). It refers to the intersection of different social relations in every concrete subject, so that, at its most basic, studying gender

Women and men as theoretical categories 81

through an intersectional lens means emphasizing that women are not only women, but also black, white, rich, poor, heterosexual, homosexual etc. I here use the term in a broad sense so as to include postcolonial feminism and black feminism, the common denominator being that they all highlight the complexities stemming from women's different positioning in power relations other than gender. Although theoretical attention to people's multiple positioning might seem a rather unspectacular undertaking, intersectionality has, as Kathy Davis puts it, 'been heralded as one of the most important contributions to feminist scholarship', even as 'a feminist success story' (2008: 67). What, then, is it about intersectionality and its propagation that rendered/renders it such an allegedly indispensable *challenge* to other feminist perspectives? I will show that, while intersectionality in its most basic terms does not need to define itself against feminist theory in a more traditional sense, the intersectionality paradigm as a whole harbours two moves, one rhetorical and one theoretical, which largely account for its pioneer status.

The background of the rhetorical move is that intersectional feminism emerged out of a disappointment among feminist women of colour with what they saw as ethnocentric and homogenizing modes of feminist thinking about women. Non-white and non-western feminist scholars (hooks, 1981; Collins, 1990; Crenshaw, 1991; Mohanty, 1988, 2003) brought to light that, contrary to what many feminist theorists seemed, in their view, to believe, not all women are white and middle class and that unless other power relations than gender are taken into account some women's experiences will be invalidated and power relations among women made invisible. It was for instance emphasized that for women who do not enjoy racial and class-based privileges, womanhood was not necessarily the most salient factor of oppression, and that ways of referring to 'women' and 'blacks' actually tended to include only white women and black men respectively, while ignoring the specific experience of black women (Crenshaw, 1991; hooks, 1981; McCall, 2005; Spelman, 1990). As well as calling attention to these modes of neglecting the specificities of non-white women's lives, intersectional feminists also pointed to modes of distortion, wherein non-white and non-western women tend to be represented as a homogenized whole, defined as the victimized Other (e.g. Mohanty, 1988, 2003).

This scrutiny of assumptions about 'women's experiences' has been crucial to the project of revealing ethnocentric biases and generally simplifying tendencies in feminist theory. Indeed, many feminist theorists, especially of the radical feminist conviction (e.g. MacKinnon, 1989), have made untenable generalizations about what it means to be a woman, obscuring the complexity and diversity caused not only by women's different positions in racial, class and sexual relations, but by the multilevelledness of power and being itself. However, the sharp dichotomy between a universalizing before and an intersectional after has been questioned by for example Davis, who emphasizes that Kimberlé Crenshaw, known for having introduced the concept of intersectionality:

> was by no means the first to address the issue of how Black women's experiences have been marginalized and distorted within feminist discourse. Nor was

82   *Challenging poststructuralist feminism*

she making a particularly new argument when she claimed that their experiences had to be understood as multiply shaped by race and gender.

(2008: 72–3)

For instance, in 1977 the black US feminist lesbian group Combahee River Collective gave out their influential manifesto making the case for a feminist analysis including issues of race, class and sexuality along with gender.

Much of the rhetorical force of intersectional arguments has come to depend upon caricature-like representations of 'earlier', 'western' or 'hegemonic' feminist theories. For example, although Chandra Talpade Mohanty, widely praised for her seminal work on western feminists' ethnocentric intellectual practices, does seek to qualify her use of the term 'Western feminism' – a term she repeatedly invokes as the subject guilty of homogenization and objectification of non-western women (2003: 18) – the end result is nevertheless that 'Western feminism' appears as much a homogeneous entity in her account as the 'Third World women' in the writings she confronts. Moreover, Mohanty's interpretations of the particular texts she scrutinizes are sometimes rather dubious. For instance, without ever substantiating her claim, she argues that these texts are based on 'the assumption of women as an already constituted, coherent group with *identical* interests and desires' (1988: 64, 2003: 21, emphasis added). Indeed, not even Maria Rosa Cutrufelli's problematic declaration that 'all African women are politically and economically dependent' (in Mohanty, 1988: 67) provides support for such a controversial accusation. Jónasdóttir and Jones point to the tendency among poststructuralist feminists to simplify and obscure the theoretical past in order to make their own argument appear as 'a necessary remedy' (2009: 34) and, in a similar vein, Hemmings highlights the frequent mode of unreflectedly contrasting oneself against the 'naïve, essentialist seventies' (2005b: 116). Perhaps Leslie McCall is right when stating that 'the social construction of all new knowledge tends to have a particular structure to it', in which 'the development of a new field is celebrated on the tomb of the old' (2005: 1783–4). The framing of intersectional feminism as a fundamental challenge to other kinds of feminism is partially owing to the rhetorical strategy of contrasting oneself against 'invented targets', to borrow Sayer's expression (2000: 68).

Anticategorical intersectionality

Besides this rhetorical element, there are also theoretical tendencies accounting for the antithetical relationship between intersectional and 'regular' feminism. McCall highlights that intersectionality can be based on different meta-theoretical assumptions, ranging from simple attention to the complex interplay between different axes of power (e.g. Crenshaw, 1991) to more radical perspectives 'that completely reject the separability of analytical and identity categories' (McCall, 2005: 1771). In the most elaborate versions of the latter approach, which McCall labels 'anticategorical', the rejection of the category 'women' comes logically from the general theoretical framework that denies categories as

Women and men as theoretical categories   83

such any analytical validity, by virtue of their empirical inseparability. It is this version of intersectionality that I take issue with here. Butler summarizes the foundational principles of this approach, when stating that 'because gender intersects with racial, class, ethnic, sexual, and regional modalities of discursively constituted identities ... it becomes impossible to separate out "gender"' (1990/1999: 6). Although this way of arguing may seem plausible at first sight, it suffers from self-contradiction. As Jónasdóttir and Jones highlight, Butler's statement that 'gender intersects with racial, class, sexual, and regional modalities' becomes absurd if it is impossible to distinguish gender analytically from other categories, 'since intersection logically implies the coming together of "parts" that are conceptually distinct from each other in some identifiable way' (2009: 41).

Some anticategorical feminists, like Wendy Brown (1997), are aware of this contradiction and, in the name of consistency, sceptical of the concept of intersectionality itself. Few wish, however, to completely reject concepts like race, class and gender: the awareness of the dangers of individualism and voluntarism is too strong. Brown is concerned with finding ways of theoretically recognizing that power relations like race, gender and class are different in kind and must therefore be attributed some kind of separate analytical existence. Yet, she does not embrace this need for analytical distinctions and make it an integral part of her theoretical framework. Instead, the necessity of distinction, albeit recognized, is conceived as fundamentally at odds with the fact that 'we are not fabricated as subjects in discrete units by these various powers: they do not operate on and through us independently, or linearly, or cumulatively [and] are not separable in the subject itself' (1997: 86). For Brown, the need for categorizations on one hand, and the empirical inseparability of categories on the other, seems to be a theoretical enigma that she can think of only in terms of a 'paradoxical moment' (1997: 93).

Elizabeth Spelman (1990) also displays a largely unresolved ambivalence about her generally disapproving approach to categorizations. She concedes that she has no trouble sorting herself out as woman *and* white; that 'What gender are you?' and 'What race are you?' 'appear to be two separate questions, which I can answer separately' (1990: 133). However, like Brown feels a need to emphasize that there are no 'discrete units' (1997: 86, 93) of gender, race etc., Spelman is careful to stress that it is impossible to distinguish the 'woman part' from the 'white part' of herself.

> If there is a 'woman part' of me, it doesn't seem to be the kind of thing I could point to – not because etiquette demands that nice people don't point to their private or covered parts, but because even if I broke a social rule and did so, nothing I might point to would meet the requirements of being a 'part' of me that was a 'woman part' that was not also a 'white part'. Any part of my body is part of a body that is, by prevailing criteria, female and white.
>
> (1990: 133–4)

In Brown's and Spelman's theoretical universes, thus, the possibility of thinking about women *as women* is conditioned on the possibility of pointing out specific 'women parts' or 'units' – that is, we must be able to separate out the 'womanness'

84   *Challenging poststructuralist feminism*

on the concrete level of existence. By that standard, of course, we will necessarily have to refute all claims about womanhood or gender as analytically distinct realities. This is a typical example of how the implicit endorsement of an actualist or flat ontology, which cannot make sense of structures and relations as real since they do not appear in pure form in the phenomenal world, leads to puzzling dilemmas and untenable theoretical claims. However, if we distance ourselves from the empiricist fixation with physical appearances and directly accessible entities, we can avoid the kind of irresolvable paradoxical moments by which Brown and Spelman are caught.

Discriminatory anticategoricalism: 'women' as a particular minefield

Before outlining how we can think of 'womanness' in other terms than an empirical entity, I want to call attention to a somewhat different mode of dismissing the category 'women' than the one offered by proponents of the anticategorical approach. Mohanty, for example, explicitly distances herself from postmodernist approaches that fail to take into account the structural reality of the power relations which categories represent. Still, she sees the specific category 'women' as inherently problematic, asserting that '[t]he phrase "women as a category of analysis" refers to the crucial assumption that all women, across classes and cultures, are somehow socially constituted as a *homogeneous* group' (2003: 22, emphasis added). This, indeed, is a radical contention, which would need an elaborate theoretical justification, since the awareness that women are different far from necessitates a rejection of 'women' as analytical category. Sayer reminds us that the search for commonalities actually presupposes diversity, which in turn becomes meaningful only from the perspective of some kind of sameness. He points out that '[t]he nature of the difference between various groups of people is more interesting than the difference between people and toothpaste partly because the former have some things in common' (1997: 457). Developing this point in relation to gender, Naomi Zack emphasizes that 'commonality ... does not ignore or suppress differences because it is the basis on which difference exist, and what we implicitly refer to whenever we say that women are different' (2005: 9). Hence, we must question the non-dialectical dualism between sameness and difference that rejections of commonality are so often premised upon.

Mohanty does not offer any theoretical defence of her categorical dismissal of 'women' as a category of analysis, considering it enough to show that some feminists have used the category in homogenizing ways, thereby rendering the problem of faulty employments of the category 'women' a problem alleged to inhere in the category as such. It is my contention that this kind of slide is constitutive of a lot of contemporary feminist scepticism towards talking about 'women' (cf. Carleheden, 2003). Ironically, Mohanty has no problem invoking other categories as highly meaningful analytical devices; notably, she repeatedly addresses the 'common social identity of Third World women workers' (2003: 163). But on what grounds does she find it adequate to appeal to this category, while categorically writing off 'women'? Might not the category 'Third World women workers', just as much as 'women', be deemed inherently homogenizing according to the theoretical standards she applies to dismiss the latter? After all, differences related to for instance sexuality and nationality risk being made invisible when women are categorized in these terms. Ann Ferguson is critical of how Mohanty's discriminatory way of dealing with categories gives analytical (and political) priority to work-related structures while neglecting the more gender-specific 'sex-affective relations' (2011: 248). Similarly, Nina Lykke notes that some intersectional feminists are 'so absorbed by feminist-bashing' and by questioning the 'primacy of gender' that they tend to emphasize class and race at the cost of gender (2007: 138).[2] This kind of discriminatory anticategoricalism, in which the category 'women' has become something of a particular minefield, can only be understood in the light of the rhetorical tendencies highlighted above.

The rejection of biological sex

The assumption that gendered relations and identities are historical/social products rather than universal or 'natural' givens is a more or less all-pervasive fundament of feminist theory and gender studies, although there is no consensus as to *how* gender is socially constructed or whether there is any pre-social ground at all for the process of construction. In the wake of Butler's influential claim that biological sex is itself discursively produced and the general 'flight from nature' pointed out in the previous chapter, the hegemonic position in contemporary feminist theory is that our tendency to divide humanity into women and men has little to do with biological reality, no matter how counterintuitive such a stance may seem. It is indicative of this lingering taboo on biological sex that the contributors of the naturalistic turn do not deal with the issue, but address the natural in very general terms.

Drawing on the critical realist theorists Carrie Hull (2006) and Caroline New (2004), I here make a case for the notion that the categorical division between women and men is necessitated by biological structures. Yet, I will also argue that the view of gender categories being biologically based is not a necessary premise for acknowledging the realness and relevance of the categories of women and men. Whether one believes a world without sex/gender categories is possible or not, it is still a fact, I argue, that women and men exist as categories pervasively structuring the world.

In Chapter 2 I highlighted that Butler's claim that there is no pre-discursive sex is a typical expression of the *epistemic fallacy*, whereby the question of what exists is conflated with the question of how we can epistemically access it. Butler is right that when we talk and think about biological sex, we have already enmeshed ourselves in culture, such that our *representations* of sex are never themselves a fact given by nature. Moreover, the way we culturally receive sex in turn shapes the way biological realities are lived. Yet, the mistake Butler makes is to derive from this that the reality of sex is exhausted by culture. It is not. As I have already argued, the fundamental support for this claim, drawing on Bhaskar's causal criterion for ascribing reality to something, is that the structure

86 *Challenging poststructuralist feminism*

of biological sex has determinate effects in the world, *whatever* we think or say about it. For instance, if we want to reproduce, we must adapt to the reality of biological sex, which prescribes that sperm and egg must meet if new life is to emerge. This does not mean everyone must be heterosexual – theoretically all fertilization could be carried out *in vitro* – but it means that the structure of sexual difference is a powerful independent reality, which sets the terms for our techno-logical transcendence of it (Soper, 1995).

Sexual difference is thus real not only to the extent that we perceive it as real and build our institutions around this notion, but in the sense of a 'natural mechanism' (New, 2004: 13) that is not a product of human activity but its basic causal founda-tion (cf. Grosz, 2011; Irigaray, 2002b). The realness of biological sex explains why the categories of women and men have existed in all known societies. As feminist theorists are quick to emphasize, gender orders differ immensely across time and space – and this is evidence to the fact that social life is not pre-determined by biological structures – but it remains the case that '[e]very society in every era has used the anatomical and reproductive dichotomy between male and female as a basis for a dichotomy in social order along productive and ritual lines' (Lewontin cited in Wilton, 2004: 80). As New highlights, '[g]ender arrangements are eminently culturally variable. But what they retain ... is that they *refer* to sexual difference' (2004: 12). For instance, although Judith Halberstam's concept of 'female masculinity' (1994) destabilizes conventional ideas of sex and gender, it does so only by referring to a pre-given sexual difference.

The idea that sexual difference is real, and naturally so, has been disputed by feminist theorists from the point of view of the existence of intersexed people, held to give testimony to the fact that sex is a continuum rather than a division (see in particular Fausto-Sterling, 2000). Butler rejects the reality of a sexual binary on the ground that 'a good ten percent of the population has chromosomal variations that do not fit neatly into the XX-female and XY-male set of catego-ries' (1990/1999: 137). As Hull highlights, this way of reasoning has strong affinities with positivism, in that both presuppose that 'theories are verified only when 100 per cent accurate predictions of empirical events can be obtained, and categories or kinds are considered legitimate only when every individual within them is identical' (2006: 87). New makes a similar observation, noting that '[b]iological kinds can never meet the essentialist criteria postmodern thinkers implicitly require' (2004: 10). From a critical realist point of view, reality is not perceived in the kind of mechanical terms tacitly assumed by Butler, whereby causality can only be conceived in terms of deterministic one-way relations between causal structures and their outcomes. Rather, a causal biological struc-ture of sexual difference may be said to exist on the grounds that it shapes a pervasive *tendency* for human beings to be either female or male. As New stresses, '[b]iology is messy and complex, and its regularities take the form of tendencies rather than laws' (2004: 10). Hull makes a similar point:

Because several processes are involved in sexual determination and differen-tiation (as is the case for all development), the relevant underlying mechanisms

Women and men as theoretical categories 87

do not operate with 100 per cent predictability. Instances of intersexuality –
overestimated and trumpeted by constructivists and poststructuralists – are
not evidence of the chaotic nature of sex, or of 'resistance' to discourse.

(2006: 95)

In other words, deviations from a general tendency does not mean there is no
structure at all, as poststructuralists tend to argue. Moreover, as Hull states:

no matter how liberally we interpret the evidence of variability provided by
intersex, some aspects of sex are indeed yes or no, on or off, 1 or 0. For
example, individuals with XY-testes can never conceive, regardless of the
amount of estrogen they voluntarily or involuntarily ingest.

(2006: 96)

Again, we can see how Sayer's 'pomo flip' (2000: 67; see p. 77) is at work in
the poststructuralist argument against the extra-discursive reality of the female/
male division. Rather than challenging mechanistic notions of causality, which
assume that there is a neat, linear relation between cause and effect, structure and
appearance, poststructuralist authors reproduce this problematic model of causality when they see intersex as evidence that there is no basic structure of sexual
difference. Similarly, because the different attributes generally related to each of
the biological sexes do not always appear conjoined on the level of individuals,
Butler concludes that the internal coherence of sex categories is entirely imposed
by culture. '"Sex" imposes an artificial unity on an otherwise discontinuous set
of attributes' (1990/1999: 146), she states, seemingly arguing that chromosomes,
gonads, hormones and genitalia have no structural relation to one another. It is a
major contribution of critical realism that it explicitly breaks with this actualist
idea of reality, according to which any irregularity at the level of events and things
is taken as evidence that there is no structure to reality. In the critical realist view,
empirical patterns are seen as caused, or produced, by the generative mechanisms
of the deeper structures of the world – biological, social etc. Yet, the stratified and
emergentist notion of reality allows for mediations and ontological gaps between
underlying causal structures and the level of concrete events and entities, such
that the latter are never a simple *reflection* of the former.

A further problem is implied by the rejection of any biological ground of
gender. In Part I, I highlighted that Butler's failure to define sexuality beyond the
discursive power regulating it begs the question of how sexual practices are to be
distinguished as sexual in the first place. Similarly, if gender is seen as having no
other basis than itself or some abstract 'power', it is unclear why we should refer
to this aspect of social life specifically as 'gender' (Soper, 1995). As R. W. Connell
states, '[w]hat makes a symbolic structure a gender structure, rather than some
other kind, is the fact that its signs refer, directly or indirectly, to the reproductive
relationship between women and men' (2002: 38). Positing such a link between
a pre-given biological ground and an emergent social and cultural gender order
does not mean that 'sex causes gender' in a determinist manner, since, as highlighted

88 *Challenging poststructuralist feminism*

in the preceding chapter, human social life has a relative independence from its natural basis, by virtue of the process of emergence. Moreover, as New (2004) puts forward, sexual difference is only one among several causal mechanisms which together produce complex, changing and diverse gender orders.

It seems, however, that the average contemporary feminist theorist eschews even such a mediated link between sex and gender, perhaps since it implies that there are constraints on the possible ways that gender can be fashioned. Hull (2006) highlights that the reasons why poststructuralist antinaturalism is so popular are partly political. As Suzanne Kessler and Wendy McKenna celebratorily establish, '[t]he possibilities for real societal transformations would be unlimited if the naturalness of gender [used here to include biological sex] could be questioned' (in Hull, 2006: 2). Hence, a sincere engagement with the natural sciences, which is not directed primarily by this kind of political agendas, may disappoint us. Yet, unless we identify the real constraints and possibilities underpinning social life, we cannot hope to develop sustainable strategies for the kind of political change that *is* possible. The 'reality principle' (Bhaskar, 1993/2008b: 55) works in such ways that if we seek to challenge male power and heterosexism by attempting to erase the biological categories of women and men, we are bound to fail.

Constructed, hence unreal?

The notion of women and men as real does not depend on an embracement of a pre-discursive ontology of sex, though. Just like race and class are real in that they are forces enabling and constraining people's lives, while having no basis in causal biological structures, gender categories can be acknowledged as real no matter how historically contingent they are held to be. Yet, as we saw in Chapter 2, in Butler's theoretical landscape the notion that gender is constructed entails that its realness is undercut. Butler asserts that, since there is no 'univocity of sex' or 'internal coherence of gender', these are 'regulatory fictions' (1990/1999: 43–4; cf. Halberstam, 1994: 125). Furthermore, apart from the fact that some people do not fit neatly into the biological categories of female and male, she holds the category 'women' to be fictive and arbitrary on the grounds that it is not 'a stable signifier that commands the assent of those whom it purports to describe and present' (1990/1999: 6) and that there is no 'substance' of 'gendered identities' (1990/1999: 22).

In addition to unjustly implying that some unnamed other feminists consider 'women' to be a 'stable signifier' and gender identities to have a substance, by this influential line of reasoning Butler also makes some questionable presuppositions about what can be considered to be real and about what categories are for. Reality, it seems, can only be conceived of in terms of coherent substances, and categories are held to be valid only if they reflect concrete reality in all its singularities. Jónasdóttir and Jones rightly contend that Butler 'conflates feminists' efforts to formulate concepts of gender and complex theories of gender systems' (2009: 39) with the 'development of a language that fully or adequately represented women' (Butler, 1990/1999: 4).

Here, despite her effort to challenge positivist assumptions about reality, in yet another version of the 'pomo flip' Butler actually reproduces them. I would contend that the radicality of the insight that gender is socially constructed lies exactly in the element that our experiences as women, men, transsexuals and queers, *although real*, are not pre-given, static entities, but products of historically determined human activity and thus subject to change. The radicality does not lie in *refuting* the reality of that which is socially constructed; that only retains the actualist, positivist assumptions of what reality is, assumptions that feminists have found crucial to dismiss, since gendered power structures could not possibly be proved to exist according to such standards. Although gender categories are socially constructed, they are not mere nominal categories only arbitrarily related to the world (Alcoff, 2000/2001, 2006; Hull, 2006). Poststructuralist theorists are known for emphasizing that our categorizations produce the world, but the Butlerian failure to wholeheartedly accept that women and men exist actually disqualifies this fundamental insight. Women and men may be social constructs, but nevertheless, as Jónasdóttir puts it, 'women and men *are* the kinds of people they are, *historically*, at present' (1991/1994: 220). Feminists have long been aware of the political dilemma constituted by the fact that when we invoke the word 'women' in order to describe, explain and challenge gendered power, this also risks reproducing patriarchal notions of the significance of sexual difference. But instead of seeking to erase this contradiction by simplified emphasis on one of its poles, we should seek to develop theoretical frameworks that can contain it – because the dilemma is real and must therefore be lived through and solved through practical struggle.

In the wake of Foucault's seminal writings, Butler and her followers have carried out an important task in highlighting how the very subjects that we struggle to liberate are themselves, at least to some degree, products of relations of power sustained by certain significatory systems that make some identities intelligible at the expense of others. The pure representational function of language is a myth and therefore the ways we use categories like 'women' and 'men', 'feminine' and masculine' will never be innocent, but play a role in determining how possibilities and vulnerabilities are distributed in the world. However, gendered identities cannot be reduced to the significatory processes through which they are produced, even if we see them as produced entirely through such significatory processes. As the notion of emergence points to, however produced these identities may be, as products they possess a relative stability, autonomy and causal efficacy of their own. It is in this sense that gender categories are not only conceptual in character but also real groupings in the world.[3] The crucial import of this is that not only do symbolic gender categories structure our perception of human beings; also, the real groupings of women and men act back upon our systems of meaning, so that these categories are necessary if we are to make sense of – and effectively change – the world.

Butler and other anticategorical theorists have acknowledged the political problems that their philosophical framework causes. What, after all, as Linda Martín Alcoff puts it, 'can we demand in the name of women if "women" do not exist and

90 *Challenging poststructuralist feminism*

demands in their name simply reenforce the myth that they do?' (2006: 143). 'Strategic essentialism' has been suggested as a way of enabling political claims in the name of groups, with the ontological existence of such groups nevertheless interrogated (Spivak, 1987/2006). And, as highlighted in Chapter 2, Butler emphasizes that precisely because the term 'gender' has been produced within oppressive regimes, it should be 'repeated in directions that reverse and displace [its] originating aims' (1993: 123). However, so long as women and men are denied an unequivocally *real* existence, we will have neither reliable nor credible criteria for judging when it is appropriate and strategic to invoke their names and not. As Alcoff argues, 'a claim can only be taken seriously – and thus have its strategic effect – when it is taken as truth in a real and not merely strategic sense' (2000/2001: 323).

In the following section I show how, from a critical realist perspective, we might think of the category 'women' – and concordantly 'men' – as real, without the implications of essentialism,[4] homogenization or ethnocentrism. The key is to understand the nature of abstraction and the relationship between structures, positions and people.

The concrete and the abstract

Sayer notes that, in popular usage, the adjective 'abstract' often refers to something vague, esoteric and 'removed from reality' (1984/1992: 87). However, besides being essential to theoretical activity in the qualified sense, abstractions are actually an inevitable part of our most mundane dealings with the everyday world. What, then, is an abstraction? It may be illuminating to have a closer look at a passage in Spelman's *Inessential woman* (1990). Aimed at revealing the absurdity of talking about women simply as women, Spelman invokes a line by the American author Gwendolyn Brooks: 'The juice from tomatoes is not called merely *juice*. It is always called *tomato* juice' (in Spelman, 1990: 186). Now, little effort is needed to disqualify this statement, for it is certainly not the case that we always call tomato juice 'tomato juice'. Sometimes – and appropriately so – we call it 'juice', sometimes 'drink', and occasionally even 'liquid'. Someone might also hold that it is utterly important to distinguish between a branded and boxed tomato juice and freshly-made tomato juice, arguing that subsuming these under the same category would be a serious simplification of reality. The simple truth is that all these words are valid ways of calling attention to the qualities of the concrete object tomato juice, but that they all operate on different levels of abstraction, which place the tomato juice in different categories. As Bertell Ollman puts it, abstraction operates 'like a microscope that can be set at different degrees of magnification' (2001: 292). Which level of abstraction we choose depends on to which aspect of reality we wish to call attention, in turn depending on the purposes of the calling of this attention. For example, if I have walked through a desert for ten hours without drinking, the most significant aspect of the tomato juice would probably be that it is a drink. By contrast, an expert on tomato juice searching for the best tomato juice in the country is likely to feel motivated to set the microscope at a much larger degree of magnification.

Women and men as theoretical categories 91

Neither in everyday life nor in scientific practice can the truth about something be simply translated it into one concept or the other, for our conceptualizations are always determined by the problem that made us approach a thing in the first place. As Ollman emphasizes, 'it is essential, in order to understand any particular problem, to abstract to a level of generality that brings the characteristics chiefly responsible for the problem into focus' (2001: 293). If we want to explain, for instance, a person's experience of discrimination, we normally do not draw attention to the fact that the discriminated person is a mammal or a Libra, while the fact that she is a woman and an immigrant will probably be held to be more significant. This judgement depends on our theories – academic or intuitive, explicit or implicit – about the nature of zoological, astrological, gendered and racial structures, which operate relatively autonomously from each other despite their unification in the specific person and situation at hand.

The word 'concrete' stems from the Latin *concrescere*, meaning 'grow together'. Sayer notes that this etymology 'draws attention to the fact that objects are usually constituted by a combination of diverse elements or forces' (1984/1992: 87). Marx puts it in a similar way: 'The concrete is concrete because it is the concentration of many determinations, hence unity in the diverse' (1939/1993: 101). The term 'abstract', for its part, originates from the Latin *abstrahere*, meaning 'draw away', referring to the activity of 'drawing away' certain aspects from the concrete whole. As Sayer states:

> an abstract concept, or an abstraction, isolates in thought a one-sided or partial aspect of an object. What we abstract from are the many other aspects which together constitute concrete objects such as people, economics, nations, institutions, activities and so on.
>
> (1984/1992: 87)

If tomato juice is a composite matter, people are even more complex, not the least since they have the capacity to reflect upon and change the conditions of their own being. However, recognizing that people are continuously constituted by a range of diverse determinations, which themselves constantly change and which people's self-reflective agency can counteract, is not valid grounds for disqualifying efforts to sort out these determinations. We can talk about 'women' without thereby assuming that women is the only thing that these persons are, or that 'woman' is a fixed category. By its very definition, the method of abstracting presumes that the concrete totality from which one abstracts is not exhausted by the abstracted element. As Berth Danermark *et al.* emphasize, 'abstractions are not there in order to *cover* complexity and variation in life; they are there in order to *deal* with just that' (1997/2002: 42).

If we acknowledge that abstract concepts, such as 'women' and 'men', are qualitatively different from lived reality, we can seek to use them effectively without any expectation that they will correspond to this lived reality in any clear-cut sense. As Sayer (1984/1992) stresses, abstractions are not problematic as such; the danger lies in making false abstractions – such as 'woman is goodness' (my

92 *Challenging poststructuralist feminism*

example) – or in not taking abstractions for what they are, that is, treating them as if they gave a total picture.[5] Nira Yuval-Davis (2006) points out the crucial fact that differences between people cannot be understood simply as a matter of identity, since they are based in social structures that are autonomous from each other and reside on a level distinct from that of our concrete embodiment and experience. Spelman and Brown are right that there are no discrete racial, gender and class parts at the level of concrete identity; nevertheless, the structures of race, gender and class have distinct existences insofar as they exercise their causal force on our lives in ways relatively independent from each other. One of the great merits of abstraction is that it is an indispensable tool for identifying structures of this kind (Sayer, 1984/1992). Indeed, we can obtain knowledge of structures only insofar as we experience their effects on an empirical level. Yet, the intellectual recognition of a gender-specific power structure was not based on any kind of straightforward discovery of an empirical entity called patriarchy, but on the creative development of new modes of abstracting certain invisible but pervasive features from the concrete reality that we could measure, observe and feel. No matter how different women's lives were, what feminists put their fingers on was that there was something quite disadvantageous about all women's lives and that this something had to do with their being women.

Structures, positions and people

If in common-sense discourse womanhood is typically thought of as a reified property contained in each female individual, the tools of critical realism allow for a radically different understanding. From a critical realist perspective, people exist only by virtue of the relations and forces – natural, social, cultural – that constitute them, through the medium of structural positions. Douglas Porpora defines the relation between social structures, positions and people like this:

> Social structures are systems of human relationships among social positions which shape certain structured interests, resources, powers, constraints and predicaments that are built into each position by the web of relationships and which comprise the material circumstances in which people must act and which motivate them to act in certain ways.
>
> (1998: 343–4)

Because of their enabling, constraining and motivating power, our structural positions make us able and inclined to act in specific ways and likely to suffer certain things. The position as woman will make its occupant disposed to act in ways commonly understood as feminine and experience things that males do not tend to experience. She will tend to earn less than her male colleagues, since those who decide her wages are in positions motivating them to discriminate against women, and in order to promote her short-term interests she will be motivated to dress in feminine clothes. Breaking with these structural tendencies is likely to cause suffering in the short run (Porpora, 1998).

Women and men as theoretical categories   93

However, and importantly, people's actions and experiences are not pre-determined by or reducible to the tendencies[6] inherent in their positions. Thus, although women are *likely* to have similar attributes, experiences and personal identities due to the tendencies produced by their common position as women, stating that women share a common position is not the same as maintaining that women are the same. The reason is twofold. First, people have a certain amount of freedom vis-à-vis their positions by virtue of their reflexivity: 'we can interpret the same material conditions and statements in different ways and hence learn new ways of responding, so that effectively we become different kinds of people' (Sayer, 1984/1992: 123; cf. Archer, 2000). This is what makes it possible for us to act back upon and change the constellation of relations of which we are made up. Second, as intersectional theorists point out, women and men as concrete individuals are never simply women and men. We exist only by virtue of our positions in an array of overlapping structures on different levels of reality. It is through these multiple determinations that we become unique and complex individuals. Not only are women and men differently positioned in social power structures like class, race and institutionalized heterosexuality; also, we are the ones we are only by virtue of natural structures transcending and conditioning these social structures and positioning all human beings in a relation of dependency on, for instance, food and love. The important and simple point that I want to make is that this multiple positioning is not the same as no positioning. Although women and men are more than women and men, they are still women and men.[7]

Conceptualizing women as those who occupy the *position* as woman (cf. Alcoff, 2006) is thus very different from reifying, homogenizing and essentializing accounts of women. To repeat Jónasdóttir's statement, '[t]o speak of what women and men are is ... actually to speak about the social conditions in and on which they act' (1991/1994: 220). It is crucial to note, however, that although the identity and experience of a woman cannot be reduced to her position as woman, the relation between the gendered position and its occupant is not one of disconnection and arbitrariness, as for instance Mohanty suggests (2003: 19). The womanhood or 'womanness' emerging from the position as woman is a real feature of women, whether they wish it or not. This is because people are what they are by virtue of the assembly of relations – biological, economic, cultural and so on – that constitute them, neither more or less.[8] In this sense, as put by Mikael Carleheden, '[t]o find one's identity is to be able to relate to one's historical situatedness' (2003: 57). Although I have not chosen my position as woman, I can only be the one I am by virtue of this position (among others). This is why it is so problematic not to recognize the reality of women's 'womanness', however much we disapprove politically of the gendered structure by virtue of which we emerge as women. Through collective struggle we may be able to change the very structure of which our position as women is part, but without a category that can take this positioning into account, such a struggle will not be possible.

The problem with the poststructuralist tendency to downplay the realness of 'women' as general category is that it rules out conceptualizations of the material relation between a woman's life and her structural gender position. As opposed

94 *Challenging poststructuralist feminism*

to Mohanty, who, in a typical actualist way, distinguishes between '"women" as a discursively constructed group and "women" as *material* subjects of their own history' (2003: 22–3, emphasis added), from the critical realist point of view the group of women has just as material an existence as individual women, insofar as the people belonging to the group are intrinsically tied to a common position in a materially (and discursively) constituted gender structure.

Conclusion

As many intersectional feminists have pointed out (e.g. Lykke, 2007; McCall, 2005), understanding the life of a particular person is not a mechanical matter of 'adding' the 'contents' of the different positions that constitute her. Theorizing is a messy and never clear-cut project, taking place in the dialectic between the concrete and the abstract, the subjective and the objective, the specific and the general, and not the least between the fundamentally processual character of concrete reality and the irredeemably static quality of the words and signs that we employ to understand and explain it. We can never single out gender from for example race and class in any neat and absolute way, since these structures are in constant transformation and only *relatively* autonomous from each other. Furthermore, the gender structure is not a global monolith, but must be studied and theorized in all its local variations. Nevertheless, it is fully adequate to think of women as a group also on a global level, because although the gender structure looks different in different locations and is continuously changing, it possesses so much internal coherence and stability so as to deserve to be thought of as one (differentiated) whole. Only from that point of view can we explain why, in all probability, it is easier for me – a female Swedish academic – than for a male Swedish academic to partially recognize myself in the life of a homeless Indian woman. It would certainly be utterly unwise to try to explain our different situations only in terms of gender, but that does not mean it is meaningless that both of us are women. As Jónasdóttir states, women's commonality has to be thought of as very 'thin' and cannot be transferred to the empirical level in any direct sense. This thin commonality implies neither a common experience nor a unified struggle, but it entails 'a common *basis* for experience and thus a common *basis* for struggle' (1991/1994: 41, emphasis added).

The reason why it would be fatal to leave 'women' behind as a feminist category of analysis is that we need it to denote women's specific relation to a gender structure the properties of which we may only then struggle to define. We should, indeed, continue to deconstruct deterministic and essentialist notions of what it means to be man or woman, but such negative relating to gender categories can never be exhaustive of feminist theorizing. We must also seek to provide positive accounts of what, substantially, it means to be woman or man in a society such as ours, however fallible and incomplete such theories are doomed to be. Following up some of the themes opened up by Jónasdóttir's ground-breaking theorization of women and men's sociosexual positioning in contemporary western patriarchy, this is what I seek to do in the remaining part of the book.

Notes

1 An earlier version of this chapter appeared in *Feminist Theory* 12(1) as 'A defence of the category "women"' (Gunnarsson, 2011a).
2 My translation from Swedish.
3 Hartwig highlights that '[u]nder the influence of Kant, the dominant modern account of the categories is subjectivist; they are interpretative/classificatory schemas or forms which the human mind ... imposes upon the world' (2007: 55). By contrast, Bhaskar (1993/2008b, 1997) and most other critical realists (see Hartwig, 2007) espouse *categorial realism*, whereby categories are not only epistemological but also constitutive features of the world – which may be more or less adequately represented by epistemological categories.
4 It should be noted that the term 'essentialist' is often used carelessly by those who are against it. Feminist theorists seem to use the term largely as a synonym for biological determinism, but it may also simply refer to the fact that something has an essence in the sense of a structure that makes it what it is, whether this essence be biological or socially constructed, eternal or ephemeral (cf. Sayer, 1997). This ties in with the notion of necessity as referring not only to necessities given by nature, but also to that which is necessary for anything to be what it is, such as the necessity for the capitalist to exploit labour.
5 Part of the background of contemporary anticategorical feminism is probably the failure of some feminists, notably of the radical feminist conviction, precisely to take abstractions for what they are, reducing the lives of men and women to their structural positions as (dominant) man and (dominated) woman (see my discussion of Mackinnon's work in Gunnarsson, 2013b). Ironically though, anticategorical feminists like Butler seem to be stuck inside the same cognitive scheme, when assuming that a category is valid only if it accounts for every concrete specificity of the thing or person it refers to.
6 I use the term 'tendency' both in the commonsensical meaning of an empirical generalization and in the more specific sense applied in Marxist and realist thought, where it is used roughly as a synonym for the generative mechanisms or powers inherent in structures rather than to denote the empirical regularities to which these give rise (Bhaskar, 1975/2008a, 1979/1998; Sayer, 1984/1992).
7 By this I do not mean that all people are either men or women in any unambiguous sense; what I claim is that those who are, are so despite the fact that their being men or women is not exhaustive of what they are and although these identities are not fixed.
8 This is not to say that individuals are but the aggregated sum of the parts constituting them; the dialectic of emergence allows for a more 'enchanted' view of the individual, in which the whole is irreducible to its parts while nevertheless being wholly constituted by these parts.

Part III

The reality of love and power: A feminist-realist depth approach

6 Loving him for who he is

The microsociology of power

Whoever he is, he is not worth all this.
And I will never
unclench my teeth long enough
to tell him so.

Alice Walker (1979/1998: 192–3)

In contemporary western welfare societies power asymmetries based on gender are not legitimate.[1] Yet, ideological and judicial norms of gender equality co-exist quite harmoniously with a persisting reality of gender inequality on all levels of society, even in the Nordic countries ruled by strong norms of gender equality. Heterosexual coupledom, based on marriage or marriage-like arrangements, is perhaps the site where this contradiction is most marked. In western societies the forming of heterosexual couples is generally based on individual choice, motivated by the mutual experience of love. Not surprisingly, this historically specific grounding of intimacy in intimacy alone has given rise to optimistic sociological accounts of democratized love. If being together is entirely a matter of the rewards each of the parties experiences from this being together, then, Anthony Giddens (1992) famously argues, the lack of equality and mutuality in love will motivate the less profiting party to end the relationship. Nonetheless, as noted in the introductory chapter, the bulk of empirical research shows that the increasing lack of significant external impetuses for staying in relationships is not a sufficient condition for providing women and men with equal negotiating power within the relationship. The most poignant expression of the poor realization of norms of equal intimacy is the wide occurrence of violence in relations whose raison d'être is supposed to be love and where there are no significant economic obstacles forcing women to stay.

In Chapter 3 I embraced Jónasdóttir's claim that sociosexuality, defined broadly so as to include women and men's practices as both desiring-ecstatic and loving-caring beings, is currently organized in a way that *'forces'* women to *voluntarily* give their love to men, even when this entails that it is exploited. In this chapter I develop an analytical framework that explains this somewhat paradoxical claim in interactionist or microsociological terms, taking the interactions in heterosexual couple relations as my object of analysis. My focus is the tension

100 *The reality of love and power*

inherent in contemporary heterosexual love between, on one hand, norms of equality and freedom of choice and, on the other, persisting inequality. Following Hanne Haavind (1984), I set out from the assumption that, in a context of an ideology of gender equality, the experience of inequality ought to be largely incompatible with the experience of loving and being loved, such that when asymmetries prevail there must be mechanisms that make them appear legitimate if the experience of love is to survive. My focus is not the kind of outright abuse to which most people would object, but the normalized asymmetrical tendencies that I hold to be constitutive of contemporary western heterosexual love. Physical violence and other forms of obvious abuse can be seen as enabled by these more general tendencies, though. Nor will my focus be the unequal structuring of tasks *connected* to the practice of heterosexual love, such as childcare and housework. At the centre of attention will be the love interactions as such.

Drawing on Jónasdóttir and other theorists of love (e.g. Djikic and Oatley, 2004; Fromm, 1956), I operate with a definition of love as the act of recognizing and affirming another person and her needs and goals as valuable in their own right, in a way not directed by one's own needs and goals. This definition mainly captures the care rather than erotic-ecstatic aspect of love and addresses love as an interhuman practice (see Chapter 9 for an elaboration on the topic of self-love). It is this interhuman care dimension of love that constitutes the focus of the chapter.[2] In line with Jónasdóttir's claim that men tend to exploit women's love, more empirically oriented scholars (e.g. Haavind, 1984; Holmberg, 1993/1995; Langford, 1994, 1999) have shown that, on the above definition of love, women tend to give more love to men than men give to women. What I seek to do here is elucidating in more detail the make-up of this asymmetrical tendency. *How, I ask, does it come about that women tend to give more love to men than men give to women, when mutual love is (supposed to be) the very raison d'être of the relationship, when the ideological context prescribes gender equality and when there are no salient external factors stopping women from breaking up a relationship in case they are not satisfied?*

My analysis sets off with an assessment of Carin Holmberg's (1993/1995) study on heterosexual coupledom, with a specific focus on her analysis of the couple interactions in terms of *asymmetrical role-taking*. The study is based on individual interviews with the parties of ten Swedish childless heterosexual couples, who are perceived by others and themselves as equal. I also draw on Wendy Langford's (1999) study based on interviews with 15 heterosexual women about love, whose findings and analytical points share considerable similarities with Holmberg's. Rather than invoking the studies as 'evidence' for my analytical framework, by means of a retroductive process[3] I demonstrate how the latter can help make sense of the empirical data. I then extend the analysis by developing a conceptualization of the link between gender identity and the gendered tendencies of loving, by examining the mediating role of expectations and gratitude and highlighting the importance of distinguishing between the subjective experience of love and the objective practice of love. Last, I show how the tension between being 'loved' for conforming to femininity and being loved for one's own sake produces different kinds of risks and possibilities, depending on which strategy women choose as a means of satisfying their need for love.

Asymmetrical role-taking: or 'loving him for who he is'

If 'giving love' means actively caring for the needs of another person in a way not directed primarily by one's own needs, it is analytically fruitful to look closer at instances of conflict between the needs and wishes of two lovers. Insofar as we are distinct persons, caring for the needs of others sometimes contradicts concern for our own needs. When the love that is the very raison d'être of the relationship is challenged by such conflicts, the ways that women and men take part in saving the experience of love from this threat can reveal the underlying structures of the relationship.

Holmberg argues that identifying patterns of role-taking can reveal what kind of power structures are at work in human interaction. *Role-taking* is a symbolic interactionist concept denoting the activity of taking the perspective of the other, to put it simply. Given that we let the perspective of the other inform our practice, I would argue that – expressed in role theoretical terms – role-taking is the essence of love. A central finding in Holmberg's study is a gendered pattern of *asymmetrical role-taking*. While the women tend to see situations from the man's perspective while relativizing their own, the men tend to take their own perspective as the neutral ground from the point of view of which the woman's standpoint is judged. It is not that the women's subjectivity is totally effaced; after all, the couples in Holmberg's study invested in gender equality. Still, when the women express dissatisfaction with their partner's behaviour they tend to see this dissatisfaction as a subjective standpoint that is relative to the more absolute standpoint of the man. They may not like what he does, but 'that's how he is'. From one point of view this may seem like something we could expect from our lover, to be accepted for who we are. Yet, the 'right' of these men to be loved for 'who they are' is premised on the withdrawing of this possibility for the women. In order for the man to be the way he 'is', the woman has to follow.

Even when aware that their partners do not like their behaviour, the men in Holmberg's study often legitimize their adherence to this behaviour by referring back to their own standpoint. One of them says he knows his partner appreciates when he buys her flowers or tells her she looks good; yet, he rarely does this because 'it is not important for him' (1993/1995: 131; cf. Thagaard, 1997). Similarly, one man says he is 'not much into talking', that he talks only when he 'has got something to say' and Holmberg notes that whether his partner wants to talk does not seem to be something he thinks about. He even states that he expects her 'not to talk to him about things that he finds uninteresting or tiring' (1993/1995: 144). Although the female interviewees are generally more interested in talking to their partners, it is telling that one of the few who is not, has tried to change in order to adapt to her partner's wishes. Although 'she finds it hard to discuss certain problems she has learnt to' (1993/1995:145).

The men's tendency to legitimize their non-adaptation by referring to what is important to themselves or to what they are like is often supported by the women.

102 *The reality of love and power*

Although they reveal frustration with their partners' unwillingness to talk, they often use statements such as 'he is a silent person' or 'he is not very interested in talking' (1993/1995: 145) in an accepting, or perhaps resigned, manner (cf. Strazdins and Broom, 2004). The limits set by the men tend to be seen as absolute features intrinsic to their personalities and the far-reaching understanding that the women practise in respect to their partners is underpinned by a playing down of their own needs and wishes. As Holmberg notes:

> She does not see that she attributes a more stable and unchangeable status to his 'personality' while her own seems possible to change. Although it is in her 'nature' to want to talk she can subordinate herself to his 'nature' of not wanting to.
>
> (1993/1995: 150)

This basic asymmetry as to how much understanding and adaptation can be expected from the woman and the man respectively is the backdrop against which evaluations of what counts as love are made. 'That he sometimes talks is interpreted by her as an expression of his understanding her. Differently put, when he refrains from defining the conversation she sees it as an expression of his love for her' (1993/1995: 150). Thus, the woman's compromising with her own wishes is the taken-for-granted norm, whereas the man's compromising with his own wishes appears, by means of a contrast effect, as an unselfish act of love. By contrast, when the women seek to break with the pattern of asymmetrical role-taking, that is when they behave like their male partners, they appear to break with the very logic of love.

'I am very demanding'

The asymmetrical role-taking not only implies that the male partner fails to see the situation from the point of view of the woman; but also, the woman herself will often identify with the man's view that her standpoint is invalid. For instance, while many women express frustration with their partner's lack of response, they often see their own behaviour as the cause of this unresponsiveness. One woman says she 'understands if he doesn't listen to her' and concedes that she 'often talks about things that are unimportant and uninteresting' (1993/1995: 147). A common standpoint of the men is that their partner is illegitimately *demanding* and this idea is often shared by the women. For example, one of the women, who would like to hear more often from her partner that he loves her, disqualifies this wish by taking up the standpoint of the man. She says that 'really, she knows that he loves her so it is unnecessary wanting to hear it sometimes' (1993/1995: 155). As Holmberg puts it:

> When she holds her wish to be unnecessary she makes herself into a demanding person. It seems that she thinks her demand is unreasonable ... Thereby she indirectly legitimizes his way of acting and diminishes herself and the wish she has.
>
> (1993/1995: 155)

Loving him for who he is 103

This pattern is manifest also in Langford's study. A fragment of the interview with Kate serves as a good example:

> Kate: I think he is very patient with me, tremendously patient, because I am demanding. I know I am demanding, because people have told me so.
> Wendy: Why do you think you are demanding?
> Kate: Erm [pause] yeh, well [pause] er [pause] because I expect attention. But I don't always get it, but erm, er, I don't really know why I am demanding.
>
> (1999: 67)

The way that Langford's simple question reveals the fragile underpinnings of Kate's idea of herself as demanding is telling. It is because people tell her that she is demanding that she sees herself as demanding and when someone questions this idea confusion arises. Nevertheless, Langford writes, '[t]his construction of women's desire for attention as lacking in legitimacy was common in the data, sometimes associated with a corresponding sympathy for the man, who was seen as long-suffering' (1999: 67).

So what if the women's demands for attention are so overwhelming as to be deemed unreasonable by most people? In light of Jónasdóttir's thesis that most women are structurally impoverished of love, it should indeed be the case that women tend to be more desperate for love than men (cf. hooks, 2000a). If women express a desperate need for attention, it is thus more likely that it is a rational response to a real lack of care rather than the result of some intrapsychic shortcoming. Moreover, men's tendency to see women's calls for approval as exaggerated must be seen in light of women's tendency to make sure men's needs for approval are satisfied. Jean Duncombe and Dennis Marsden highlight that 'men have powerful if unacknowledged needs of the emotion work that women perform for them' (1993: 236; cf. Benjamin, 1998: 84; Firestone, 1970/1979: 122; Jack, 1991: 59). In this way, men can live their lives under the illusion that they are not dependent on approval from their partners, thereby undermining sympathy for and identification with their partner's similar needs. As Holmberg observes: 'He does not need to ask her for affirmation since she is actively giving him that. This may be a reason why he holds these ways of expressing love to be less important. He does not know what it means to be without them' (1993/1995: 159).

When the women identify with the man's perspective at the cost of their own, this can be seen as a way of 'resolving' a conflict between two persons by transferring it into the woman herself. However, occasionally the women in Holmberg and Langford's studies air their own standpoint more univocally, such that the conflict between them and their partner emerges more clearly. Yet, it seems difficult for the women to stick to their differing point of view when met by resistance from the men; then, the dynamic of male identification often reinserts itself. Just as both the women and men in Holmberg's study are prone to see the woman as 'too demanding', the women often identify with their partner's view of them as 'difficult and hysterical' (1993/1995: 160). When the men get angry, contrarily,

104 *The reality of love and power*

this appears as a legitimate and rational reaction; often men's anger is not even perceived as anger. One of the women in Langford's study tells about an incident in her marriage, when her husband wanted to have sex while she did not. When she explained to him why, his response was: 'That's nothing but emotional crap' (1999: 97). As Langford argues, the man seemed to be blind to the fact that his own way of reacting was no less emotional than hers. Langford pinpoints the logic of this widespread dynamic: 'men's accusations that women were "irrational" implied a deviation from a norm which was assumed to be manifest in men's own point of view and which therefore, paradoxically, did not require examination or rational explanation' (1999: 96). The subjective nature of the man's standpoint is thus disguised. The normative structure underpinning this asymmetric way of demanding accountability resonates with a long history of feminist theorizing about Woman as the deviant, subjective Other, defined in relation to the allegedly genderless, objective male centre.

Yet, this structure cannot be reduced to a set of ideological notions. In my analysis, one reason why both the women and the men tend to see the woman as the cause of their common conflicts is also that she is mostly the one putting problems on the agenda (cf. Dempsey, 2001). Since, in the normal structure of asymmetrical role-taking, she already carries the conflicts within herself, the man will not experience that there is any problem – until the woman gives air to her subjectivity in an uncompromising manner. In this way, when the woman points to a conflict, this often appears as if she causes the conflict. Hence, as Holmberg notes, the strategy of 'starting' a row is a double-edged sword:

> By quarrelling she shows that it is serious, which leads them to talk to one another. On one hand she achieves what she really wanted, which was not to quarrel but to talk to him. On the other hand she is seen as 'the troublesome' or 'the hysterical' by him since she is the one starting the rows.
> (1993/1995: 163; cf. Langford, 1999: 95)

There is nothing objective about the notion that she is the cause of conflict, however; it is underpinned by flawed conceptions of causality, leading to unjust evaluations of whom to blame. The man does not see that the woman's dissatisfaction is something he is a part of creating; to him, it is his problem only in the sense of him undergoing it, not in the sense of his responsibility.

Women as technical problems

Holmberg sums up the logic underpinning asymmetrical role-taking:

> [H]er personality and demands are seen as relative to his personality and demands. These in a sense appear as absolute. She is the one expected to change her attitude to household work, to what their discussions should be about and to her wish to be courted. He, however: 'is like that', 'does not think about that', 'does not like talking' etc. He and his way of being just 'are'.

Loving him for who he is   105

She is the other' who should arrange herself according to what is possible to demand from him.

(1993/1995: 191)

Holmberg's concept of role-taking needs to be a bit more differentiated, however. Holmberg herself rightly notes that the men are often aware of their partner's standpoint (1993/1995: 190), which they could not be unless they had somehow 'taken' it. I would argue that this is actually mostly the case; the crucial point is that the man's tendency to delegitimize the woman's perspective causes a disjunction between his being informed about her standpoint and his feeling motivated to let this information influence him. It does not move him.

In my interpretation there is a lot of role-taking going on by the men in Holmberg's study. Whether we want it or not we are dependent on other people's wills, so even the person who is interested only in manipulatively pursuing his own egoistic interests, has to adapt to other people's agendas in order to do exactly this. Michael Schwalbe's distinction between analytical and receptive role-taking is useful here. Schwalbe argues that the kind of role-taking that is constitutive of what he calls the 'masculinist self' can be characterized as analytical. It implies '[dealing] with women as technical rather than moral problems', that is 'in the ways necessary to overcome women's resistance as objects' (1992: 42). Receptive role-taking, contrarily, means to receive the other as subject, which involves feeling with the other so that 'the facts of an other's feelings can become the facts of our own existence'. 'When we truly feel with the other', Schwalbe argues, 'we are forced to reckon with the weight of the other's feelings as equal to our own. It is this, it seems, that men so often fail to do vis-à-vis women' (1992: 37).

The men in Holmberg's study often seem to experience themselves as somehow nonparticipating targets of the moods of their partner. This discloses a failure to feel with her; they do not emotionally identify with her so that her distress becomes theirs, thereby compelling them to take action. Instead, their role-taking seems to stretch only so far as to allow them to get rid of the troublesome situation they find themselves in by virtue of their relation to the woman standing before them. One man pictures two alternatives, when in a row with his partner: 'say I'm sorry' or 'let her have it her way' (1993/1995: 168). The role-taking implied here is based on his understanding that she is angry with him and if she is to become calm he must do something. His action is motivated not by care for the subjectivity of his partner, by a desire to make her feel good, but by the instrumental ambition to 'overcome her resistance as object' since it stands in the way of his own wellbeing.

The gendered mediation of love: expectations and gratitude

How, then, do we explain the gendered tendency outlined above? What is the causal link between a person's gender position and her/his way of role-taking, of loving and not loving? Following Haavind, Holmberg emphasizes that the wish to have one's gender identity affirmed is a crucial driving force in heterosexual love. In this sense, insofar as femininity is constituted by a more caring attitude

106 *The reality of love and power*

towards others than masculinity, women will tend to voluntarily take part in asymmetrical role-taking. As Holmberg states,

> women have internalized the gender hierarchy as a part of their gender iden-
> tity. A consequence of this is that women's choice of strategies for action put
> them in a subordinated position in relation to men and at the same time it is
> precisely through this subordination that they are affirmed as women.
>
> (1993/1995: 45)

Still, I think it is misleading to put too much emphasis on the affirmation of gender identity as such, especially in a context that is largely gender-neutral on the level of intentions. I would argue that the primary motivating force for people in love relationships is to be validated as persons, that is, to be loved. It is only because our existence as persons cannot be separated from our gender identity that the wish to be affirmed as woman or man – or some other gender identity – becomes such a force. If a woman behaves in ways generally perceived as mascu-line, her primary problem will not be that she is not validated as woman but that she is less likely to be experienced as a lovable and desirable person than women who conform to prevailing standards of femininity. As Schwalbe says:

> [our] needs for love, inclusion, acceptance, and material support – needs
> which must be met to sustain feelings of esteem, efficacy, and coherence – are
> usually met by conforming to the expectations of others who are similarly
> bound to gender ideologies and practices.
>
> (1992: 32)

The issue of expectations is crucial in the context of love. It is in the nature of love that it cannot be given on demand; love's power to prove our worth comes from the fact that it makes someone care for us although she does not have to. As Arlie Hochschild (2003a) highlights, the feelings of gratitude that fuel our love are evoked when we feel that we are given something 'extra', something we cannot demand or expect. The fact, then, that expectations on women and men differ, not only due to norms but also to actual behavioural tendencies, means that what induces gratitude, appreciation and love is also gendered. Tove Thagaard combines Jónasdóttir's theory of love power with Hochschild's analysis and concludes:

> One consequence of male exploitation of women's love power may be that
> the husband more or less takes his wife's love for granted, and will thus not
> appreciate her consideration of him as a gift. Since the wife is not in a posi-
> tion to count on corresponding love, even small signs of love from her
> husband may be considered gifts.
>
> (1997: 359)

For example, in Holmberg's study, 'that he sometimes talks is interpreted by her as an expression of his understanding her. Differently put, when he refrains from defining the conversation she sees it as an expression of his love for her' (1993/1995: 150). Hence, while the woman's compromising with her own wishes is the normal state of affairs, the man's accommodation to the woman's needs appears, by virtue of its exceptionality, as an expression of love. The other side of the coin is that, when a woman behaves like men normally behave, she will generally appear more unloving than the men. In this sense, a symmetrical subjective experience of being loved may co-exist with an actual asymmetry of loving, while an actual symmetry may appear as if the man is dominated by a 'demanding'– even 'egoistic' (Lagarde, 2001; Langford, 1994; Tormey, 1976) – woman, due to the contrast with the expectations built into the feminine position. Since feeling loved generally makes us love back, the gender-differentiated parameters for what counts as love also implies, with Haavind's words, that 'the way feelings of love are called forth in another person is different for men and women' (1984: 144), the general rule being that '[w]hen women engage in the same activities as men they are rewarded less' (1984: 139). Put more concisely: women generally need to love more than men in order to be loved.

The above argument depends on a distinction between a subjective and an objective dimension of love. It implies that even though a person feels loved by her partner, if this is not based in her partner's practically realized care for her needs but by a lack of expectations to have her needs valued, her feeling of being loved will not have the effect of love proper; that is to say, it will not effectively empower her as person. Being personally empowered is conditioned on the actual experience that others value our distinct needs and aims, in practice. Conversely, a man who feels unloved only because of his strong sense of entitlement will still be empowered if his needs and wishes are actively cared for. In this sense, Schwalbe's statement that we generally have our needs met by conforming to expectations needs qualification, since the appreciation we receive by successfully embodying femininity is far from fully-fledged. Being validated as feminine person is paradoxically conditioned on the readiness to set aside one's own person.

In the following section I pinpoint how this structural contradiction shapes women's quest for love in heterosexual coupledom, creating dilemmas for both conformists and resisters.

The costs and benefits of conforming

The *conformist* strategy, in its idealized form, would be for the woman to identify with her partner's needs and wishes to the extent that they are experienced almost as her own. This strategy can be highly rewarding on two conditions: that the woman experiences that she *chooses* to put aside her own needs and that she is valued by the man for doing this. The experience of choice preserves her dignity as a person, because even if she makes herself into an object existing for the needs of others, this stems from her own wish. A great advantage about this strategy is that the woman avoids the risk of discovering that her partner's appreciation of her is premised on her not expressing parts of herself that contradict his aims.

108 *The reality of love and power*

By *choosing* to put her own needs aside, she can rest in the belief that she would still be loved *if* she chose not to.[4] The disadvantage, however, is that her belief that she is loved for her own sake will never be verified.

More acute problems may arise if the two conditions pointed out above are not met. First, if the woman submits to the wishes of the man because she experiences it as the only way of being 'loved', her dignity will be undermined. As Jónasdóttir highlights, the essence of love is that it is practised in a way not determined by the goals of the lover, but that 'the object in receiving love win the capability of "shaping" himself or herself and his or her goals' (1991/1994: 73). It is by virtue of this quality of love, I contend, that it has the force of empowering us as persons, since being a person is the antithesis of being an object or means of someone else's purposes (Smith, 2010). Langford notes that if one is loved only on the condition of suppressing one's self, the love will not have the desired effect. She describes the vicious circle that her interviewee Hannah repeatedly found herself in: 'Through engaging in self-objectification, Hannah ... became implicated in a process of losing "herself" which was motivated, quite paradoxically, by the desire to regain the feeling that she was loved "for herself"' (1999: 103). This process, which was common in Langford's data, also tends to be self-reinforcing, since it weakens the woman's self-confidence, thereby making her ever more dependent on the man's affirmation.

Second, the counterproductive character of this strategy gets even more marked in case the woman's efforts to please her partner does not have the desired effect of being appreciated. Sarah, another woman in Langford's study, is very unhappy with her relationship but has great difficulties leaving. The awareness of her own submissiveness to her abusive partner undermines her worthiness, making her feel unworthy of love. In this way, her current partner – who at least has not left her – appears to be her only hope of being loved, which compels her to continue her efforts to please him. Put in the terms of expectations and gratitude, her feeling of being unworthy of love will make her grateful even for the smallest crumbs of love. And the more she downgrades her own worth by being grateful to her abuser, the less worthy of love she will appear not only to herself but also to him. It is hence likely that the more Sarah annihilates her self by subordinating herself to the will of her partner, the more he will disrespect her, since there is simply no *person* there to respect and love.

The risks and promises of resisting

The *resisting* strategy involves the struggle to have one's own needs and wishes honoured, even when they contradict those of one's beloved. The great possible gain here is that, if the struggle succeeds, the woman will *know* that her being valued is not premised on her being *useful*. She will feel loved in her own right. The risk, however, is that her struggle for recognition does not succeed. If she ends up being experienced as 'too demanding' and 'unreasonable', not only her partner's love for her but her love for him is threatened. We should not underestimate the existential and practical significance of the latter in a context where entire living arrangements depend on love. Here, one way for her to save both her experience of him and his experience of her as reasonable and lovable is to fall back upon the conformist strategy, by validating his view of her demands as unreasonable. As Holmberg notes about the instances in which the woman gets angry only to later take up her partner's invalidating stance toward this anger, 'it seems that she seeks to make his limit to her anger more comprehensible by seeing herself as demanding and hot-headed' (1993/1995: 163). By sacrificing the validity of her own feelings, she saves the image of her partner as reasonable and lovable and thereby also justifies the 'investments' she has made in him (cf. Haavind, 1984: 161).

If, instead, the woman sticks to her demands for symmetry in spite of the man's resistance, she risks being left. In the first place, such a demand for symmetry will not be easy to pursue without intellectual and affective feminist resources that help highlight asymmetries that tend to be obscured in the gendered structure of expectations. Yet, feminist consciousness is not enough, since it does not take away the crude risk of being left unloved, in a context where the chances are small of finding another man who will accept demands for symmetry. As Duncombe and Marsden highlight, 'faced with feminist challenges in their personal lives, men commonly react by denying they have a problem, a way out being to seek validation in another heterosexual relationship with a "less demanding" woman of more traditional views' (1993: 233; cf. Ferguson, 1989: 80; hooks, 2002: 43–4).

Moreover, in case the woman does find a man who is genuinely reciprocating, she will still be structurally subordinate to him by virtue of his status of rare exception. Both know that he could get, patriarchally defined, a 'better deal'. As Hochschild notes, gendered norms about what to expect and what to be grateful for are not only matters of ideology, but grounded in a 'pragmatic frame of reference' deriving from comparisons between what one has and what alternative options exist (2003a: 116). When unusually equality-oriented men are not especially appreciated for being more considerate than one could generally expect from men, they might thus feel unappreciated. Paradoxically, then, their forbearing from taking advantage of their privileges is likely to be connected to a remaining feeling of entitlement (cf. Pease, 2010), which undermines the equality that was intended. For what is at stake is love and appreciation as such, and if men expect more love and appreciation than women for their being equally loving and full of appreciation as women, we are back where we started.

Conclusion

I have sought to pinpoint the mechanisms whereby women tend to give more love to men than they get in return in heterosexual coupledom, despite the lovers' adherence to notions of equality and despite the fact that the experience of mutual love is the raison d'être of such coupledom. While Holmberg sees women's wish to have their femininity affirmed as the basis for their subservience, I have argued that gender identity is not the primary 'good' in heterosexual interactions, but rather a crucial vehicle by means of which we become loved. It is the need to be loved that is the basic force in these interactions.

110 *The reality of love and power*

We need love because love is what empowers us as persons. Thus, conforming to expectations built into the feminine position empowers us insofar as it will tend to ensure that we are loved. Yet, I have shown that the love women get by adhering to gendered expectations is in a way also disenabling them as persons, since it is premised on women being useful for others rather than valued in their own right, that is being loved in the proper sense of the term. This contradiction structures women's quest for love and compels them to balance between the risks and gains involved in conforming to subordinate femininity on one hand and those involved in resisting asymmetry on the other.

That the experience of being loved is largely based on the experience of being better treated than one could demand or expect, helps explain why feelings of mutual love can co-exist rather smoothly with actual practical asymmetries concerning who cares more for the other. From the point of view of the differences between how women and men generally behave, and thus between what is expected from them, women will simply tend not to be as appreciated – or loved – for their actual acts of love as much as men. This leaves us with the peculiar contradiction that a woman may feel unsatisfied with the reciprocity in her relationship with her male partner, while still experiencing that his lesser acts of concern are more valuable as a sign of love since they are not to be expected. Yet, drawing a distinction between an objective and subjective dimension of love, I have argued that even if she does not feel dissatisfied, asymmetries will be damaging to the woman's sense of dignity as person.

In this chapter I have focused on the unequal 'exchange' of love between women and men in heterosexual coupledom. It should be noted, however, that the love that women offer men under these exploitative conditions is an alienated kind of love and, to this extent, men cannot be said to be truly personally empowered by this sociosexual order either. If we operate with a definition of interhuman love as practically affirming the needs and goals of the other, we may want to elaborate somewhat on the notion of wherein a person's needs consist: do women really meet men's sociosexual needs when subordinating their own needs to theirs? I have already stated that love is necessarily a business going on between two *persons* and that someone who reduces herself to an instrument for the other will therefore tend not to be very lovable. Nor, I would here like to add, will she be very capable of loving, in the real, non-alienated sense of the term. This is basically because, as the oft-repeated truth has it, love of others essentially depends on love of oneself (Bhaskar, 2002b). Fundamentally, the act of self-negation damages others too, since they are rendered the cause of the other's self-negation and lose out on the possibility of being enriched by the kind of love that is given freely in a more qualified sense than the compulsive voluntariness characteristic of women's love under patriarchy. Hence, to fully realize their human potential, men are not in need of women who adapt to them, but of women whose independent subjectivities are unconstrained by urgent need. In the rest of Part III I develop these ideas, thereby deepening and complicating somewhat Jónasdóttir's account of sociosexual exploitation.

Notes

1 An earlier version of this chapter appeared in *Love – a question for feminism in the twenty first century*, edited by Anna G. Jónasdóttir and Ann Ferguson. London/New York: Routledge (Gunnarsson, 2014).

2 It should be noted, though, that given the dialectical relation between erotic ecstasy and care, no neat distinction can be drawn between them; the experience of erotic ecstasy is indeed premised on the fact that one's erotic-ecstatic needs are cared for by someone else and/or oneself. It is in this sense, in my view, that we should understand Jónasdóttir's claim that 'loving *care* showed to the desiring individual as a particular person' (2011: 56, emphasis added) is what charges sociosexuality with power. Also, as for the dualism between self-love and love of others, as I expand on in the ensuing chapter this dualism is in my view *fundamentally* illusory, despite the fact that it crucially structures the current order of sociosexuality.

3 The method of retroduction is central in realism. It is the mode of inference whereby a known phenomenon is explained by 'postulating (and identifying) mechanisms which are capable of producing them' (Sayer, 1984/1992: 107).

4 Haavind argues that in a context ruled by an ideology of gender equality '[t]he essence of femininity is to make inequalities appear as equalities' (1984: 147) and that the chances for a woman of having her femininity confirmed will be greatest 'if she herself contributes to making this relative subordination appear as something else than subordination' (1985: 21, my translation from Swedish).

7 Love
Exploitable resource or 'no-lose situation'?

Is love an exception, the only one, but of the first order of magnitude, to the law of masculine domination, a suspension of symbolic violence, or is it the supreme – because the most subtle, the most invisible – form of that violence?

Pierre Bourdieu (1998/2001: 109)

The very existence of love, if taken seriously by social theorists, ought to put the final nail in the coffin for lingering conceptions of human beings as self-contained entities only contingently related through interactions of exchange.[1] The hallmark of love is that it dissolves the boundaries between people and their interests, such that the pleasure of our beloved is our pleasure, her pain our pain (Weitman, 1999). By virtue of this unification of the aims and longings of lovers, the dualism of giving and getting is destabilized, and with it conceptions of human interaction as a matter of exchange. What characterizes love is that it makes the act of giving not an expenditure, but itself a gift. One might of course try to conceive even of love as a practice in which the giving is motivated by the anticipated rewards this will bring the giver. Yet, as already highlighted, once we introduce such an element of instrumentality, we are no longer talking about love (Djikic and Oatley, 2004; Fromm, 1956; Jónasdóttir, 1991/1994, 2011).

Since women are generally the ones with chief responsibility for caring and loving, it is no surprise that feminist scholars have been at the forefront of deconstructing atomistic notions of selfhood, highlighting the error implied in ignoring that relations are not something we choose to enter, but something of which we are made (Hartsock, 1983; Noddings, 1984/2003; Radden, 1996). Not only have feminist theorists highlighted that models of human beings as self-enclosed and self-interested individuals can hardly make sense of the unconditionality implied in typically feminine activities of caring, but, as already touched upon, feminists have also revealed that men's paradigmatic experience of self-sufficiency could not be sustained without the largely invisible need-tending labour that women perform (cf. Duncombe and Marsden, 1993; Jack, 1991; Rubin, 1983).

Yet, while scholars within the field of feminist ethics in particular (Kittay, 1999; Noddings, 1984/2003) have highlighted the fulfilling aspects of caring for others, thus questioning zero-sum accounts of human interaction, as should be

Love: Exploitable resource or 'no-lose situation'?   113

clear from the assessment of Jónasdóttir's work and the analysis in the previous chapter, feminist scholarship on love and care also displays an opposing tendency. While, in the malestream imaginary, the ego(t)istic zero-sum games taking place in public have traditionally been comfortably complemented with notions of family life as a harmonious 'haven in a heartless world' (Lasch, 1977), one of the most central elements of feminist critique has been precisely to reveal that, although the family may be a haven for men, it is generally not so for women. Efforts to de-romanticize both motherly and heterosexual love and reveal them as damaging traps for women have thus crucially involved an introduction of a degree of zero-sum thinking to areas commonly understood in non-conflictual terms. From different theoretical perspectives feminist theorists have emphasized that love is not a blissful win-win game, but that women's love of men and children, contrary to dominant beliefs, often happen at the *expense* of women. From de Beauvoir via the radical feminists to empirically oriented sociologists, the argument has been, simply put, that women, at least in their relationships with men, generally love too much for their own good (Atkinson, 1974; de Beauvoir, 1949/1989; Ferguson, 1989, 1991; Firestone, 1970/1979; Frye, 1983; Haavind, 1984, 1985; Langford, 1994, 1999).

Jónasdóttir continues this tradition of thinking of love as conflict, only in a much more systematic and theoretically refined way than her predecessors. While adhering to the view that love must necessarily be practised in a non-instrumental way, she nevertheless conceives of it in terms of exchange. In her view, theorizing love in terms of 'exploitation' is fruitful precisely because it can make sense of the sociosexual bond 'as a relationship of exchange', where something is 'taken and given, won and lost' (2011: 52). At the same time, she highlights the potential of sociosexual relations to dissolve the dichotomy between self-interest and altruism (2011); more than this, she seems to acknowledge that this dichotomy is partly cancelled out even in exploitative sociosexuality, inasmuch as it is empowering for women not only to be loved but also to love: '"Woman" needs to love and to be loved in order to be sociosexually empowered, in order to be a person' (1991/1994: 224). Jónasdóttir also directs attention to Schlomo Avineri's interpretation of the passage in *The economic and philosophical manuscripts*, where Marx deals with the sexual relationship between man and woman as one revealing 'the extent to which man's *need* has become a *human* need; the extent to which ... the *other* person as a person has become for him a need' (1844/2007: 101). For Avineri the passage conveys the view that 'the basic structural principle of sexual relations' offers the paradigm of a fully humanized future, since '[s]exual relations are at once necessary and spontaneous; they are also other-oriented *par excellence*. Man's need for a partner in the sexual relationship makes his own satisfaction depend on another person's satisfaction' (Avineri cited in Jónasdóttir, 1991/1994: 210).

When referring to Avineri's interpretation of Marx, Jónasdóttir seems to endorse the view that sexual relations have a *fundament* of non-antagonism. However, in my view she does not sufficiently elaborate on the tension between this idea and the notion of love and sexuality as a win/lose relation. This is all the more unfortunate since this unaddressed tension underpins not only Jónasdóttir's work, but feminist thought more generally. On one hand, feminists are eager to

114 *The reality of love and power*

question masculinist ideas of self-contained selves opposed to one another. On the other, the notion that women's loving care for others may stand in conflict with their own interests partly draws on the idea that human beings stand opposed to one another. As far as I am aware, no one has approached this analytical tension in an elaborate way. When the potentially depriving aspects of loving are highlighted, this is typically done from the implicit starting point that, basically, loving – and not only being loved – constitutes a vital part of an enriching life. Yet, it is rarely suggested how we might integrate this positive notion of loving with the idea of love as something like a scarce resource that can be depleted and that, consequently, we might be interested in withholding.

The point of departure of this chapter is that I find plausible both Jónasdóttir's view of love as exploitable and notions of love as essentially transcendent of such oppositions between giving and getting, by virtue of its self-generating qualities. It is my contention that the tension between these different approaches to love echoes not only contradictions in common-sense notions of love, but also real contradictions in the world. For one thing, it is intimately connected to the tension inherent in human sociality itself, stemming from the fact that human beings are both distinct from and mutually constitutive of one another. In the following I compare Jónasdóttir's account of sociosexual exploitation with Bhaskar's theorization of love as a 'no-lose situation' (2002b: 190). Treating their respective perspectives as representative of two equally persuasive but seemingly contradictory ways of thinking about love, I seek to show how they can be reconciled. I begin by presenting Bhaskar's philosophy of metaReality and the essentially harmonious or non-dual concept of love that he develops within this theoretical framework. Then, with the help of Bhaskar's general ontology of metaReality, I sketch a conceptualization of how love can be thought of both as intrinsically a 'no-lose situation' and as a power that can be alienated, exploited and accumulated for the benefit of some and at the cost of others, and I show that contradictions between the different approaches reflect contradictions in the present world.

MetaReality – realism's self-transcendence

In order to understand Bhaskar's conception of love, we must first have a look at the general meta-theoretical framework underpinning it. Bhaskar argues that the philosophy of metaReality 'accepts but goes beyond' (2002c: 8) original critical realism, yet also concedes that there is a sense in which the former challenges the latter. As we have seen, a crucial tenet of the critical realist ontology is that the world is stratified. The different strata or levels of reality are part of a totality, insofar as they are intrinsically related to and emergent from each other, but each stratum also possesses a distinct ontological existence, so that one cannot be reduced to the other. In his philosophy metaReality (2002a, 2002b, 2002c; Bhaskar with Hartwig, 2010) Bhaskar builds on this ontology of stratification and emergence by introducing a distinction between three realms or strata of being, which are distinct in terms of their relation to the issue of identity/non-duality as opposed to difference/duality: (i) *absolute reality* or *metaReality*, (ii) *relative reality* and (iii) *demi-reality*, characterized respectively by *non-duality*, *duality* and *dualism*. The level of absolute reality or metaReality is what constitutes the ground-breaking element of this new philosophy of Bhaskar's. This non-dual level, he argues, is the primary reality or truth from which the other levels emerge and on which they depend. And acknowledging the fact that it is an ingredient in all kinds of realities has important implications for how we should conceive of the constitution of our current dualistic modes of being.

For Bhaskar, original critical realism is correct but partial, insofar as it deals only with the realm of the relative. The philosophy of metaReality instead focuses on that which transcends relativity and Bhaskar contends that, in a sense, 'realism about transcendence leads to the self-transcendence of realism' (2002c/2012: 11).

> The idea of meta-Reality[2] is designed to capture a level of truth which cannot be conceptualized in normal realistic, that is dualistic terms – in this sense [it is] beyond reality; but [it is] not therefore unreal – [it is] beyond reality in the sense of transcending or surpassing the dichotomies in terms of which reality is normally understood.
>
> (2002b: 51)

Among the dichotomies – or rather distinctions – transcended by the concept of metaReality is that between the epistemological and ontological, which was central in the development of original critical realism, while constellationally unified in dialectical critical realism (see pp. 15–16). Bhaskar himself registers the 'irony that there is a level of social being at which the whole premise of my previous work, existential realism, breaks down'. Yet, he emphasizes that the existence of a non-dual *level* of being, where distinctions between subject and object, truth and reality etc. are not valid, does not imply they are inadequate when applied in relative reality; only that 'there are *aspects* of reality that cannot adequately be thought in a realistic way' (Bhaskar with Hartwig, 2010: 182, emphasis added).

Hence, at the level of the absolute or metaReal, which is part but not exhaustive of everything that exists, all is one. The core argument Bhaskar gives for this is that 'it is difficult to see how ultimately any two things in the world could be related in some way unless in some mode or point they are interconnected, and in that moment of interconnection, they are identified' (2002b: xiv). For example, he contends that we cannot possibly understand another being unless in some way we can see ourselves in the other, which in turn we could not do unless we were in some respects part of her or him (2002c). Similarly, taking the example of the subject/object distinction, he contends that on a fundamental level this distinction is untenable, since 'in perception the subject is always a part of the field he perceives, and while he is perceiving the field, the field is part of him, his perception, his consciousness, his awareness' (2002b: 89).[3]

Bhaskar is careful to emphasize that this concept of identity or oneness differs from common atomistic-empiricist ideas of identity as 'punctiform and undifferentiated' (in Bhaskar and Callinicos, 2003: 22). MetaReality is 'a philosophy of a rich differentiated and developing identity that constellationally embraces non-identity

116 *The reality of love and power*

and difference' (Bhaskar with Hartwig, 2010: 72; cf. Ollman, 1971/1976).[4] To clarify this stance, Bhaskar reminds us that we normally have no problem allowing that a person can be 'both one and the same, and differentiated and developing', at the same time and without elementary contradiction (in Bhaskar and Callinicos, 2003: 22). As already noted, this acknowledgement of the co-presence of unity and difference is constitutive of critical realism also in its original version, since without it one cannot make sense, for instance, of the process of emergence. It is also the basis of dialectical critical realism, according to which 'differentiation is a necessary condition of totality and diversity of unity' (1993/2008b: 270).

Although realist and Marxist dialectics differ greatly from the postmodernist school of so-called difference feminism, they have significant overlaps in that both question accounts of totality and unity that deny or supersede difference, such as is the tendency of Hegel's system of thought. For instance, the French philosopher and 'difference feminist' Luce Irigaray challenges 'the artificial and authoritarian unity' (2002b: 10) of phallogocentric modernism, arguing that identity should not be 'determined by the same understood as an equivalence between two terms' (2002b: 81). Unlike Bhaskar, Irigaray is at pains to reject the idea that difference can be contained within a wholeness. Yet, inasmuch as Bhaskar endorses a notion of totality as partial, open and changing, and 'containing' only in a relative or loose sense, I see the outlook of dialectical critical realism as remarkably similar to Irigaray's, although Irigaray lacks the elaborate and stratified ontology endorsed by Bhaskar and is likely to be antipathetic to his effort to capture reality within logical categories (see interview with Hirsch and Olsen, 1995). The fact that Irigaray addresses questions of social being partly in spiritual terms makes her work even more aligned with Bhaskar's philosophical project seen as a whole. In Chapter 9 I draw on this interesting overlap, when seeking to elucidate a way of transcending the current contradictions of love.

The co-presence of unity and differentiation, Bhaskar argues, is valid for the universe as a whole and he articulates this universal embrace as the 'cosmic envelope' (2002b: x). In human and other beings, this absolute level, by virtue of which the universe is one, exists in the form of what he calls the 'ground-state', each being's deepest singularized expression of the whole; in Mervyn Hartwig's interpretation, 'the state that is present in all other states' (2012: xiii). At this level we are immediately connected to every other being and what we are in our ground-state constitutes our most essential and real being, our 'transcendentally real self' (Bhaskar, 2002c: 91). Although the non-dual quality of this level may be – and currently is – suppressed and dominated by the levels emerging from it, this is the basic source of our agency in the world, so that without it we could not be or act. This corresponds to the way that all causality ultimately stems from the non-dual ground of the world, characterized by love, creativity and freedom (Bhaskar, 2002b).

However, the world in which we act and live as distinct embodied selves is one of relativity and duality, without which there could be no change or development. Relative reality is 'the world of becoming' (2002b: xxiii), governed above all by various principles of attraction and repulsion. Yet, this level, at which our selves are contained in our bodies, depends on the more fundamental level of non-duality, accounting for our intrinsic relatedness. In the sense that non-duality is ingredient in everything, metaReality not only signifies the non-dual ground of being, but also 'the constellational unity of non-duality and duality' (2002b: 83). Non-duality, Bhaskar states, is the 'fine structure or deep interior' of the world of duality (2002b: 188). Were this not the case, we could not exist, because 'to be is precisely to be related' (2002c: 238) and, as pointed out above, relating necessarily implies some aspect of identity or oneness. Although relativity and duality are necessary features of all embodied life, Bhaskar contends that it is possible to expand the field of non-duality into this realm, by loving, unconditional modes of being that transcend dualities and differences.

The causally efficacious illusion of 'demi-reality'

In the present epoch, however, the incentives for affirming and expanding the realm of non-duality are highly marginalized. In our world, the unavoidable duality of relative reality has turned into dualism, antagonism and split. This is what Bhaskar calls *demi-reality*, characterized by master–slave relations and instrumentalist modes of being. He argues that, really, demi-reality is an illusion, in the sense that it has no real object; at the same time, it is real inasmuch as illusions are causally efficacious. This theme of a constellational unity of realness and illusoriness is anticipated in dialectical critical realism (1993/2008b), where Bhaskar introduces a notion of, in Hartwig's terms, 'real emergent false levels of being', whose very reality·is constituted by a denial of its reality or truth, so that there is a 'falsity *in* something *to* its essential nature' (Hartwig, 1993/2008: xxiii). In fact, Bhaskar actualizes this notion already in *The possibility of naturalism* (1979/1998), one of the magna opera of the early phase of critical realism, when discussing Marx's concept of mystification. Apart from the kind of mystification that Marx identified in fetishism, whereby historically specific value relations appear as the natural qualities of things, in line with Norman Geras (1971; cf. Arthur, 2009), Bhaskar highlights that Marx also operated with a different concept of mystification:

> in which, to put it bluntly, he identifies the phenomena themselves as false; or, more formally, shows that a certain set of categories is not properly applicable to experience at all. This is best exemplified by his treatment of the wage form, in which the value of labour power is transformed into the value of labour – an expression which Marx declares to be 'as imaginary as the value of the earth', 'as irrational as a yellow logarithm'. ... [T]his mystification is founded on a characteristic *category mistake* – that, *intrinsic to* the wage–labour relation, of reducing powers to their exercise.
>
> (Bhaskar, 1979/1998: 52, emphasis added)

With this idea of ontological falsity or half/demi-reality, Bhaskar can be said to qualify somewhat his causal criterion for ascribing reality to something, which has been so pivotal for my refutation of poststructuralist claims that the socially constructed has a fictive character to it. Capitalism, for instance, is certainly real in that the ideas underpinning it are causally efficacious in the world, with disastrous

118   *The reality of love and power*

material effects. Yet, unlike relations that are real in a more invincible sense, its efficacy in the world is dependent on a negation or suppression of the realities on which it depends; hence, its false character. As I elaborate on in the next chapter, demi-real structures' simultaneous *dependence* on and *negation* of basic necessities is what lends to them what I call an 'ontological fragility', constituted by dialectical contradictions which can be resolved only when these constitutive realities are no longer denied.

If at the level of relative reality we are relatively distinct embodied selves, in demi-reality we are egos, apprehending ourselves as 'existing separately from and in opposition to all other I's' (Bhaskar, 2002b:38). This ego is an illusion, insofar as it is an abstraction from 'a much deeper and broader totality' (2000: 3), which it must deny in order to exist. We *are* not opposed to or separate from one another, since at a primary level we are inexorably related to that which is external to us at the level of our embodied selves. Hence, the idea that I am an ego depends on a suppression of some of the realities that constitute me. It should however be noted that the emergence of the ego structure is no random event. Bhaskar highlights that the features of relative reality constitutes a real basis for our mis-identification with our ego, so that 'underlying this ... mis-identification would be a real truth that we are indeed as embodied personalities spatio-temporally separate and qualitatively distinct from all other beings'. This truth of separateness is false, he stresses, only when taken as the whole truth (2002b: 84).

Despite the illusoriness of the ego, since in the present world we tend to act as if we were egos we do in one sense emerge as beings separate from and opposed to each other. Bhaskar's important point, though, is that relating as an ego to other egos implies not only alienation and split between people, but also necessarily alienation and split within oneself. This is because the non-duality between people is the ultimate reality from where everything else stems, even the wars of demi-reality. Thus, by denying or hurting another person one will necessarily deny or hurt the fundamental part of oneself that is part of her. This kind of split or inconsistency between a person's ground-state and her embodied personality, Bhaskar contends, constitutes the original alienation of the human being.

Drawing on Marx's notion of the world as the 'inorganic body' of humans and Baruch Spinoza's idea that 'the body-actual of each is part of the body-cosmic of all', Collier offers an argument similar to Bhaskar's (2003: 15). Rational self-advantage is inherently cooperative, he argues, since the more we make the 'outside' world a part of ourselves, the stronger or more expanded we become. In line with Bhaskar's view of the differentiated oneness of the universe, he states:

> Insofar as we interact causally with all of nature, but to different degrees, the body-cosmic has no clear boundaries ... but it can be said to be extended to the degree that direct and indirect causal interaction between the body-actual and its world is increased – not just *any* interaction, however, but that which serves to maintain the equilibrium of the system. The more we are sensitive to the world around us, and the more we control it, the more it is part of us.
>
> (2003: 13)

Hence, although in a sense there are no limits between self and that which is not self, whether this non-duality becomes effective depends on the stance taken by the self, in turn conditioned by – although not pre-determined by – the current social organization. By not blocking this natural connectedness by means of conditionality, contractuality and other restrictions, we open ourselves up as much as possible to the powers of the world. Hence, contrary to what we tend to believe *as* egos, it is when we shed our ego that we are as most powerful (Bhaskar, 2002b).

The hope for overcoming the demi-real structure of the present world lies precisely in the fact that the energy used in oppressive and exploitative ways ultimately stems from our ground-states, which are characterized by free, loving creativity whose essence is incompatible with dualism. Nothing could actually be without modes of existence that transcend dualities and dualisms, Bhaskar argues. For example, he highlights that there could be no war without the solidarity of the people involved. By contrast, there could be solidarity without war, and this expresses the asymmetrical relation between non-dual and dualistic modes of being, accounting for the greater power, ultimately, of non-duality. Contradictorily, however, the dualisms of demi-reality currently dominate and occlude, while parasitizing upon, the non-dual energy of metaReality. Here we can see a clear parallel to Marx's theorization of capitalism: under capitalism capital has come to dominate the very grounds of its existence, namely labour power. However, the fact that labour power is, really, more fundamental than capital constitutes the hope for the destruction of capitalism. Similarly, male authority, as conceived by Jónasdóttir, could not be without women's love, a theme which Bhaskar himself actualizes, when stating that feminism 'articulate[s] the interests of those who are excluded from what they essentially constitute or sustain' (2002c: 27).

In line with his non-atomistic concept of identity and unity, Bhaskar emphasizes that a world where non-duality reigns is not a world totally void of contradictions in the weaker sense of the term; without some kind of contradiction there would, indeed, be no development. Demi-reality, however, is constituted by contradictions in the more qualified sense, relating to 'the tension experienced by blocks, constraints, a dualistic play of forces', constituting an absence which one is prevented from absenting 'by something outside or inside yourself or your environment' (2002c: 60–1). Whereas the contradictions of a relative reality shed of its demi-real superstructure are also characterized by some kind of absences which prompt for their fulfilment, Bhaskar highlights that if 'there is no constraint on a process of fulfilling that absence, then there is really no tension involved' (2002c: 60). Hence, development can occur harmoniously. He stresses that even a eudaimonistic society,[5] in which the flourishing of each depends on the flourishing of all, will be located in the world of duality. Hence, in such a world too 'there will still be challenges and conflicting points of view'. Yet, 'they will be resolvable' (Bhaskar with Hartwig, 2010: 191).

Love as the fundament of existence

In the philosophy of metaReality love plays a crucial role. 'Love', in Bhaskar's terminology, 'is the totalizing, unifying, healing force in the universe. And, just

120   *The reality of love and power*

by virtue of there being a "universe" (one-verse), it is the most powerful force in being' (2002b: 175). Hence, the central place of love is intrinsically connected to the fundamental role of non-duality/unity/identity in Bhaskar's general ontology. Just as non-duality is primary to both the duality and dualism which parasitize on it, love is the fundamental driving force of all emotions, including fear, hate and anger.[6] We cannot but love, Bhaskar argues, in the sense that there is always some element of love in everything we do, since without the cohesive and energizing force of love we actually could not or would not be motivated to relate to anything or anyone. Human love is thus by no means confined to love for another human being, but, beginning with self-love, it radiates in ever-widening circles to encompass all human beings, all beings and finally the cosmic envelope, the sphere in which the ground-states of all beings are interrelated (2002b: 181).

If we are in touch with and affirmative of the non-dual level of being at which the 'outside' world is part of us, unconditional loving will be the spontaneous attitude towards the world. Conditional or contractual ways of loving will constitute an anomaly, since *'loving is a no-lose situation'*, such that 'when you give love, you become more love and even if you receive no love back, you are still more love than you were before'. And since love is self-generating and self-sufficient, 'the more love you give necessarily the more love you will get', although this positive reward must of course never be the reason for loving (Bhaskar 2002b: 190). In my interpretation, love's privileged ontological status as *basis* stems from this unique self-generating quality. 'Love', Bhaskar argues, 'is unique in both that it attracts itself, and in this way attracts sustenance from the rest of being, and also in that it is entirely self-sufficient'. This is why '[y]ou do not have to give a justification for love. Rather, everything has to be justified in terms of it' (2002b: 198).[7]

As this conceptualization of love indicates, Bhaskar's philosophy of metaReality is inspired by eastern spiritual systems of thought, hence the characterization of Bhaskar's later work as his 'spiritual turn'. Bhaskar is careful to point to the everyday character of the transcendence implied by non-duality, though. Very simple acts like reading a book imply some kind of transcendence of the duality between the reader and the read, he argues. And the above conceptualization of love does, I believe, resonate deeply with some aspects of the most ordinary experiences of love. Every person who has been in love knows about the radical collapsing of dualities, between lover and loved, between giving and getting (Weitman, 1999). Love as an endless source, expanding the more you pour from it, also seems to be a phenomenon to which many people can relate.

In the world of oppression, alienation and dualism in which we live, non-dual modes of using our loving energies are systematically undermined, though, and 'conditional, false, selfish, possessive, clinging, oppressive forms of love' dominate (Bhaskar, 2002b: 175). These demi-real forms of love are products and generators of dualism and antagonism, and are as such opposed to love in its fundamental or absolute form. It follows logically from the philosophy of meta-Reality that dualistic loving alienates not only the lover from the loved, but also the lover and the loved from themselves. Hence, this kind of loving is not a no-lose situation. Contrary to what is often believed, loving in conditional, selfish

Love: Exploitable resource or 'no-lose situation'?   121

and clinging ways does not protect the lover from anything or make her gain something; instead, it hurts her.[8] The reason is that, given that love is what we ultimately and invincibly *are*:

> if you place a condition on love you thereby take some of it back and thereby lose some of your own love, and become less of what you are, diminish yourself. Moreover, in placing a condition on love, you automatically impose a constraint on yourself, and so on the coherence of your action; and instead of being clear you become cloudy and murky.
>
> (2002b: 191)

By virtue of our non-dual ground-states, *we cannot not love*; therefore, the only way of being consistent with oneself, of being whole and free, is by shedding all that which is not love, such as the elements of fear and egoism in possessive and oppressive forms of love. As Bhaskar puts it, we can either 'maximize the energy at our disposal by being and doing things only which are consistent with our ground-state' or we can 'drain or block or interfere with it by utilizing that energy in ways which drain and dissipate it' (2002b: 57).

In the end of the previous chapter I raised the idea that the love women give to men from a standpoint of submission is a deprived kind of love, and I will elaborate on these issues further on. In relation to this, it is important to make clear that, for Bhaskar, unconditional love is not the same as or even compatible with submissiveness or self-denial (cf. Gross, 1993). He emphasizes that non-dual loving can have all kinds of practical expression, including toughness and breaking up relationships. Most importantly, '[l]ove means, depends upon, loving yourself' (2002b: 181). Bhaskar stresses that at the level of relative reality, where human beings appear as singularized embodied selves, love is not some co-dependent oneness obscuring the differences between lovers. As already stated, his concept of identity is always identity-in-difference. Hence, the identity of my ground-state and yours is one respecting and including our distinct singularities, so that love is also always associated with 'a conatus for autonomy' and 'a respect for difference and independence' (Bhaskar 2002b: 216). This ties in with Irigaray's (1992/1996, 2002b) conviction that true and non-oppressive love must be based in an acknowledgement of the irreducible difference between self and other (see Chapter 9). In a similar way, the feminist psychoanalytical theorist Jessica Benjamin cautions against a 'false closure' of the basic existential contradiction implied in acknowledging the other as something outside of one's own control. 'The defensive assumption of identity' with the other, she states, 'conceals the real strain of acknowledging the other. Acceptance of this strain is a condition of acknowledgement, not an invalidation of it' (1998: 98).

Although unconditional love is the basis of being, there are nevertheless great obstacles to the realization of unconditional loving in a world of demi-reality, where people emerge as egos disposed to relate instrumentally to one another. By virtue precisely of the essential interconnectedness of all beings, the alienation of one person constitutes an obstacle also to other people's possibilities of realizing

122 *The reality of love and power*

their ground-state of unconditional love. That is why a world structured by dualism and split tends to reproduce hate, fear and greed, and possessive and other conditional forms of love. However, even within the confines of demi-reality we have the capacity for struggling to become more at one with our ground-state and shed all that within us which negates this fundamental being of ours. The motor in this process is the realization that we cannot in fact reach satisfaction if we stay within the confines of our ego, that possessive loving, for instance, cannot give us that which is the motive behind possessive loving. This kind of revealing of the illusory character of demi-reality is the ground for struggling to 'expand the zone of love and decrease the zone of the negative emotion parasitic on it' (Bhaskar, 2002b: 216; see Chapter 9).

The illusoriness of patriarchal reality

There are considerable differences but also affinities between Bhaskar's and Jónasdóttir's approaches to love. The point of convergence is that they both conceptualize love as a creative, energizing power or force, fundamental to human life. The main divergences can be derived, as I see it, from their different foci and levels of abstraction. While Bhaskar focuses on the transcendent and universal quality of love (which is not restricted to the realm of the human), Jónasdóttir theorizes the historically specific configuration of practical human love in contemporary western societies. Whereas Bhaskar's main project is to highlight the non-dual and loving component of all our doings in the world, Jónasdóttir takes what might be considered the opposite course, highlighting how conflict and exploitation are constitutive elements of normal loving encounters in societies characterized by formal freedom and women's relative economic independence. Finally, while Bhaskar avoids any systematic treatment of how issues of sexuality and gender structure love in demi-reality, these are of course pivotal concerns for the feminist theorist Jónasdóttir, who sees *sexual* love as the structural axis around which other love practices revolve. The latter is clearly connected to the fact that Jónasdóttir is primarily concerned with love as an embodied human practice, whereas Bhaskar treats love mainly as the fundamental force or principle that underpins such practices. Finally, while Bhaskar sees love as essentially a no-lose situation and approaches the issue of gender and love only insofar as he depicts the typically feminine mode of 'intuitively, tacitly, holistically' caring for the 'relative needs of … husband and children' as a model for a less dualistic society (2002c: 99), this is clearly not Jónasdóttir's way into the subject. In her account, women's impoverished condition is a matter precisely of the fact that they 'love too much' (1991/1994: 224). Given that I find both Bhaskar's notion of love as no-lose situation and Jónasdóttir's thesis that men exploit women's love highly resonant with widespread intuitions, how might these apparently opposed accounts be reconciled?

Bhaskar's framework, as I interpret it, does not preclude a theory such as Jónasdóttir's; in fact, Bhaskar explicitly contends that there are 'oppressive forms of love', which are nevertheless love, to the extent that they too are based in non-dual forms of love (2002b: 175). Yet, from the perspective of the philosophy of

Love: Exploitable resource or 'no-lose situation'? 123

metaReality, patriarchal love and its emergent twin properties of male authority and female sociosexual powerlessness would only qualify as *causally efficacious illusions*, rather than as realities in the fundamental sense. Male authority, female sociosexual poverty and the exploitation which they both depend on and sustain are real inasmuch as our collective belief in them informs our practices, which construct the reality in which we must act. Yet, they are only half-real, since they negate necessities on which they depend. The basic structure of human existence, which underpins the totality of human life, is our interconnectedness, implying that we cannot be empowered at the expense of others. It is only men's empowerment as *egos* that necessitates women's powerlessness, and since the ego is constituted by a curtailing of the transcendentally real self on which it depends, for this more basic self the empowerment of the ego is really a disempowerment.

This is not a challenge to the realness of male power, but a complexification of its ontology. The distinction between the demi-real and that which is real in a more sustained sense helps make sense of the dual or paradoxical character of the ontology of loving encounters between women and men. The fact that many women find hard to accept the idea of these encounters as imbricated in an exploitative process cannot be reduced to a matter of romantic duping or some other form of pure false consciousness; it must also be understood as an effect of the fact that, on the most basic level, love *is* fundamentally unexploitable and transcends all categories of opposition. This, I believe, is one important reason why women generally enjoy loving men, even when it deprives them of their strength and dignity; there will always be elements of non-duality that are worth 'everything'. While Bhaskar emphasizes that even the most appalling events in the world depend on love, there is another side of the coin, namely that the rewarding character of the non-dual elements of exploitative processes tend to make people love their exploited situation and thus make them unmotivated to opt for change. As Sandra Lee Bartky highlights, there is a way in which 'women's provision of emotional sustenance to men may *feel* empowering and hence contradict, on a purely phenomenal level, what may be its objectively disempowering character' (1990: 114). I would only add that this feeling of empowerment cannot be totally written off as illusory, but has its true components too.

The contradictions implied by the demi-real status of patriarchal love also reverberate through the ontology of male authority, a theme I elaborate on in the next chapter. There is an influential common-sense discourse suggesting that women are actually stronger and better than men, that *really* men would be nothing without women, while women would be quite alright without men. 'Women have always known how men need love, and how they deny this need', as Firestone states (1970/1979: 122), pointing to the fragility of men's demi-real self-sufficiency and their real need for women's love (cf. p. 103). When Catharine MacKinnon, in her ground-breaking theoretical account of feminist consciousness-raising (see Chapter 9), seeks to conceptualize the ontological status of male power, she implicitly touches upon the theme of demi-reality:

> Consciousness raising has revealed that male power is real. It is just not the only reality, as it claims to be. Male power is a myth that makes itself true.

124 *The reality of love and power*

To raise consciousness is to confront male power in its duality: as at once total on one side and a delusion on the other. In consciousness raising women have learned that men are everything, women their negation, but the sexes are equal. The content of the message is revealed as true and false at the same time; in fact, each reflects the other transvalued.

(1989: 104)

As I elaborate on elsewhere (Gunnarsson, 2013b), the main difference between MacKinnon's and Bhaskar's accounts of this duality is that, by lack of a notion of being as distinct from the epistemological level, MacKinnon's framework fails to acknowledge the asymmetry between the realness and illusoriness of male power and her claim that male power is both real and a myth is bound to remain a closed paradox. She overlooks the fact that the realness of male power is *based* in the basic vital powers of women, as well as on the denial of this fact, whereas women's basic power and equality with men is a matter of an eradicable human ontology. Hence, male power is not 'total' and the two levels of reality are not on an ontological par.

In his writings on the worker's alienation under capitalism, Marx points to the inversions implied in the capitalist process of production, one of which is that 'the more values [the worker] creates, the more valueless, the more unworthy he becomes' (1844/2007: 719). Similar inversions are constitutive of patriarchal sociosexuality. For example, in contemporary western patriarchy one of the most powerful sociosexual resources a woman can possess is the power to induce desire in men. This constitutes a typical ground for arguments to the effect that women really have more power than men – 'a woman can turn a man's head', 'she's a femme fatale' etc. The paradox, however, is that this female power typically turns into vulnerability, in the sense that the male desire that it provokes has an authority of its own, which comes to dominate the sexual power of the woman in much the same way as capital comes to dominate the labour power that is its source. Women generally do not have the means or authority that they need to control their own sexual power; the sexuality stemming from the woman, once made use of or let free, tends to confront her as 'something *alien*', as 'a power independent of' and opposed to her, to use Marx's words (1844/2007: 69).[9]

In this sense, the sociosexual poverty from which women tend to suffer, explaining many women's eagerness to love men who do not reciprocate, is indeed real, albeit only in the sense that it has causal effects in the world. The exploitative process drains women of their self-esteem, so that, I would put it, their basic need for love tends to be distorted into a craving for love.[10] The other side of this coin is that, within the demi-real logic of male authority, men's love – however poor in the real sense of the term – comes to be more valuable and potent than women's. Although women's love is the real creative source of men's surplus worthiness, just as labour is the real creative source of surplus value (Dussel, 1988/2001), male authority seems to stem from the creative powers of men themselves. This appearance is underpinned by the fact that women's eagerness to love men forms a structure that tends to grant men access to women's love, so that the helplessness men would suffer without this love is concealed.

The necessity of conflict in the present world

As already touched upon, Bhaskar's vision of a society liberated from the demi-real structures of oppression and exploitation is not one of absolute, undifferentiated oneness – or emptiness. The harmony of such a society would not be based on lack of intentions or drives to develop, but on the kind of non-duality envisioned by Marx and Engels, where the free development of each is the condition of the free development of all (Bhaskar, 2002b, 2002c; Marx and Engels, 1848/2010). As Bhaskar argues already in *Dialectic* (1993/2008b), all life is constituted by development, which he conceives of as the absenting of absences. The need for love, in both its caring and erotic-ecstatic senses, is at base level the absence of fulfilled sociosexuality. Our need for love – not only to be loved but also to love – is what relentlessly pulls us towards other people and makes us love and be loved. In a society where love (along with other social relations) were not organized in dualistic ways, the fulfilment of the need for love, that is the absenting of the absence of love, would not be such a difficult project as it often is within current societal structures, especially for women. This is, indeed, logical, because if everyone needs love and if no one really loses anything by loving, then it cannot be an impossible equation that people could fulfil their needs for love rather effortlessly and harmoniously. If people generally and women especially were not confronted by so many constraints on the process of fulfilling the need for love, the urge to fulfil this need would not be as marked by desperation and clinging attachment. And, as we saw in the previous chapter, desperate seeking for love is often the least efficient way to find oneself loved. That is perhaps the real tragedy of women's condition.

Although Bhaskar emphasizes again and again the supremacy of non-dual, unconditional modes of being, he also states that 'as long as there remains negative incompleteness in the world', in the sense that there are severe structural constraints on the process of fulfilling our relative needs, of completing incompleteness, 'you will have to employ modes of behaviour which are not only non-dual, but themselves contradictory, conflictual, antagonistic and so forth' (2002c: 67). A well-known example of how women can use their sociosexual power and men's sociosexual needs in conflictual ways for the sake of peace is depicted in Aristophanes' classical Greek drama *Lysistrata*, where the women successfully engage in a collective sex strike to force their men to stop making war against each other. There is, indeed, a sense in which the conflictual mode of Lysistrata and her sisters could be said to be an expression of unconditional love, in that it was for the best of the whole community. In that sense, the dualistic play of forces involved in the sex strike was constellationally embedded in non-duality.

Along similar lines Bhaskar argues that, despite the ills of a world structured by egos, some people would actually need to strengthen their ego, if only as a means of letting it go. 'Some of us have very weak egos. If we are not in our ground-state the ego can just as easily be too weak, as too strong' (2002c: 105). It is more harmful, he contends, to have no self-love at all than to love oneself as an ego opposed to other egos.[11] These statements open up a space for conceptualizing

126   *The reality of love and power*

the necessity for women to break with the caring tendencies inherent in femininity and start thinking a bit more of themselves. Insofar as this implies a rupture with women's characteristic 'capacity and willingness to boost egos' (Langford, 1994: 97), such female self-centring can actually be said to be a more authentic expression of love, since it helps dismantle the male ego that is premised not only on its alienation from other people, but also from its own transcendentally real self.

I earlier offered a definition of love as the act of recognizing and affirming another person and her needs and goals as valuable in their own right. I here want to qualify this definition somewhat by emphasizing that, if the needs and goals stem from the ego structure, affirming them does not amount to love in the qualified sense; this is rather the characterization of alienated love. We may instead turn to Milton Mayeroff's suggestion that '[t]o care for another person, in the most significant sense, is to help him grow and actualize himself' (in Noddings, 1984/2003: 9) and conclude that tending to someone's ego wants and needs serves such growth poorly. Hence, women who actively work to make sure men feel safe within the illusory boundaries of their ego are really less loving than women who threaten this safety, by standing up for their own needs for growth and actualization.

Women indeed occupy a privileged position from which to undo the male ego, since it has come into being only by suppressing the female self. As I showed in the preceding chapter, on an individual level this kind of assertiveness on the part of women is a risky project, though, precisely since the male ego is the privileged reality and value in the society in which we live. Efforts to dismantle egos will tend to meet resistance from men, whose ultimate source of power in this struggle is to withdraw the 'hard currency' of their love. Thus, as I elaborate on in Chapter 9, women need to build up the existential-authoritative resources that give them the power to 'stand off' from men, so that men's need for women's love is laid bare and women's negotiating power strengthened.

The historical need for such conflictual attitudes does not mean that change is not in men's interests, as I discuss more thoroughly in the next chapter. Although the male ego may be powerful and privileged within the parameters of demi-reality, the fact that it is conditioned on split and alienation means that it is ultimately disempowering. Inasmuch as demi-real, patriarchal modes of loving block, drain and interfere with the energy of our ground-states, in a world where women's loving energy were allowed to flow freely rather than being conditioned by its being *of use* to men, there would actually be more love for men by which to be empowered. The productive forces of love, like those of labour, are augmented in a world in which the free development of each is the condition for the free development of all.

In an article about the western 'importation' of female care workers from the Third World, Hochschild gives expression to a sense of puzzlement over the issues highlighted in this chapter. While arguing that in the current global economy of care we can speak of love as an 'unfairly distributed resource – extracted from one place and enjoyed somewhere else' (2003b: 22), she hesitates when examining this statement a bit closer. The love that Rowena Bautista, the US-based Filipina nanny that Hochschild has followed, gives the children of her employers is clearly premised on her own children's being deprived of their mother's love.

Love: Exploitable resource or 'no-lose situation'? 127

Yet, Bautista surely does not stop loving her own children just because she is in the USA caring for – and developing genuine love for – other children. Hence, Hochschild asks, can love really be thought of as a 'scarce resource'?

> In some ways, this claim is hard to make. The more we love and are loved, the more deeply we can love. Love is not fixed in the same way as most material resources are fixed. Put another way, if love is a resource, it's a *renewable* resource; it creates more of itself. And yet Rowena Bautista can't be in two places at once. Her day has only so many hours. ... In this sense, love does appear scarce and limited, like a mineral extracted from the earth.
>
> (2003b: 22–3)

I think this passage summarizes very succinctly the problematic addressed in this chapter. It points to the crucial tension inherent in human love, in my view emerging from the tension between the spiritual[12] and material aspects of love and, more generally, from the constellational unity of non-duality and duality. Although the essential quality of love is non-dual and as such unbound and inexhaustible, the practical, embodied realization of this boundless quality is always constrained by the relative and bounded nature of our embodied material existence. Whereas love is essentially a qualitative matter, to the extent that its human realization is linked to using our exhaustible bodily energies in certain ways, a quantitative element enters the picture. By virtue of the energizing and transformative quality of love, however, the rate of exhaustion and exploitation cannot be reduced to a quantitative matter of how much bodily energy or time is used in our loving practices; one peculiar thing about love is, indeed, that when immersed in it our physical energy often seems unlimited. It is somewhere here, in the tension between the non-dual and unbounded on one hand and the dual, relative and materially bounded on the other, that we need to centre our analysis both of the contradictions – in the weak sense of the term – of practical human love as such and of the historically specific oppositions in which love is immersed in demi-reality.

Jónasdóttir specifies that:

> to say that the human capacities to love and labour are *exploitable* is to say that these are living sources of energy which can be released as it were in a person or a group of persons and be used as human powers in the sense of abilities to bring about developmental effects in some physical (non-human) material and/or in another person or a group of persons.
>
> (2011: 51)

It is the material-organic-energetic embedding of these powers, I would contend, that makes it possible for some people to appropriate them from others, so as to materialize new emergent entities of power that acquire a relatively independent existence and come to dominate the basic powers through which they ultimately derive their force. Also, it is this material embedding of our love practices that accounts for the fact that loving, when practised under oppressive conditions,

128 *The reality of love and power*

may be exhausting one's powers. Yet, as I elaborate on in the next chapter, the *constitutive* element of love's particular force to empower us as persons is a matter of human subjectivity or consciousness and this crucially constrains the extent to which it can be exploited.

Conclusion

Again, we see how the stratified and dialectical conception of being offers a way of complexifying our accounts of reality. The idea that reality is comprised of distinct yet internally related strata helps make sense of the many paradoxes, contradictions and dualities that life has to offer, such as the ambiguity between the reality of women's basic power and equality with men on one hand and their powerless vis-à-vis men on the other. Instead of just juxtaposing such contradictory levels of reality, so that their interrelation is bound to be understood in terms of an enigmatic paradox, the critical realist framework also offers tools for elucidating their different nature, thereby enabling a more exact analysis of the relation between them. Crucially, ontological contradictions are often hierarchically structured, by virtue of the fact that some dimensions of reality are more basic – and hence real – than others since they are necessary also for the existence of other levels, whereas some parts of reality have no necessary link to the (re)production of life as such. Even though, *within* the confines of demi-reality, women's relative powerlessness and men's power are real, this reality will always be fragile, since it is founded on suppressing the more basic realities on which it depends.

The contradictions of contemporary love, stemming from its organization along different axes of reality that are internally related yet in tension with one another, seem to have been extrapolated into an unfortunate theoretical split between cynical and naïve approaches to love. We have here another example of dialectical antagonists, who seem to be opposed to one another but who are in fact fighting on the same reductionist and one-sided terrain. These theoretical adversaries need to be integrated into a coherent whole, which can account for and make sense of lived contradictions, instead of focusing only on one of their poles. Not only need feminist theorists pay more attention to the necessary, rewarding and liberatory dimensions of love, if their critical edge is to appear credible for the majority of women (cf. hooks, 2002); malestream theories of love, such as Bhaskar's, also need to take into account feminist scepticism about too optimistically embracing love. As I have sought to show, Bhaskar's framework does not contradict theories such as Jónasdóttir's; still, I believe it may appear to do so to many readers and to this extent there is a need for further efforts to theorize the often painfully experienced relation between the damaging and beneficial aspects of women's loving. In this chapter I have initiated such a bridging endeavour. By reconciling Bhaskar's non-dualistic view of love with Jónasdóttir's concept of love as an exploitable power, by means of Bhaskar's general meta-theoretical framework, I have sought to offer a more integrated account of the unintegrated forms of love that dominate our conflict-ridden world. In the remaining part of the book I elucidate some further consequences that my introduction of the metaReal has for our understanding of the contemporary conditions of sociosexuality. This will involve an identification of the lacunas in Jónasdóttir's theory, emerging from the fact that she does not delve deep enough into the reality of love and human interconnection.

Addressing the problem of heterosexual love under patriarchy, Virginia Held comes to the conclusion that '[i]n trying to live with a recognition of the importance of both fighting and loving, women will have to accept a kind of schizophrenic existence'. She claims that for women '[a]n integrated stance toward the world is a distant goal to be sought, a luxury they cannot yet afford (1976: 182). In a way, then, it seems that Held dooms women to the kind of split existence that Bhaskar holds to be detrimental to the project of liberation. This, however, is probably too hasty an interpretation. After all, Bhaskar argues that a world of dualism requires dualistic ways of being. On a deeper level, however, the 'schizophrenic existence' posited by Held, if embraced in a non-dual fashion, could perhaps be seen as the most non-dual and integrated stance possible for women in present society, since it is the only one *at one* with the position that women occupy. The female position as we know it is constituted by severe contradictions, however half-real one set of their poles is. Denying that would imply a splitting of women from a part of themselves as they are constituted in this world. Bhaskar's conception of metaReality as the constellational unity of non-duality on one hand and duality and dualism on the other allows for a transcendence of the gulf between dualistic 'fighting' and non-dual 'loving'. In line with this, the challenging task for women is to love men's ground-states unconditionally, while struggling against those aspects of men that contradict their loving ground-states, without losing sight of the fact that what is at odds with men's ground-states is also emergent from them.

Notes

1   An earlier version of this chapter appeared in *Journal of Critical Realism* 10(4) as 'Love – exploitable resource or "no-lose situation"'? Reconciling Jónasdóttir's feminist view with Bhaskar's philosophy of meta-reality' (Gunnarsson, 2011b) © Equinox Publishing Ltd 2011.
2   'MetaReality' was originally spelt with a hyphen, 'meta-Reality', but in his later publications Bhaskar dispenses with the hyphen. I follow the later mode of spelling, except when quoting the older literature.
3   This is another argument offered by Bhaskar for the case that all is one:

> [A]ll being, in virtue of its being part of one universe, which even considered materially we believe emerged from a single spark, lightening flash or big bang (or perhaps some originating primordial sound or stirring in the void), must be bound together or share the properties of every part of it in common in virtue of the unity inscribed in the universe's beginning and/or its interconnectedness as a whole.
>
> (2002b: 69)

It is indeed quite easy to claim the chronological priority of unity; another example that can be drawn on here is that of the child being first unified with the mother before differentiating from her. The question remains, however, how this chronological or diachronic aspect ties in with the ontological or synchronic one. I would argue that they are ultimately inseparable. For instance, oneness is ontologically more basic than difference

130 *The reality of love and power*

not only in the temporal sense of the emergence of a person; also, the extent to which a child can exist, here and now, as a differentiated, singular being is premised on the extent to which it experiences unity with its caretakers. Unity, trust and love are the foundation of the child's autonomy.

4 Bertell Ollman argues for a corresponding 'dialectical conception of identity' (1971/1976: 266) and challenges the idea of identity and difference as mutually exclusive. He cites Marx, who stated that '[i]t is characteristic of the entire crudeness of "common sense" … that where it succeeds in seeing a distinction it fails to see a unity, and where it sees a unity it fails to see a distinction' (in Ollman, 1971/1976: 265) and, like Bhaskar, he argues that identity is primary to difference and that this was also Marx's view.

5 'Eudaimonia' is Greek for 'happiness' or 'flourishing' and a central concept in Aristotle's ethics. Bhaskar often uses the term 'eudaimonistic society' to denote the kind of society envisioned by Marx, in which each person's development or flourishing is entailed by that of all others.

6 Michael Hardt and Antonio Negri endorse a similar view, arguing that evil is 'love gone bad', rather than lack of love (2009: 193).

7 Bhaskar's idea of love and connection as ontologically primary can be related to Nel Noddings' (1984/2003) view that the most basic reality is one of relatedness. Against the existentialist idea of aloneness as the fundamental human reality and anxiety as the primary affect, she suggests that joy, accompanying the recognition of relatedness, is the basic affect that requires no other reason than being itself.

8 Bhaskar's line of thought ties in with Erich Fromm's (1947/1990) claim that human constructivity is primary to our potential for destructivity, insofar as any violation of the life forces of others is a violation of the principles on which our own lives are based.

9 In an earlier study (Gunnarsson, 2004) I interviewed women about their sexual experiences with men. While it was common for the women to feel that something was *taken* from them when they had sex with men, they also expressed a feeling that this experience was somehow *erroneous*, somehow not fully anchored in reality. This experiential ambivalence can be understood as reflecting the ontological contradiction between demi-reality and its constitutive base.

10 Put in Bhaskar's terms, the basic need for love, which is part of the relative realm, can be understood as an absence prompting for its fulfilment, but – if non-dually-embraced – with 'no constraint on … [the] process of fulfilling that absence' (2002c: 60; cf. 1993/2008b), whereas the demi-real craving for love is constituted by a more marked dualism between absence and the possibilities of absenting it.

11 Here Bhaskar's view of the ego differs from that of Buddhist feminist Rita Gross (1993), who argues that the weak self is as much an ego as the dominating self (see p. 157).

12 Here I operate with a definition of the 'spiritual' as that which does not follow the laws of relative, material reality, but pertains to consciousness, understood as fundamentally transcendental and non-dual.

8   Men in love
The work of repressing reality

> Masculinity is structured through contradiction: the more it asserts itself, the more it calls itself into question.
>
> Lynne Segal (1990: 123)

In this chapter I look closer at the contradictions produced by the fact that the demi-real level of sociosexual exploitation negates the logic of the basic forces on which it depends, and locate the consequences these contradictions have for *men*. Expanding on the theoretical themes raised in the previous chapter, I argue that men's pursuit of their interests as created *within* exploitative sociosexuality is at odds with their more basic needs and emancipatory interests. Whereas within the parameters of demi-reality men have a salient interest in continuing to base their personal authority on exploitative practices that (re)produce female socio-sexual poverty, these practices create contradictions which block the possibilities for men to be empowered in a fuller and more sustainable sense.

I begin by discussing the notion of contradiction and, more specifically, *internal contradictions* and its sub-species *dialectical contradictions*. I show that the patriarchal sociosexual structure can be theorized as constituted by dialectical contradictions that create dilemmas not only for the exploited, but for the exploiters too. I flesh out some paradigmatic dilemmas confronting men in patriarchal sociosexuality and argue that the strategies to manage them within the confines of continued exploitation necessarily produce new contradictions that require manoeuvring. I introduce a couple of notions articulated in Bhaskar's dialectical critical realism, in order to elucidate how contradictions of this kind can be understood only in relation to the constraints emerging from the basic necessities of reality. Finally, I discuss the implications of these discussions for how men's interests in patriarchal sociosexuality should be conceived, and highlight that Jónasdóttir's framework fails to take into account the complex and contradictory character of men's interests, by lack of a depth ontology of love.

Dialectical contradictions

One of the peculiarities about the capitalist system which Marx sought to explain was that the more values the worker creates the more valueless or worthless she

132　*The reality of love and power*

becomes, since the more she realizes her productive powers within the confines of the capitalist system the more exploited she will be (1844/2007). This is not something that just 'happens' to be so, but a necessity emergent from the internal contradictions of capitalism. Not surprisingly, contradictions are a crucial theme in dialectical critical realism. The dialectical-emergentist ontology, which thematizes relations in which internal connection coincides with distinction, is also what allows for a coherent understanding of the oppressive and alienating dialectical contradictions that are constitutive of our society. Bhaskar defines *contradiction* as 'a situation which permits the satisfaction of one end or more generally result only at the expense of another: that is, a *bind* or constraint'. While contradictions often exist between entities external to one another, in the *internal contradiction* the constraint comes from within rather than without (Norrie, 2010). It is 'a *double-bind* or self-constraint (which may be multiplied to form a knot)' (Bhaskar, 1993/2008b: 56). The *dialectical contradiction* is a kind of internal contradiction that is constitutive of oppressive and exploitative power structures. In dialectical contradictions existential interdependence coincides with opposition or split, 'in the sense that (at least) one of their aspects negates (at least) one of the other's, or their common ground or the whole …, so that they are tendentially mutually exclusive, and potentially or actually transformative' (Bhaskar, 1993/ 2008b: 58). Here, as Norrie puts it, the two poles of the contradiction 'appear to be, but are not, distinct' (2010: 70). Following what he sees as Marx's manifold conception of contradictions, Bhaskar also introduces a notion of *generative separation*, in which basic existential contradictions are tied up with structural oppositions, producing a contradiction at the core of the human being.

The situation in which the worker finds herself under capitalism is a dialectical contradiction insofar as the possible ways for her to satisfy her basic needs are simultaneously to the detriment of these needs. Whatever she does to pursue her goals, this will obstruct the fulfilment of these goals. If she abstains from selling her labour power, in order not to be exploited, it is likely that she will not be able to satisfy her basic needs for food and shelter. If she does sell her labour in order to have these needs met, she will be exploited of the life forces that the selling of her labour was meant to secure. In Chapter 6 I elaborated on how women in heterosexual coupledom are faced by similar contradictions by virtue of their position in patriarchal sociosexuality. In general terms, there is a systematic pattern positioning women in situations in which that which they must (within the parameters of demi-reality) do in order to be produced as worthy persons simultaneously tends to undermine their worthiness. Put differently, the sociosexual relations through which women are compelled to satisfy their need for love are structured in a way that deprives them of the personal power and worthiness that their loving and love-seeking is about.[1] On one hand, it is in the women's interests to submit their own subjectivities to the needs of their male partners, since this will increase the chances of being 'loved'. On the other hand, the love they receive by suppressing who they are is not love in the qualified sense and will therefore not empower them very effectively as persons. Hence, on a deeper level it is in their interests to assert their own distinct needs and wishes, because only

Men in love: The work of repressing reality   133

then can they be loved for their own sake rather than for being useful and comfortable for others. Yet, this is a risky project, since the current patriarchal sociosexual structure positions women in such a way as to appear unloving, and thus unlovable, if they break with the feminine tendency of subordinating their own needs to those of others. Hence, the risk is that this strategy ends up in not being loved at all.

The exploiter's burden

On one level, the privilege of exploiters is that they do not need to cope with the contradictions internal to the system by means of which they come to be dominant. Contradictions are 'pushed down' to the exploited so as to become their problem. Even, by virtue of their control over the means by which other people can exercise their powers, exploiters are in a sense liberated also from the most fundamental constraints of life, stemming from our being inevitably needy and dependent. For example, as pointed out in Chapter 6, men's paradigmatic experience of self-sufficiency and their tendency to be unaware of their own needs for affection and recognition is underpinned by women's tendency to take responsibility for men's needs. As Benjamin states, 'the historically masculine subject … has always been constituted by its disavowal of dependency on the maternal, the subordination and control of what it needs' (1998: 84). However, due to its reliance on denial, this subject is inherently fragile. As Andy Moye hints, men's unawareness of their vulnerability is never absolute, so while they 'expect women to provide them with sexual and emotional security, … women are in turn feared for having a powerful insight into men's insecurity' (1985: 51; cf. Segal, 1990: 212). This points to the 'ontological fragility' of men's personal strength as produced in patriarchal sociosexuality; on a fundamental level even exploiters find themselves captured by contradictions that require management.

It is a well-known fact that the capitalist cannot wholly ignore the needs of workers, if he is to exploit them. Most notably, the worker must earn enough so as to be able to reproduce herself, so that she can continue working; unless her basic needs for food and shelter are met, there will be no labour power to exploit. However, as Christopher Arthur points out, the reproduction of labour power cannot be restricted to the satisfaction of crude biological needs, if it is to be effective; the humanity of the worker must also be respected at least to a certain extent:

> [T]he problem of capital is that it needs the *agency* of labour. It is not really a matter of reducing the worker to the status of a mere instrument of production, like a machine, or like an animal whose will has to be *broken*. It is a matter of the *bending* of the will to alien purposes. … The former 'subjects' of production are treated as manipulable objects; but it is still a question of manipulating their activity, not of depriving them of all subjectivity. … Thus, even if Marx is right that the productive power of labour is absorbed into that of capital to all intents, it is necessary to bear in mind that capital

134 *The reality of love and power*

still depends upon it. Moreover, the repressed subjectivity of the worker remains a threat to capital's purposes in this respect.

(2001: 29–30)

The capitalist's necessarily ambivalent relation to the subjectivity of the worker constitutes a dialectical contradiction in the sense that the poles contradicting each other also presuppose one another. For the capitalist, the value of workers lies in their human capacity to work, but by its structurally necessitated disrespect for human needs the logic of capitalism tends to destroy the humanity on which this capacity is premised. In this sense, the more freedom workers enjoy, the greater their potential productivity will be, although of course the potential will also be greater for rebellion. This contradiction forces capitalists into a balancing act between repression and democracy, and the more they succeed in reducing the risk of rebellion by ideological means, the freer they can let workers be. As I elaborate on below, as with the sociosexual contradictions already highlighted, this contradiction can be understood only by reference to a 'natural ontological order' (Collier, 2002: 166) of human needs and powers. It is based on absolute limits imposed on capitalism, stemming from the fact that the living powers to be exploited possess their own distinct logic, which constrains the possible ways they can be realized, used and moulded. The power of the capitalist, hence, is never total.

Now, while Arthur is right that a stifled subjectivity is detrimental to the productive power of workers, I would argue that freedom is not as essential to labour as it is to love. When it comes to many kinds of labour, it is indeed possible to break the will of the worker to quite a high degree, without severe loss of productivity. The efficacy that is lost with the disinvolvement of the worker's will can be compensated for by the efficacy enforced by threat and violence. By contrast, when it comes to sociosexual exploitation, repressing the subjectivity of the exploited is more essentially problematic for the exploiter, since love power is rooted in the subjectivity of its practitioner in a more absolute sense than labour power. While it is possible to force someone to work, it is impossible to force someone to love. One cannot even buy love. To repeat Jónasdóttir's insight, the 'extreme vulnerability' of 'sexual goods/values' stems from the fact that 'they cannot be bought, and still less extracted by force', but must be offered voluntarily (1991/1994: 107; cf. Lynch, 2007). A lot of the practical aspects of sociosexuality are indeed laborious, and as such they can be forced or bought from people, as in sexual violence, prostitution and care work. Yet, the essential quality of sociosexuality which lends it its force to empower persons is the loving element by means of which we give of ourselves to someone *spontaneously*, because we want to or cannot help but to, because we hold the other person worthy thereof.

Thus, insofar as love cannot be demanded or forced from someone and inasmuch as we need love, we are also dependent on other people's freedom. If we lived in a world where we had total control over all other human beings, there would be no one left to empower us personally-existentially. We would be everything and no one. Inspired by the Hegelian master–slave dialectic, Benjamin writes insightfully

Men in love: The work of repressing reality 135

about the ultimate vanity of efforts to empower oneself by controlling others, by making them into objects constructed to fulfil one's own wishes:

> In order to exist for oneself, one has to exist for an other. … If I destroy the other, there is no one to recognize me, for if I allow him no independent consciousness, I become enmeshed with a dead, not-conscious being.
>
> (1988: 53)

The free will and consciousness of the other, which in one sense constrains our own existence, is also its fundament.

I suggest that the dialectical contradictions of demi-real sociosexuality be seen as the emergent dualistic expression of this basic tension in the human situation. This view aligns with Benjamin's conceptualization of sexual domination as effectuated by the splitting or breaking down of the basic human tension stemming from the fact that our independent existence can come about only if we are recognized as independent by others, on whom we therefore depend. 'True independence', she states, 'means sustaining the essential tension of [the] contradictory impulses [of] asserting the self and recognizing the other. Domination is the consequence of refusing this condition' (1988: 53). This denial of dependency results in 'the transformation of the need for the other into domination of him' (1988: 54). The fundamental tension of relative reality between the mutually constituting poles of autonomy and dependency is broken down and transformed into a split or polarization between the male, autonomous subject and the female dependent object.

Men's dependence on women's freedom

While the undemandability of love tends to cause painful dilemmas for women deprived of love, as highlighted in Chapter 6, what is perhaps more intriguing is that it also causes dilemmas for men, whose exploitation of women's love is ultimately dependent on women's freedom. As Octavio Paz states, 'the emergence of love is inseparable from the emergence of woman. There is no love without feminine freedom' (1993/1995: 85).[2] Elaborating on this insight Mike Featherstone highlights that love 'depends upon the capacity of the woman not only to attract, but to choose and reject' (1999: 3). In an important sense, then, sociosexual exploitation is premised on the relative freedom of the exploited, since the creative human powers to be exploited will be undermined if the subjectivity of the exploited is stifled. Hence, a woman who is not reduced to the function of being of use to men will actually have more to give the latter. Consequently, men do have an interest in restructuring their personhoods so as to no longer base it on their structural control of women.

At the same time, men have a perseverant demi-real interest in remaining structurally in control of women, since patriarchal male personhood is premised on a secured collective access to women's vital powers. As Jónasdóttir states in a parallel to the capitalist's structural compulsion to exploit labour, men *must* partake in sociosexual exploitation 'if they are to remain the kind of men that historical circumstances force them to be' (1991/1994: 225). In her reading of Jónasdóttir

136   *The reality of love and power*

Valerie Bryson (2011) criticizes this parallel, pointing out that the compelling mechanism is more definite for the capitalist than for the man, since the capitalist will cease to exist completely as capitalist if he stops exploiting labour. Here Bryson is indeed right that the choice at hand for a capitalist is much more of the 'either/or kind'; either you are in or you are out. However, although biology will secure that a man remains a man even when produced as unmanly, and while masculine identity is more negotiable and shifting than capitalist identity, the former is more intimately linked to the existential core of a person than the latter. Hence, in one sense its force may actually be stronger. Failing to exist as a masculine self is more likely to be experienced as a failure to exist as a human being as such.

Michael Schwalbe (1992) states that it is via conforming to the relatively egocentric, uncaring 'masculinist self' that men tend to have their needs for approval satisfied, so if this self is threatened this will tend to be experienced as a threat to survival. The fabric of contemporary paradigmatic masculine selves, I would contend, simply cannot harbour the unavoidable existential risk of being rejected. On a deeper level, men would benefit from facing this risk, for it is only in its light that they can be truly empowered by not being rejected, and it is only from the point of view of the vulnerability entailed by this risk of rejection that we can be really receptive of the power of love. Yet, within the confines of demi-reality it is rational for men to cancel out their vulnerability, by means of exploiting the privilege of a structurally secured access to women's sociosexual powers.

The sociosexual contradiction wherein men are both burdened by and dependent on women's independent subjectivities has its patriarchal 'solution' in men's authority and entitlement to determine the limits to women's freedom and self-expression. The patriarchal sociosexual logic of contemporary western societies produces men who want women to be free, but only to the limit where this freedom serves men's needs. This claim can be linked to Ann Cahill's argument that it is misleading to conceptualize women's subordination to men in terms of objectification; rather, the relation is one of 'derivitization', whereby women are treated as subjects, but subjects whose status is derived from the usefulness they have for men (Cahill, 2011). In my view, the reason why the exploitative logic of this sociosexual arrangement is often hard to track down is precisely that it depends on female agency and subjecthood.

Here, then, emerges a pervasive tension in men's sociosexual structure of interests, between promoting women's freedom, on one hand, and controlling women, on the other. In the following discussion I pinpoint some dilemmas produced by this contradiction. I also locate typical patriarchal ways of managing these dilemmas, demonstrating that these solutions are necessarily ridden with their own contradictions, due to the impossibility of escaping the fundamental structure of human interrelatedness.[3]

The double-edged sword of control

Following Jónasdóttir, I have emphasized that in order for sociosexual actions to empower us as persons, they need to be performed voluntarily. Jónasdóttir does

Men in love: The work of repressing reality 137

not elaborate on to what extent women's love of men can be seen as truly voluntary in a context of oppressive structural constraint. Her central point is that, much like the worker exercises her formal freedom when she sells her labour, women do not have to be forced to submit to men's sociosexual needs, but do so willingly. It is only that this willingness is produced by conditions that leave women with few realistic alternative ways of fulfilling their need to love and be loved, so that the willingness cannot be equated, as I see it, with freedom in a fuller sense. Jónasdóttir (1991/1994) states that women are *alienated* from their voluntarily given love under current exploitative sociosexual conditions and this, I argue, implies a structural kind of unfreedom that can be coupled with voluntariness in the immediate sense of the term. However, it is my contention that true freedom and voluntariness – and the true sociosexual-existential empowerment stemming from it – can only come about under non-alienated conditions, in which women and men exercise shared control over the structures by means of which they are compelled to realize their sociosexual capacities and fulfil their sociosexual needs.

Yet, besides the fact that men exercise a structural control over women that tends to secure their access to women's voluntarily given love, we know only too well that men also often use more direct modes of control in order to enjoy women's (and children's and other men's) sociosexual capacities. I write *sociosexual* even in this case, emphasizing the intersubjective dimension, for it is not an object that is wanted in situations of sexual coercion, in my view. There must be something about the social and intersubjective powers of sexuality that is sought, since sexual stimulation on a mere physical level can easily be pursued on one's own (cf. Cahill, 2011). While there are sexual perpetuators motivated by sadistic inclinations, it seems that the most common kind of sexual control and abuse is one where the free and mutual sociosexual interplay somehow fails. In cases where men's structurally secured access to women's freely offered socio-sexual powers is put at risk, the contradictions constituting men's situation can mostly be easily detected. Overt force or money may then have to substitute for the structural sociosexual power men commonly enjoy, however incomplete the empowerment derived from *taking* sexual 'goods' turns out to be.

Even the most univocally sadistic sexual acts can in fact be interpreted as an alienated effect of the basic interdependency of subjectivities. As Benjamin states, domination is an alienated form of differentiation. With the denial of the dependency of one's own self on the other, the basic tension between self and other breaks down. Domination, distance, idealization and objectification, Benjamin states, can then be employed as means of recreating the tension on which any sexual satisfaction depends, and may as such stand in for the satisfaction created by the tension involved in surrendering to the true otherness of the other. However, although the tension produced by this alienated kind of differentiation can give temporal pleasures, it 'is destined to repeat the original breakdown unless and until the other [recognized as independent from oneself] *makes a difference*' (Benjamin, 1988: 68, emphasis added).

Whereas many radical feminists see men's violence against women as the engine of patriarchy (mostly failing to explain *why* men have an interest in being

138 *The reality of love and power*

violent), from Jónasdóttir's perspective violence is rather a symptom of the under-lying exploitative structure (1991/1994: 195). When women do not give that which men expect and which is moreover constitutive of paradigmatic male personhood as currently produced, seeking to take it by force may seem the only solution. This is much like capitalist societies based on the 'voluntary' entering into labour contracts use overt force when workers challenge the 'normal business'. As Benjamin says, '[v]iolence is the outer perimeter of the less dramatic tendency of the subject to force the other to either be or want what he wants' (1998: 86). It is important to stress that, mostly, men are not motivated to control women by some kind of wickedness. The main mechanism, in my view, is that, by virtue of the normalization of their exploitation of women's love, men tend to feel *entitled* (cf. Pease, 2010) to a greater share of ecstasy and care than women, such that when women challenge the exploitative pattern this will, by means of a contrast effect, tend to appear unfair (cf. Chapter 6).

However, as should be clear from the earlier discussion, the empowerment men get by using direct force or money to appropriate women's sexuality is an alienated kind of empowerment. While it is possible to control another person's body, the psychic or spiritual dimension that is constitutive of the existentially empowering force of sociosexuality cannot be controlled. I contend, thus, that being sociosexually empowered by means of overt control works only if underpinned by illusion. Even if it is indeed common to achieve intense sexual satisfaction and empowerment in a temporary and superficial sense by treating another person as non-person, it is revealing that most sex-buying men want the prostitute to pretend she enjoys having sex with them. Often they are not even primarily inter-ested in sex, but in being cared for and listened to – yet without all the problems and risks implied in interactions with non-prostitutes. As Lauren Joseph and Pamela Black highlight, research shows that '[s]ex workers are often expected to display or feign sexual arousal or sexual pleasure for their clients' gratification as well as provide emotional, therapeutic-type services to the men' (2012: 491). One prosti-tute in Teela Sanders's study even says that '[n]inety percent of the job is chatting, therapy' (2006: 2436). Whether sex-buyers want care or no-strings-attached sex, what they have in common is that, as Celia Smyth Anderson and Yolanda Estes put it, they 'seek … a prostitute in order to avoid the inconvenience of sexual relations with another *subject* … [Buying sex] delivers a woman-thing without the responsibility of dealing with a woman' (1998: 154–5). I would also suggest that if a man experiences that a woman he has bought or forced himself upon *nevertheless* truly enjoys him and wants him, this might constitute the ultimate proof of his irresistible value as person and man.

Reality biting back

Since the natural ontological order of sociosexuality is such that sociosexual 'goods' need to be underpinned by loving care (by definition voluntarily given), if they are to satisfy our need to be empowered as persons (Jónasdóttir, 1991/1994, 2011), contradictions inevitably arise when sociosexual actions are

Men in love: The work of repressing reality   139

enforced. In dialectical terms, although the empowering force of love is existentially dependent on the freedom of its practitioner, in the emergent patriarchal sociosexual order women's freedom comes out as *opposed* to men's empowerment. '[O]ntologically extravagant' is the expression Bhaskar uses to characterize societies, such as the present, constituted by dialectical contradictions of this kind (Bhaskar with Hartwig, 2010: 193). The contradiction between the demi-real and its basis can also be thematized as a contradiction between false and real necessities. Whereas the internal connection between freedom, love and existential empowerment is an ontological truth or natural necessity – it stems from the inner structure of love and humanness – the internal relation between male authority and structural control of women's love is what Bhaskar (1993/2008b) terms a *TINA necessity*, which is really false, although taking on the character of a real necessity when acted upon and sedimented in our institutions. TINA is short for 'There is no alternative', which refers to Margaret Thatcher's way of arguing for the necessity of a monetarist solution to the economic problems of the UK.

Bhaskar elaborates on how acting on a false TINA necessity is bound to create a contradictory meshwork of dilemmas and repressions, which he articulates as a *TINA compromise formation*, where the idea of compromise formation, like that of the reality principle, is borrowed from Freud (1901/1938).[4] If practices which violate or contravene natural necessities 'are to survive and be applicable to the world in which we ... act', Bhaskar states, they 'require some defence mechanism, safety net or security system, which may well, in systematically related ensembles, ... necessitate supporting or reinforcing connections, in the shape of duals, complements and the like' (1993/2008b: 116, emphasis removed), such that a complex internally related constellation of contradictory practices and ideas emerges.[5] The idea is that for *any* practice or system to work it *must* in some way, however covertly, adapt to the natural necessities mediated by the reality principle. We *cannot* ultimately contravene the basic order of things, if we want to have our intentions fulfilled, because any practice is dependent on forces of natural necessity which impose their own, invincible conditions. For instance, and as already highlighted, if women seek to find autonomy by denying their need for love, they are bound to fail. The reality of one's neediness is destined to make itself heard and necessitate new defence mechanisms and compromises with reality, if the whole project is not to fall apart.

Whereas the TINA necessity of basing one's independence and power on the denial of vulnerability is one strategy women may use to get out of subordination, for men it is constitutive of what they *are* in patriarchy. However, men's self-sufficiency can emerge as real only insofar as they secure their supply of love by means of the structural control they exercise over women's loving. The safety net implied by this structural control is itself unsafe, though, and physical violence and coercion is just the most extreme way whereby men compensate for the fragile ground of their ontological security as constituted in patriarchy. The naturalization of men's violence against women then in turn works to safeguard the necessitarian guise of the status quo. In this way, the initial falsity of the patriarchal project produces 'a tangled web of contrivances that somehow hold the project

140 *The reality of love and power*

together without resolving a basic problem', as Norrie puts it. 'Things may work for a while, but reality has a habit of biting back' (2010: 106).

When Jónasdóttir states that 'men today are dependent on an exploitative "traffic in women" if they are to remain the kind of men that historical circumstances force them to be' (1991/1994: 225), I would say that she in fact articulates a TINA necessity integral to the TINA compromise formation that the patriarchal totality comprises. Men are not *really* forced to exploit women in order to sustain themselves. Yet, the connection between the specific kind of male personhood that depends on exploitation, on one hand, and, on the other, being a male person in the basic sense acquires a necessitarian semblence, underpinned by practices that punish those – men and women – who reveal it as false.

Put in more everyday terms, the idea of TINA compromise formation is articulated in the common wisdom that one lie necessitates further lies in order not to be revealed. To refer back to the discussion above, the extreme expression of patriarchal sociosexuality where men 'extract' women's sociosexual powers by direct force, thereby denying the basis of sociosexual power in freedom, necessitates the effectuation of further falsity if it is to 'work'. The basic existential tension is that, whereas men need women to be free if they are to be chosen and hence personally empowered by them, women's freedom also means they may not be chosen, loved, desired. When men control women to get what they need, they must thus somehow repress this reality of control if the empowerment is to be successful. The fact that a woman does not engage in a sexual interaction because she wants to, but because she is forced to or paid for it, must be somehow denied, and this creates a web of inconsistencies constitutive of the man's ontological security. To a certain extent, this dynamic is at work also in more normalized exploitative heterosexual bonds, in which the man is unaware of his dependency on his partner, as well as of the fact that she does not offer him her love simply because he is esteemed as a lovable individual, but because she is in more or less desperate need of a man who can bestow her with the worthiness emerging from his structural position as man. The fragility of men living in this patriarchal mode stems from the fact that there is always a risk that these illusions be revealed as such.

Men's ambivalent interest in women's pleasure

Jónasdóttir argues that in contemporary western patriarchy men tend to realize their sociosexual capacities through the pursuit of erotic ecstasy, while women are more likely to channel their sociosexuality through care. These two tendencies are internally linked in the sense that men's historically determined possibilities for ecstasy depend on women's care for them, whereas men's relative lack of care for women hampers women's ability 'to practice ecstasy on their own terms, that is, as self-directed and self-assured sexual beings' (Jónasdóttir, 1991/1994: 102). As Sichtermann suggests, women 'are not allowed to develop their own feelings of desire and therefore remain dependent on the desire of others' (1986: 77), a claim that can be aligned with Benjamin's (1988) analysis

Men in love: The work of repressing reality   141

of women's tendency to constitute their 'own' self through its submergence in male subjectivity. Within current sociosexuality, hence, the most accessible way for women to live their sexuality is through men's desire for them. It is indeed possible for women to desire in more self-directed ways that are relatively independent of the desire of the man and, as stated in the introductory chapter, this possibility seems to have expanded during the last decades. Yet, as the lingering phenomena of the Madonna/Whore syndrome and the sexual double standard indicate, the overall tendency is still that women's sexuality must be sanctioned by male desire.

The gendered splitting of ecstasy and care, which must be considered a demi-real phenomenon, comprises a dialectical contradiction inasmuch as it represses the fact that, fundamentally, ecstasy and care are internally related aspects of one and the same capacity for love. Men, I would argue, have strong interests in women's experiencing ecstasy and pleasure, insofar as this is sociosexually empowering for men themselves. Significantly, pornographic plots often involve a woman beside herself with ecstatic pleasure (Moye, 1985) and men's magazines follow the same pattern of bolstering the reader's confidence that he will be able to give pleasure to women (Rogers, 2005). Importantly though, a crucial element in these plots is that the woman receives pleasure *because of the man*, so as to confirm *his* sociosexual power. It is less common to see women practising ecstasy in ways not caused by or derived from the desire of the man.

The logic at work here can be depicted as patriarchal, inasmuch as the man's interest in the woman's experiencing pleasure does not stem from his care for *her*, but from the flattering light it throws upon himself. In the previous chapter I drew on Avineri's claim that sexuality offers a paradigm of mutuality, in that '[m]an's need for a partner in the sexual relationship makes his own satisfaction depend on another person's satisfaction' (Avineri cited in Jónasdóttir, 1991/1994: 210). Although I agree with Avineri that this interdependency of the interests of lovers points to a non-dual core to sexuality, which is of great political significance, as Held puts forward, Avineri fails to distinguish between mere interdependence and genuine mutuality. She states that:

> although the man may gain pleasure from the states of arousal or satisfaction of the woman, if the latter states are considered primarily as factors contributing to his greater pleasure, the resulting value of his initial pleasure, increased by the pleasure which her pleasure gives him, is still an egoistic value.
>
> (1976: 173)

The widespread phenomenon of faked orgasm (Wiederman, 1997) – indeed, a TINA mechanism – is an excellent illustration of this skewed kind of reciprocity. When women pretend to feel pleasure in order to please the man, it becomes alarmingly clear that the primary function of the woman's pleasure is often to empower the man rather than herself.

We can elucidate the patriarchal mechanisms crystallized in the faked orgasm by relating Jónasdóttir's framework to Schwalbe's analysis centring on 'the

142   *The reality of love and power*

masculinist self', the paradigmatic masculine identity produced under patriarchal conditions. Although not specifically addressing sexuality, Schwalbe touches negatively upon the theme of pleasure and satisfaction, arguing that the existence of the masculinist self 'is premised on not caring about women's pain' (1992: 43). Like Jónasdóttir, he stresses that the uncaring tendency inherent in masculinity is structurally brought about, rather than an expression of individual men's immoral inclinations. The masculinist self 'simply cannot survive the demands of enacting an ethic of care when trying to resolve conflicts with women' (1992: 43) and a collapse of the masculinist self will be experienced as a collapse of selfhood as such, when the latter is premised on the former. In light of Schwalbe's argument, I posit that men's relative inattention to women's pain or lack of satisfaction is not rooted in indifference, but quite the reverse. Especially in contemporary western societies, where love and formal freedom play such a fundamental role, the fact that a man might be unable to please a woman threatens his personal existence. However, rather than taking in women's full subjectivity – i.e. receptively role-taking – and responding to their dissatisfaction as a means of realizing the wish to please, the strategy equipping the masculinist self is to block out the parts of women's subjectivity that indicate that there is something hurtful about this self. Given that the masculinist self is premised on 'remaining insulated from [women's] pain', Schwalbe states:

> [i]f this pain were to be fully felt, its roots in the patterns of domination that sustain masculinist selves in other ways might become obvious. The pain that men cause women would then become men's pain and men would be motivated to destroy the masculinist self causing it. A suicidal dilemma is thus avoided by avoiding receptive role taking.
>
> (1992: 42)

Here, then, we can identify another patriarchal contradiction and its patriarchal 'solution'. In order for men to be ecstatically empowered in a full sense, which does not depend on blocking out aspects of reality that can become part of one's own expansion, they need to feel that their sociosexual practices enable pleasure, wellbeing and ecstasy in their partners as well. When this mutuality does not prevail, the strategy of repressing the reality of the woman's lack of satisfaction may be employed, often with active aid from the woman herself, due to her structurally weak position. In case the woman is not cooperating, as pointed out in Chapter 6, there is the strategy of explaining her reaction in terms of her own defects, structurally enabled by the fact that men will mostly have no problem finding another woman who is more cooperative. Only if the majority of women were to start behaving in less submissive ways, would men be *forced* to monitor their own part in the conflicts they have with women, if they wish to remain in the warmth of their love. Again, though, the male contentment founded on such repression is inherently fragile, since the truth of female dissatisfaction always risks being revealed. Moreover, the price to pay for a satisfaction that is premised on ignoring the dissatisfaction of the woman is a circumscription of the sociosexual energies flowing from the woman to the man, for the suppression of the less

Men in love: The work of repressing reality 143

pleasant parts of a woman is also a suppression of her irreducible subjectivity, which is the creative source of the power the man is out for.

Male emancipation

In her book *The will to change: men, masculinity, and love*, US feminist theorist bell hooks states that '[p]atriarchy is the single most life-threatening social disease assaulting the male body and spirit in our nation' (2004: 17). While acknowledging men's responsibility for oppressing women, hooks argues that on a deeper level men lose out as much as women from living in a society which, in her view, prevents the possibility of love between women and men. Although this notion is not uncommon among lay people, it tends to be cautioned against by feminist theorists. This is not surprising, since it appears paradoxical that men are damaged by a system that privileges them. Also, those who do subscribe to the idea that current society is oppressive of men tend to be antifeminists, either in the sense that they see women and men as equally oppressed, thereby neglecting the asymmetry between them, or that, even, they see men as oppressed by women (see Messner, 1997). Much like feminists have avoided biology in order to remain on a safe distance from biological determinism, there may be a reluctance to acknowledge the damages done to men in patriarchy, since this is associated with a neglect of men's oppression of women.

Moreover, the flat ontology implicit in the poststructuralist and antirealist thinking currently in vogue makes it difficult to sustain a notion of men as being oppressed by an order which privileges them, since it is premised on the idea that there is a level of the self stretching beyond the socially constructed order. As already argued, such a reductionist view of the self rids us of the possibility of coherently claiming that the current construction of women is undesirable and oppressive, since this presumes that women have needs – for worthiness, autonomy, respect, love – which are not products of social construction. If they were, we could just as well seek to deconstruct women's need for worthiness as a struggle against the practices negating it. Empirical data also provide massive support for the existence of a level of the self that is irreducible to current social determinations. As Caroline New states, 'we know enough about human potential and influences on human development to be able to describe situations or types of social environment which tend to hurt or limit people, whatever the cultural context' (2001: 739).

New highlights that the interests men have in reproducing the current gender order are themselves products of this order, which negates the deeper interests men have by virtue of their basic humanness.

> While men are frequently the agents of the oppression of women, and in many senses benefit from it, their interests in the gender order are not pregiven but constructed by and within it. Since in many ways men's human needs and capacities are not met within the gender orders of modern societies, they also have a latent 'emancipatory interest' in their transformation.
>
> (2001: 729)

144   *The reality of love and power*

New's characterization of the complexity of men's interests can be related to my discussion of dialectical contradictions and the theme of demi-reality. New contends that 'the very practices which construct men's capacity to oppress women and interest in doing so, work by systematically harming men' (2001: 731), actualizing the theme of an emergent level which comes to dominate its basis, producing a generative separation at the core of men's being. She takes the example of how the structural demands on men to control emotions circumscribes their human potential (cf. Farough, 2004; Schwalbe, 1992). This constriction of men is more often seen as an aspect of male privilege, New points out, since '[t]he control of emotions is closely linked to the control of women' and more generally to the ability to function well in capitalist, patriarchal organizations (2001: 740). Yet, 'because of the human natural capacity for empathy and identification which is crucial to social life', it is in men's emancipatory interests, she argues, to create a gender order that not only meets men's own needs better, but also the needs of others (2001: 745). To connect this line of thought with mine, the male withholding of affection that is constitutive of patriarchal sociosexuality (cf. Illouz, 2012) gives men power in the sense of a certain control over the course of events. Yet, it undermines the more encompassing and sustainable personal power that stems from *being in relation* or *communication*, to as high an extent as possible, with the forces outside of one's embodied personality. To this extent, true freedom and empowerment[6] involves not only control, but also surrender. As Collier states, power comprises not only our active powers to affect the world, but also our 'passive powers ... to be affected by more of the world in more ways' (2003: 15). There is also an important sense in which we are empowered by giving, by meeting other people's needs. As articulated in Marxist thought, human emancipation involves not only having our needs met, but also realizing and developing our capacities; in fact, these are two aspects of the same dialectical process.

New distinguishes between conservative and emancipatory interests. She defines conservative interests as interests in preserving the status quo, arguing that most women also have conservative investments, since 'they construct themselves to find what satisfactions they can' within the current gender order (2001: 737). This mechanism was laid bare in Chapter 6, where complying to a patriarchal style of femininity made sure women were at least loved in what we might now term a demi-real sense. New does not offer any definition of emancipatory interests, but I suggest that whereas her notion of conservative interests corresponds roughly with the patriarchal strategies to *manage* patriarchal contradictions, as depicted above, emancipatory interests are what is at stake in the feminist *resolution* of them.

As New highlights, feminists have an interest in acknowledging the harms done to men in patriarchy, since the 'complexity of interests' that this creates constitutes one of the central hopes for change (2001: 736). She points to the mutual entailment of men's and women's emancipation, highlighting that the consequences of what she calls the 'systematic mistreatment of men' (2001: 729), in particular the blunting of their capacity for empathy and intimacy (cf. Connell, 1987), possibly 'inhibits men's

Men in love: The work of repressing reality 145

aspirations for the richer relationships of equality, leading them to settle for the maintenance of the "patriarchal dividend"'. If this is so, she deduces, 'the mistreatment of men would be directly opposed to the interests of women' (2001: 744).

Conclusion

I have argued that, on one level, the privilege of exploiters is that they do not have to deal with the contradictions inherent in the structures producing their dominant positions. Yet, the harmony achieved by 'pushing down' contradictions, so that they are borne by the exploited, is a false one, always at risk of revealing itself as such. Therefore, within the context of patriarchal masculinity men's sense of security depends on the continuous holding at bay of contradictions that tend to tear, so to speak, reality in opposing directions. Following on from my discussion in the previous chapter, I pursued the argument that, on an essential human level, men are hurt by engaging in practices which hurt women. The structural power men enjoy by virtue of their exploitation of women's love is constituted by ontological falsities and consequent contradictions, which always threaten to crumble this power. The personal authority men acquire by virtue of the alienated love offered to them by women is a meagre substitute for the deeper and hence more robust personal strength that stems from being involved in equal and free relationships with others. In this sense, men's deepest human interests coincide with women's: to eliminate women's illusory – yet causally efficacious – overdependence on men, by putting an end to exploitation, thereby augmenting the 'productive forces' of love by which to be empowered. Yet, the cost of giving up control is that women are granted the possibility to realize their sociosexual powers in ways unwanted by men. This is the fundamental existential contradiction that men have been able to suppress – if only ever partially so – by means of their structural power; in non-exploitative sociosexuality they too have to face it. As Benjamin says, 'our need for the other's independent existence demands we bear' contradictions of this kind (1998: 98).

The time is due for feminist theorists and activists to start embracing the complex and multi-layered structure of gendered interests and its roots in the basic ontology of the human situation, where unity overrides division. Although exceptions exist (apart from New, see e.g. Dowd, 2010), feminist theory and politics are too entangled in the zero-sum accounts of human interaction, which are really a product of the oppressive order against which we (should) struggle. It may seem counterintuitive to care for the wellbeing of our oppressors, when patriarchal male wellbeing is premised on the negation of women's wellbeing. Yet, if we acknowledge that ultimately women's and men's emancipation depend on one another, the conclusion that must be drawn is that if we reduce men to their current harmfulness, we lose the possibility of identifying and actualizing the range of human forces that could work in the service of feminist transformation.

146 *The reality of love and power*

Notes

1 The same sociosexual contradictions structure non-heterosexual women's interactions with men, but they are expressed differently. By not entering sexual bonds with men, to a certain degree women can avoid the specific dilemmas facing women involved sexually with men. Yet, as is all too familiar, the very situation of being a woman who does not direct her sociosexual energies mainly towards men produces unworthiness, since the specific female worthiness attributed to women in patriarchal sociosexuality is attained by loving and being loved by *men*, but also due to the general disrespect and unlovingness shown towards non-heterosexuals in current society. Furthermore, to a less intense degree the dilemmas facing women in heterosexual coupledom face all women in their interactions with men in friendship, kinship, work etc. This elucidates the *structural* character of the exploitation analysed in this book; as long as the structure is not transformed, all women are affected by it, regardless of the choices they make.

2 We might only want to qualify this heteronormative statement somewhat, so as to state that there is no *heterosexual* or *lesbian* love without feminine freedom.

3 These conditions can be analysed in terms of the extent to which they advance or 'become fetters on the existing productive forces' (Marx and Engels, 1845/1970: 102) of love. On one hand, by virtue of their 'immiserated' sociosexual position, women are structurally compelled to develop their sociosexual capacities, since these are what they have to offer in their negotiations with men, by lack of the authority enjoyed by the latter. Hence, to a certain extent, men's structural possibility of exploiting women of their love is likely to have augmented women's sociosexual forces. On the other hand, however, under circumstances in which women's love will tend to be exploited, there will be constraints on women's willingness and ability to develop their capacity for loving. The love that women 'voluntarily' offer men from a stance of compulsion is likely to be split by resentment and alienated by urgent need. The powerlessness experienced with regard to the unequal conditions and consequences of sociosexual interactions alienates women from their love and tends to render it a matter of negotiation, thereby constraining its power. Only if women are able to freely love men, instead of loving them from the stance of desperation produced by sociosexual poverty, will their 'productive forces of love' be emancipated from their fetters.

However, the greatest impoverishment of the sociosexual forces of humanity is constituted by the fettering of men's capacities for love, brought about by their sociosexual position. In the current sociosexual order men do not *need* to develop their capacities for love to a very high extent in order to be loved. It is only when their access to women's life forces is structurally conditioned on their own active loving that men will have a salient interest in developing their nurturing and other-oriented capacities on a large scale. Hence, on the demi-real level both women and men are locked inside a structure of antagonism which produces interests of *not* loving, although ultimately both women and men would be most effectively empowered as persons in a eudaimonistic structure, in which loving and caring for others do not happen at the cost of oneself, but is experienced as the 'no-lose situation' that love essentially is.

4 Merriam-Webster's (2013) definition of *compromise formation*, in its original Freudian sense, is 'a psychic product, symptom, symbol, or dream form that expresses simultaneously and partially satisfies both the unconscious impulse and the defense against it'.

5 Norrie defines Bhaskar's TINA compromise formation as 'a set of ideas and/or practices which are brought together to guard the vulnerability in the initial false necessity, and which themselves assume their own false necessitarian contradictory guise' (2010: 106).

6 I do not ultimately distinguish between freedom and power, such as tends to be done in atomistic modes of thinking, where power is conceived of as 'control over' and freedom as 'freedom from' what is outside of oneself. With the dissolution of the dualism between self and the world, this distinction is no longer tenable.

9 Reality and change

Be the change.
    Mahatma Gandhi

In this book, in particular in the two preceding chapters, ontological tensions between different levels and degrees of reality have been at the forefront. Although this sort of philosophical exercises may perhaps seem detached from the concerns of practically oriented feminists, I would contend that this is not the case. An ontological tension of this kind is in fact at the heart of the feminist project. On one hand, feminists claim that there is a social order constructing men as more powerful and valuable than women, and that this order is not a matter only of ideas and 'prejudices', but *real*. On the other hand, the meaningfulness and political-ethical import of this analysis depends on the notion that the construction of women as less valuable and powerful than men somehow contradicts a more fundamental reality, where women are as valuable and capable as men.

Within feminist scholarship probably no one exposes this tension as clearly as MacKinnon, however without being able to contain it theoretically. MacKinnon contends that in a way male domination leads to a 'distortion' of women's selves, indicating that there is something about women beyond male domination, which can and should be liberated. However, she cannot theoretically ground this idea, for, in her radically social constructionist – or reductionist – view, '[i]f the reality of [the] damage [done to women] is accepted, women are in fact not full people in the sense men are allowed to become'; hence, 'on what basis can a demand for equal treatment be grounded?' (1989: 103). This unresolved ambiguity concerning the reality of the socially constructed is also expressed in her claim that 'male power is real' but 'not the only reality'; it is 'a myth that makes itself true' (1989: 104) (see also Gunnarsson, 2013b).

Although MacKinnon insists on the totality of men's power to construct the reality of women and sexuality, the idea of distorted selves and the understanding of male power as a myth making itself true depend on a notion of a deeper and truer reality. Similarly, Butler's somewhat hesitant inclination to see gender as a fiction is premised on an idea of a less fictive reality; indeed, this is the reason for her hesitance. I have argued against the idea of the socially constructed as a

148 *The reality of love and power*

fiction, highlighting that it robs us of the grounds for arguing that the constraints of gender are real, as opposed to a matter of our imagination. However, through the course of the book I introduced a sense in which the socially produced gender order is in fact illusory, although real inasmuch as it is causally efficacious – a myth that makes itself true. Hence, the Butlerian and MacKinnonian vacillation between notions of the socially constructed as *the only reality* on one hand and a *fiction* or *myth* on the other has some adequacy to it. Yet, by lack of a specified ontology, in which natural necessities are distinguished from contingent social orders, neither Butler nor MacKinnon can account for this tension, nor for how its two poles are related.

The way we make sense of ontological tensions like this has crucial implications for our conception of transformation. The more adequately we pinpoint the structure of social reality, the more adequately we can grasp how it may be changed. In this chapter I delve deeper into the issue of how a feminist transformation of the exploitative sociosexual structure can come about, and of how the theorization of such a transformation is related to the way we understand the fundamental structure of social being generally and of sociosexual existence specifically. I begin by recapitulating and elaborating on my earlier discussion of Bhaskar's conception of the real as comprised by different layers and degrees of realness, and discuss the ontological complexity this lends to social reality. The main part of the chapter then deals with the issue of how women, whom I see as the principal agents of feminist transformation since their interest in it is more urgent and actual than men's, can find a way out of the current contradictions of love. I sketch a dialectic between two modes of feminist struggle, where the first aligns with more traditional collectivist conceptions of feminist politics, whereas the second, which draws in particular on the depth ontology of metaReality but also on the work of Irigaray, can be said to be ultimately spiritual in character.

The real and the 'really real'

In original critical realism Bhaskar applies the causal criterion for ascribing reality to something, meaning that anything effecting material change in the world can be judged real. The empiricist notion that only that which can be directly experienced is real precludes an identification of power structures, since these cannot themselves be seen, heard or felt. Hence, Bhaskar's alternative reality criterion is crucial from a feminist viewpoint, indeed, for any critical and emancipatory project. Although the structure systematically privileging men at the expense of women cannot be directly experienced, it can be included in the realm of the real on the basis of the empirical tendencies it produces.

From the point of view of the causal criterion for reality-ascription, everything is part of reality, even absences (1993/2008b) and illusions (2002b), since these too affect the course of events. However, the idea of real illusions carries with it the implication that this kind of realness is only 'half', as conveyed by the concept of demi-reality, introduced in Bhaskar's philosophy of metaReality, but anticipated already in dialectical critical realism with the idea of falsity *in* being.

Reality and change 149

The illusory or false quality of the demi-real lies in that its reality is premised on denying aspects of what is in fact its reality. By contrast, the 'really real', to use Arthur's expression (2009: 178; cf. Dussel, 1988/2001),[1] is not compromised by such suppressions – which inevitably create contradictions and splits – but in harmony with its true ontology based in natural necessity.

This differentiated conceptualization of the real and the idea of the constellational unity of realness and illusion are crucial for a more exact understanding of the anatomy and dynamic of the reality of gendered power. The widespread nature-phobia in feminist theory rules out such a complex, dialectical conception of the real, though, since it precludes an identification of necessities that cannot be constructed away. Whereas Butler shies away from any idea of natural necessity, it is a decisive strength of Jónasdóttir's framework that it is grounded in the necessities of socio-sexuality. It is only insofar as we *must* involve ourselves sociosexually with others, if we are to survive and thrive as persons, that the structure of sociosexual exploitation can be reproduced. At the same time, sociosexual necessities also put important constraints on the ways that sociosexuality can be organized and, hence, on the scope of men's power. Men's patriarchal power is based on women's vital powers and as such men are ultimately dependent on women. Moreover, inasmuch as women's love power is constituted by their irreducible and ultimately uncontrollable subjectivity, it can be appropriated only if women are in some sense free.

Still, Jónasdóttir fails to draw out the full consequences of her acknowledgement that human sociosexual existence is structured by invincible necessities. Most centrally, she does not distil the implications of the fact that the kind of male power that is premised on the powerlessness and constriction of women is inherently fragile, due to its contravention of the basic logic of sociosexuality, and that, as such, this power is not 'really real'. This power is at continuous risk of being torn apart from within, due to the contradictions produced by the fact that *the realness of male authority is constituted by the suppression of its true ontological ground*, which is not men's personal qualities but their exploitation of women's vital powers. This 'ontological fragility' of men's power as produced under exploitative sociosexuality means that, ultimately, men have an interest in refraining from basing their personal power on exploitative practices that secure their access to women's sociosexual powers, and restructure their selves in a way that does not suppress their dependency on others.

The dialectical relation between the 'really real' and the demi-real is what should be laid bare by critical social science. When male authority and female powerlessness are *explained*, that is when their 'truth[,] … real reason(s) … or dialectical ground' (Bhaskar, 1993/2008b: 394) are identified, they are also demystified. This demystificatory process implies the simultaneous acknowledgement of the realness of male authority and female powerlessness, on one hand and, on the other, the demonstration that they are illusory in the sense that their realness depends on the suppression of their constitutive ground, the fact that men exploit women of their power. The very acknowledgment of this real ground of male authority destabilizes its existence – its realness – insofar as the causal efficacy of male authority depends on the illusion that it stems from the personal qualities of men.

150　*The reality of love and power*

This process of demystification, of 'elucidating one reality by disclosing its foundation in and determination by another', as Norman Geras puts it (1971: 77), was the project of Marx's analysis of capitalism, taking as its point of departure the *puzzling* appearance of capitalism, the fact that 'capitalist society necessarily appears to its agents as something other than it really is' (1971: 71). As Geras emphasizes, by this Marx did not mean that the way capitalism appears is a subjective matter or arbitrary fiction, sustained by the misconceptions of agents. Its appearance is objective in the sense that it is *in its nature* to '*present... itself* as something other than it really is', he states, invoking Maurice Godelier's claim that '[i]t is not the subject who deceives himself, but *reality* which deceives *him*' (in Geras, 1971: 79). This stratified and dialectical conception of reality, which allows for the constellational unity of realness and falsity, is of utmost importance to feminists, since it helps theoretically make sense, for instance, of women's ambiguous experience that their powerlessness is both real and not real.

Importantly though, as obscure as it might sound, the reality of women's power and equality with men is 'more real' than their powerlessness, since, unlike the latter, it is not premised on suppressing constitutive aspects of itself, but a necessary feature of the human ontology. This ontological claim is the foundation of my following outline of a twofold mode of feminist struggle, which can help dismantle the reality of male patriarchal power.

Female withdrawal: laying bare men's dependency

The hope for a feminist transformation of sociosexuality lies in the fact that male patriarchal independence is illusory, in the sense of being *really* dependent on women's powers. The implication is that men's true vulnerability and dependence on women would be actualized, if women pursued a relative withdrawal of their caring and erotic energies from men. This would equilibrate women's and men's respective power to determine the conditions under which they love: men would have to love more if they are to be loved and women would be loved more for loving. However, just as a worker cannot displace the power imbalance between herself and her employer on her own, women cannot pursue such a transformatory withdrawal as an individual project. Only if women withdraw on a collective scale will men be rid of the possibility, articulated by Hochschild's 'pragmatic frame of reference' (see p. 109), to compensate one women's withdrawal with the availability of others.

But, given my emphasis on women's sociosexual poverty and the neediness it tends to generate, how is such a female withdrawal to be brought about? Here too the importance of collective action comes to the fore. A central aspect of women's withdrawal from men is that it frees time and energy for women to increasingly invest their sociosexual energies in one another, thereby building up their reservoirs of personal worthiness relatively independently from men. If a sociosexually impoverished woman seeks to challenge the power imbalance by withholding her love from men (cf. Illouz, 2012; Strazdins and Broom, 2004) without alternative forums for sociosexual empowerment, she will not *really* be ready to dispense

Reality and change 151

with men's love. Rather than finding a way out of the contradictions that cause her pain, she is thus instead likely to find herself in an ever tighter contradiction, in which dependency co-mingles with isolation. As Hochschild notes, the kind of 'armoured self' implied by this strategy hardly constitutes a radical challenge to the current order of love: 'Instead of humanizing men, we are capitalizing women' (2003a: 29; cf. Illouz, 2007, 2012). Seen from a metaReal point of view, it is a strategy locked inside the logic of demi-reality.

An authentic female withdrawal must involve a genuine de-actualization of women's dependency on men, and this can come about only if women direct more of their caring and erotic energies towards one another, a theme that is recurrent in feminist thought (Ferguson, 1989; Haavind, 1984; Irigaray, 1977/1985; Rich, 1980/1983). Such a redirection of women's sociosexual power from men to women can be relative and combined with living heterosexually. My broad conception of love and sexuality means that this kind of sociosexual reorganization does not involve only straightforwardly sexual interactions or romantic love. As famously argued by Adrienne Rich (1980/1983), we can think of the erotic bonds between women as a continuum, rather than an on/off matter. The crucial thing is that women displace the centrality of men in their life (cf. Medina-Doménech *et al.*, 2014) and start prioritizing one another more strongly.

Yet, this sociosexual reorganization can also take the form of political lesbianism, the conscious choice to practice lesbianism, often involving the effort of previously heterosexual women to transform their structure of sexual desire (Atkinson, 1974; Douglas, 1990; Imray, 1984; Leeds Revolutionary Feminist Group, 1979/1981; Radicalesbians, 1973). Turning away from heterosexuality does not necessarily have to be a conscious effort, though; it can also be the spontaneous consequence of a process of consciousness-raising, whereby the true reasons and implications of one's attraction to men are revealed and rejected, not only on an intellectual level but on an affective too. I want to stress, however, that political lesbianism that is not anchored in one's actual desires (see Imray, 1984; Kitzinger, 1987: 139) is in my view unproductive. If a woman longs to be sexually with men, this need must be taken into account if she is to be emancipated. One might perhaps defend the strategy in terms of sacrificing one's own heterosexual pleasure for the sake of the political cause of transforming the sociosexual structure more generally, but the risk is significant that this strategy will create tensions that sooner or later cause it to break down.

The idea that women need to break with the male-centredness fostered by patriarchy is also constitutive of the practice of feminist consciousness-raising, which was of immense importance, practically and theoretically, in the development of second wave feminism. As theorized most comprehensively by MacKinnon, feminist consciousness-raising is 'the collective reconstitution of the meaning of women's social experience' (1989: 83), taking place when women break their isolation from one another and share their experiences without male interference, so as to find out that what they thought were their own private problems are in fact systematic features of being a woman in patriarchy. The idea of consciousness-raising focuses on the epistemological process of reorganizing one's experiences.

152 *The reality of love and power*

MacKinnon states that 'the process redefines women's feelings of discontent as indigenous to their situation rather than to themselves as crazy, maladjusted, hormonally imbalanced, bitchy, or ungrateful' (1989: 100). This process of redefinition is politically crucial, in that identifying the broader structures that produce women's painful experiences is a premise for taking action against them. Perhaps more centrally, it helps women regain a sense of worthiness and self-love, earlier undermined by their experience that it was *they* who were faulty. As MacKinnon puts it, '[i]t is validating to comprehend oneself as devalidated rather [than] as invalid' (1989: 100). Although there is a crucial cognitive-intellectual dimension to this process of redefining one's worth, it could not come about without the loving energies produced when women gather, often standing in stark contrast to an earlier lack of care and recognition. Hence, consciousness-raising too is essentially a sociosexual process.

Women's strategy of redirecting their sociosexual energies from men to one another takes place in the nexus between dualism and non-duality, illustrating Bhaskar's idea of their constellational unity. In a patriarchal society based on men's structural access to women's sociosexual energies, a female withdrawal of this kind doubtless has an antagonistic touch to it (cf. Daly, 1978; Frye, 1983; Haavind, 1984). Such a withdrawal, in particular if pursued on a large scale, works as a structural force that actualizes men's need for women, otherwise masked by women's accessibility. Yet, as in the case of Lysistrata and her sisters, engaging in a sex strike to make their men stop warring (see p. 125), seen from a deeper vantage point this withdrawal is an act of love and unity, since it augments the conditions for women and men to enter non-antagonistic bonds with one another. Having regained a sense of worthiness, freeing them from the desperate stance produced by sociosexual poverty, women will be able to love men more genuinely (cf. hooks, 2002). Also, the female withdrawal helps dismantle the male ego, which fundamentally disconnects men from others. Although the vulnerability this actualizes may feel disempowering, it is really the source of a more encompassing sociosexual empowerment of men too, inasmuch as it expands men's channels of connection with others.

Getting to the root of causality: a depth mode of feminist transformation

The strategy outlined above aligns with feminism's tradition of taking issue with the liberal-individualist tendency to see women's vulnerability as a personal shortcoming and its overcoming as an individual responsibility and possibility. This stance is grounded in a particular social ontology, whereby people's possibilities and vulnerabilities are seen as largely produced by social structures, contrasting with the tendency in present society to see people as self-sufficient entities with no intrinsic connections to one another or to wider social forces. The structural depth ontology of original critical realism underlabours the feminist project, in that it similarly ontologically prioritizes the structural conditions of human doings, since the causal roots of these doings are held to reside there. The implication of this approach is that if we want to achieve change, we must direct

Reality and change 153

our energies at transforming these structural conditions, rather than acting from the point of view of our immediate individual inclinations, which are generated by and for the most part reproductive of these structures.

Still, there is an important sense in which the mode of struggle outlined above is essentially about transforming women themselves. When, in a patriarchal context, women turn increasingly to one another, the primary effect is the transformation this brings about in the women, both in terms of their awareness of the nature of their condition and in terms of their capacity to respect and value themselves. While I have argued that a crucial momentum of this strategy lies in the indirect effects it has on men, paradoxically, these effects come about only if women let go of their preoccupation with changing men and focus on themselves.

A central component in Bhaskar's philosophy of metaReality is the principle of the *primacy of self-referentiality* and *self-change*. It accommodates to the necessities prescribing that 'your response to the situation you are in [is] the only thing that you can immediately affect' (Bhaskar, 2002b: 241) and underpins my continued elaborations on feminist transformation. For some, this principle may seem to contradict the structural focus of the classical critical realist ontology so as to implicate an apolitical stance, since it takes us back to the individual. Bhaskar rejects this interpretation, however. Referring to the internal relation between self and society[2] and the fact that we can only ever act *ourselves*, he argues that we must redirect our focus towards ourselves *so as to* become more efficacious social transformers (2002b; Bhaskar with Hartwig, 2010).

This idea of changing the world by changing oneself can be understood in terms of Bhaskar's idea of *holistic causality*, introduced in dialectical critical realism (1993/2008b), and the closely connected notion of *metonymic causality*, presented in his work on metaReality (2002b). These concepts of causality draw on the fact that, despite splits and differentiation, the world is a unified whole. Hence, changes in a part of the whole can effectuate a reorganization of the whole. Importantly though, as I interpret it, if we act in a way detached from the non-dual ground of being, by virtue of which everything is internally connected, this causal mode will not operate, but be blocked by the splits of demi-reality. Hence, the order of priority, according to Bhaskar, is to first become aware of and take responsibility for the ways that the heteronomous orders of demi-reality are anchored in ourselves (which we can be sure they are, by virtue of our being part of an interrelated whole) and struggle to dissolve this element of the demi-real, by seeking to 'disconnect if from its source' in our own ground-state (2002b: 361). Our possibilities for 'creat[ing] that platform from which we alone can truly initiate change' (2002b: 32) stand in proportion to the extent to which we can clear ourselves from the causal efficacy of the illusions of demi-reality and be in touch with that basic level of ourselves that is characterized by love, clarity and freedom. For '[n]o action', Bhaskar states, 'is more effective than single-pointed action from the ground-state, no action is stronger than that which expresses the binding power of love' (2002b: 353).

Somewhat paradoxically, this further deepening of the traditional structural critical realist ontology, based on the identification of a basic causal stratum that

154 *The reality of love and power*

underpins the structures of both demi-reality and relative reality, takes us back to the level of the individual, albeit on premises radically different from those of liberal individualism. The crucial difference is that, when liberal individualism sees people as only externally related and free insofar as others do not affect them, in the philosophy of metaReality the power and freedom of the individual becomes stronger the more she realizes her essential interconnectedness with other people and the cosmos.

Although female self-transformation is an integral part of the feminist project, it has been a defining feature of feminism to displace responsibility from women onto men and the structures underpinning their power. For too long women have been forced to carry burdens that are not really theirs, and it has been a central feminist imperative that responsibility be attributed to where it belongs. It may therefore prove disturbing to suggest, as I do here, that women need to redirect their energy from blaming and demanding to taking responsibility for their own role in sustaining the current order. This, it should be noted, is not to say that women are to blame, but a realistic, strategically motivated move, drawing on rather than working against necessities that cannot be circumvented. The mode of feminist transformation that I sketch in the rest of this chapter is based on the depth causality of the philosophy of metaReality and Bhaskar's 'understanding of emancipation as the shedding of heteronomous orders of determination to release the good or true enfolded within them' (in Bhaskar with Hartwig, 2010: 72). It also draws on Irigaray's ontology of human relationality and on feminist work on strategies for transformation in love. This essentially spiritual mode of reorganizing the sociosexual structure by working 'downwards' and inwards stands in a dialectic relationship to the mode of collective withdrawal sketched above. The two modes overlap inasmuch as both involve a kind of withdrawal from men and are focused on transforming women themselves, but they are also different in character, in particular in that the mode of practice outlined below can be pursued by individual women in any setting.

Women's anger

To start elucidating the character of this depth mode of feminist transformation, let us take the reaction of anger, which many women experience as an effect of living the contradictions of patriarchal love. For Bhaskar, negative emotions like anger is one way in which the oppressive order of demi-reality is mediated by our personal mode of being. Whereas anger is in a sense a natural reaction to the ills of exploitation, as humans we have a capacity to choose how to respond to it. In line with spiritual traditions like Zen Buddhism, Bhaskar argues that unless we want to offer further fuel to the reproduction of dualism, we must refrain from acting out our anger in an unmediated fashion and instead turn inwards to explore its *interiority*. It is not that anger and other negative emotions should be banned; quite the contrary, for inasmuch as the root source and driving force of all negative emotions is always love,[3] one must accept and be attentive to one's anger so as to locate its non-dual 'deep interior'. 'Going into the deep interior of the heteronomous

Reality and change   155

element', Bhaskar suggests, we can 'trace it back to the ground-state it is parasitic upon, disconnecting or dissolving it or allowing its reabsorption within the cosmic binding force of love' (2002b: 353). Having done this, we are better equipped to express the intentionality behind our anger in a clear and loving way, which is likely to be constructively responded to.

This is a phenomenology that is at the heart in particular of meditative practices, but to a certain extent it is also constitutive of the methods of more profane therapeutic traditions. The primary message delivered in the bestselling feminist advice book *The dance of anger* (1985/2004), by therapist and psychoanalytical feminist theorist Harriet Lerner, is that if women who live with men are really interested in efficaciously changing their situation, they need to focus on taking responsibility for where *they* themselves stand, for who *they* are, rather than vainly trying to change the man by complaining and blaming. 'If feeling angry signals a problem, venting anger does not solve it', Lerner states. Rather, '[v]enting anger may serve to maintain, and even rigidify, the old rules and patterns in a relationship, thus ensuring that change does not occur' (1985/2004: 4, emphasis removed). Whereas the alternatives for managing anger are traditionally portrayed as a choice between suppressing it or acting it out loudly, she argues that these seemingly opposed routes are in fact similar, in that in both cases the angry person fails to take responsibility for what her anger signals about *herself*. Hence, their equal unproductiveness.

Lerner argues that the key to transformation is that women learn to use the power their anger represents as a tool for clarifying and strengthening themselves – who they are, what they want – instead of using it on blaming others. In line with Bhaskar, she highlights that it is only from a platform of inner clarity and strength, which we attain when we focus on the nature of our own feelings and needs while letting go of the idea that others must be in a certain way, that we can communicate our feelings and needs in a clear, open and loving way, which is likely to be clearly, openly and lovingly responded to. Here we see at work a kind of causality that is not premised on instrumentally trying to control that which is outside of ourselves. Instead, it is based on transforming ourselves – or, rather, on being more in touch with what we really are – in a way that will necessarily have effects in others, since their selves are constellationally embedded in ours and ours in theirs.

Lerner uses several examples from her own therapeutic practice, which show the radical transformation that tends to be brought about when women make this subtle shift of focus from others to themselves. The core idea is that women should 'reclaim the power that is truly ours – the power to change our own selves and take a new and different action on our own behalf' (1985/2004: 39), instead of futilely trying to exercise power over men's will. As Bhaskar states, focusing our energy on things beyond our immediate control, 'shifting ... the blame on to another agent or the situation itself, immediately disempowers the agent, dualistically splitting and undermining his response' (2002b: 241). Lerner takes the example of a woman who was not 'allowed' by her husband to go to a seminar and used her energy trying to make her husband '*want* her to go' (1985/2004: 38),

156 *The reality of love and power*

instead of exercising the power she had to decide for herself whether to go or not. It is understandable that the woman felt hurt and abandoned – unloved – in this situation and wanted her husband to care more for her needs and rights. No matter how wrongly one is treated, however, Lerner stresses that we must accept that 'we cannot ensure that another person will do what we want him or her to or see things our way, nor are we guaranteed that justice will prevail' (1985/2004: 39). The message she communicates is that we need to develop an ability to endure this fact, if we are to be able 'use our "anger energy" in the service of our own dignity and growth' (1985/2004: 10), which must underpin any effective struggle against injustices. It is precisely by virtue of anger's root in love that it can be thus used, in my view. The reaction of anger is fundamentally a signal of love: *the reality of who I am and therefore also of who you are has been violated and that is wrong*. However, it is in the nature of anger that when we feel it, we tend not to be in touch with its basis in love, but instead get carried away by anger's own emergent dualistic play of forces, so liable to accumulation. The task, then, is to resist being carried away and instead continuously struggle to reconnect with the ontological fundament of our anger.

When the women in Lerner's analysis use their anger as a signal that something is wrong and search within themselves for a way of remedying this ill, they get in touch with the love for themselves which must sustain any efficacious self-assertion, *the kind of self-assertion that is not immediately dependent for its efficacy on the other's validation*. The paradox is that when we let go of the other and can endure that he may not be the way we want him to, we are more likely to get the love we need, since love emerges only from a stance of freedom.

Diseffectuating the illusion of female powerlessness

The strategy of collective female withdrawal operates mainly on the causal terrain of relative reality. It challenges male power by targeting the ways that the basic powers and needs we have as embodied sociosexual beings are organized. The depth mode of transformation instead intervenes mainly in the causal stratum of the ground-state and the cosmic envelope, characterized by its transcendence of relativity. In this realm, women, like men, are already and essentially in communion with other people, in a way that makes their need to *get* something from others de-actualized. If women get in touch with this fundamental reality of theirs, they can, even in relative material isolation from other women, find a way to empowerment relatively independent from men. When Lerner states that women should reclaim the power that is truly theirs, she seems to draw on the implicit notion that women's powerlessness is a causally efficacious illusion that can be challenged, if women give up their unnecessary attachments to things outside of themselves, which occlude this reality. Women's – all people's – basic autonomy and non-violability is linked to the fundamental ontological fact that, whatever we feel, think or do, we *are* singular beings relatively autonomous from others. This is a reality that cannot be erased and to which even oppressive practices must adapt, however covertly and exploitatively.

Reality and change   157

It has been a recurrent theme of this book that men's power in the current sociosexual order pertains only to an ego self, whose reality depends on a denial of its constitutive base. It has been more obscured from view that the paradigmatic female self in this order is also an ego self, whose mode of constitution complements that of the male. As Buddhist feminist Rita Gross highlights, while women tend to be 'self-less' in the sense of being over-identified with others, this does not mean they are not invested in an ego in the deeper sense of 'any style of habitual patterns and responses that clouds over the clarity and openness of basic human nature' (1993: 162). I would contend that whereas the male ego is constituted by the suppression of dependence and vulnerability, the characteristic female ego under patriarchy is based on a denial of its ultimate reality of relative *in*dependence and power. As we have seen, Bhaskar emphasizes that the non-dual totality of being is not at odds with but founded in the irreducible singularity of its parts, including human beings, and that true connection is always associated with 'a conatus for autonomy' (2002b: 216). While men tend to derive their sense of security and strength from the illusion of being more separate than they really are, women tend to base theirs on over-identifying with others, in a way that covers over their immutable distinctness (cf. Benjamin, 1988, 1998; Chodorow, 1978; Irigaray, 1992/1996, 2002b).

It is perhaps easier to grasp the ego character of the hyper-autonomous masculine self, since it so clearly entails the separation and opposition associated with the ego structure. However, making oneself smaller than one really is also reproduces opposition and separation, inasmuch as a non-dual relation can emerge only from the platform of being at one with one's own reality (cf. Irigaray, 1992/1996, 2002b). If a woman is not in touch with her own distinct reality, she will have nothing to offer to a relation which is not already derivable from the person with whose reality she over-identifies. Depending too much on others also means that one is likely to approach them from a stance of urgent need, which, ultimately, renders them means rather than ends to us. And, as already highlighted, treating someone as a means is opposite to love.

While feminist theory has traditionally taken issue with the hyper-individualism fostered by patriarchy and stressed the constitutive relational character of human existence (Hartsock, 1983; Noddings, 1984/2003; Radden, 1996), it is also characterized by its emphasis of the need for women to become more individuated (de Beauvoir, 1949/1989; Benjamin, 1988; Irigaray, 1992/1996, 2002b; Medina-Doménech et al., 2014). From the point of view of the dialectical conception of unity-in-difference, this does not necessarily represent an inconsistency. Rather, many feminist theorists have sought to come to terms with the patriarchal female/male split between relationality and independence, by highlighting their mutual constitution (Benjamin, 1988, 1998; Chodorow, 1978; Irigaray, 1992/1996, 2002b; Radden, 1996). Within the field of feminist therapy theory, this duality is captured by the notion of 'autonomous relationality' (Radden, 1996: 72).

Discussing how women may find a way out of subordination in love, Rosa Medina-Doménech, Mari Luz Esteban-Galarza and Ana Távora-Rivero highlight the importance of 'an individuation of women's subjectivity' (2010: 24), based

158   *The reality of love and power*

on mourning 'the sense of loss that accompanies the discovery that we are separate subjects who interact with others, and not subjects stuck to other subjects' (2010: 13). Women, they argue, need to cultivate a 'care of the self', as a necessary condition for 'the task of channeling our energies and influencing our becoming as subjects capable of learning to satisfy our needs without expecting to resolve them through a confused demand of the person(s) we love' (2014: 170). That this is often difficult and associated with grief is an expression of the causal efficacy of female powerlessness. If a woman's sense of identity and mode of relating to others is based on an over-identification with the needs and powers of others, her own independence and power will paradoxically appear as a threat to her existence. Hence, on the level of demi-reality women have an interest in making themselves smaller than they are, in order to remain sheltered by the power of the other, premised on the relative powerlessness of themselves (cf. Benjamin, 1988). This threat of independence is fundamentally illusory, though, and this will mostly become clear when women start acting in ways less directed by their attachments to others, work through the emotions that arise, and note that they are quite alright.

Irigaray, Bhaskar and the ethics of letting go

The theme of love's necessary basis in the irreducible difference between self and other is at the centre of Irigaray's later work (1992/1996, 1994/2001, 1999/2002a, 2002b).[4] Although Irigaray, being largely inspired by Derrida and Lacan, is commonly seen as a postmodernist theorist, her later writings are clearly realist (Stone, 2004) in that they identify as a central task of humans to return to and cultivate what we really are. Tying in with Bhaskar's idea of emancipation accommodating the reality principle, she states that we need to be 'faithful to what is by nature – including in the subject as such' (2002b: 113), rejecting any opposition between the natural and the cultural and instead arguing for the importance of basing human culture on the simultaneous allegiance to and transcendence or 'spiritualization' (1992/1996: 31) of nature. Despite Bhaskar's and Irigaray's vastly different academic styles and foci, as noted in Chapter 7 their works overlap in interesting ways. Irigaray's dialectical theorization of the mutual constitution of difference and relation, her focus on ontology, her claim that negativity pertains to being itself (e.g. 1992/1996: 35) and her thematization of the spiritual make her work crucially affiliated with Bhaskar's. A cross-fertilization of their ontological frameworks and approaches to love could thus prove productive.

Bhaskar's work points to how non-dialectical notions of both unity and difference tend to cause split and separation, by their inability to account for the constellational unity of relation and distinction (1993/2008b). Irigaray similarly critiques the closed concept of unity that she holds to dominate western thought, arguing that it is conducive of the kind of false unity between humans that is based on one subject's appropriation of or projection of himself onto the other. She contends that the kind of unity which is in harmony with our true ontology, and will thus be a real unity, 'remains open and leaves each term its specificity and autonomy' (2002b: 78), since it is 'difference itself which will provide us with the necessary

Reality and change 159

mediations' for a continuously (re)constructed connection (2002b: 70). The ethical implication of this ontology is that we must respect the other as truly other, as a reality that cannot be appropriated to fit our own reality. If, Irigaray states, both poles in a relation (and especially between woman and man) are not acknowledged in their irreducibility, a genuine relation will not be possible. Instead, one of them will 'seek in the other the lost whole, the complement of its amputated being, the instrument of its division or of its reunification' (2002b: 79).

Like Bhaskar, Lerner and Medina-Doménech *et al.*, Irigaray maintains that we must turn more of our attention inwards, towards our own reality, in order to be able to enter into true relation with an other. Otherwise we are only 'artificially open, cut off from [our] reserve of life' (2002b: 166). Connecting with this source of our existence, which is the premise of a real, living relation, depends on 'the withdrawal of the other in their self and my withdrawal in my self', a gesture which, Irigaray emphasizes, 'does not exclude but accompanies the opening to the other' (2002b: 163). Much like Bhaskar endorses a rechannelling of our energies towards ourselves and the interiority of our reactions, Irigaray thus advocates a 'return to self' (2002b: 91), a restoring of 'the integrity of intimacy with oneself' (2002b: 150), as a necessary premise for intimacy with the other. For it is only from the point of view of 'being faithful to our own Being' (2002b: 157) that we can bring ourselves into relation with the other.

Irigaray (see especially 1999/2002a) and Bhaskar are both influenced by mystical spiritual traditions, in particular of the eastern kind, in which this turning inwards is a crucial component, in contrast to the externalizing tendencies of modernity. In line with these traditions, both also advocate an ethics of surrender – of letting go and letting be – as the way both to genuine love and to liberation more generally. For Irigaray, this letting go is essentially the act of letting the other be other, uncontrollable and impossible to contain in our own being. It is also the gesture of letting go of 'the lure of an immediate fullness' (2002b: 157) that neglects the gaps in being, tying in with Bhaskar's idea of surrendering to and searching the non-dual roots of what is, rather than trying to correct it.

Bhaskar addresses this theme in terms of the need to let go of *desire*, defined as the closed, instrumental stance in which we are attached to anticipated results of our actions, rather than being present in the moment (2002b). Thus defined desire is at work in the mode of seeking relational satisfaction by trying to make the other into something we want him to be, instead of acting in accordance with our own inner reality and being open for whatever unfolds from that. This stance of desire disempowers us, since it rids us of our openness to the moment and the potentials it harbours. This is why, Bhaskar states, 'generally you must act intentionally without desire, that is attachment to results and consequences, if those desires or the intentionality they express are to be realised in the world' (2002b: 235). It is not that we should erase the directionality of our being in the world, but when we close down the future by evaluating it in terms of how well it fits our idea of what it should be like, we block ourselves from the forces of reality as they *are* and so narrow our possibilities of being fulfilled through them. This truth is perhaps most salient in the sociosexual dimension of human existence, where

160 *The reality of love and power*

failure to be open to the moment and to the irreducible independence of the other is unlikely to produce much love and eroticism.

Both Irigaray and Bhaskar highlight that the letting go which allows us to be at one with being in its present becoming involves letting go of our conceptions of reality, '[s]ilencing what we already know', as Irigaray says, 'in order to let the other appear, and light ourselves up through this entry into presence irreducible to our knowledge' (2002b: 165). Bhaskar emphasizes the importance of 'unthinking' (2002b: 145) in order to get in touch with the healing power of basic reality, arguing that '[a]ny received belief, any repetitive pattern of thought or action, will inevitably divide/separate/split/alienate, and perpetuate the state of dilemmatic being which is characteristic of an alienated world' (2002b: 32–3).

When letting go of our conceptions of how things are or ought to be, we open ourselves up to an empowering reality that is commonly conceptualized in spiritual terms. Yet, without explicit spiritual references, Medina-Doménech *et al.* emphasize the need for women to 'stop thinking about relationships only in terms of what they give or don't give you and instead become able to discover new aspects of those relationships', conveying a sense in which there is something *beyond* which opens up when we give up ingrained patterns of relating (2014: 163). In her essay on feminism and heterosexual love, Virginia Held (1976) endorses a similar approach. Discussing the particular character of the revolution of love, she makes a case for a non-antagonistic struggle on this arena, whereby women explore ways of cultivating the seeds of genuine love that already exist between women and men, thus tying in with Bhaskar's notion of expanding the non-dual from within, rather than fighting its dualistic superstructures. She acknowledges the feminist need to engage in antagonistic struggle and concedes that some revolutionary ends may perhaps be achieved with means contradicting these ends. Yet, in correspondence with Bhaskar's idea that in the endeavour of expanding the zone of love and non-duality 'there must be no dichotomy or split between means and ends' (Bhaskar, 2002b: 327), she maintains that such a separation between vision and the method of realizing it cannot underpin the particular revolution of love, whose 'ends must themselves be its means' (1976: 183). Like Medina-Doménech *et al.*, Held contends that in order for women to succeed in this non-antagonistic struggle devoted to the present, they need to detach themselves from their history and abandon 'most traditional interpretations of what makes a relation satisfactory' (1976:180). Although neither Medina-Doménech *et al.* nor Held expand on this theme, what they seem to say is that, when women are caught up in the binds of expectations and resentment produced by the past, they partake in blocking the possibility for something other to emerge, here and now.

Breaking the circle of unworthiness

I have argued that women live their sociosexuality through a dialectical contradiction, whereby their search for worthiness tends to produce unworthiness. The urgency generally characterizing women's need for love under current sociosexual circumstances makes them ready to accept exploitative conditions which undermine

Reality and change 161

their worthiness, since the love they get under these conditions is premised on their being useful for others, rather than valuable in their own right. Although I stick with Jónasdóttir's claim that we need to be loved by others in order to emerge as worthy persons, I contend that the critical factor in the production of female unworthiness is not men's failure to love women, but women's failure, implicated by compromising with oneself in order to be loved, to show *themselves* esteem and respect – love. On a general level, the capacity for self-love is a product of being loved by others and this causal connection is very salient when we are children: our capacity to value – and know – ourselves emerges from being valued and seen, in our own right, by our caretakers. Yet, depending on how successful the emergence of self-love has been, as adults the interdependency between being loved by others and loving oneself has less tightness to it. Just as the person as such is relatively autonomous from the relations constituting her, her capacity to empower herself through self-love is relatively autonomous from its basis in others' love. This ontological hiatus is, I argue, what needs to be exploited in the service of women's sociosexual emancipation. hooks is right when stating that women in patriarchy tend to be '[d]eprived of the means to generate self-love' (2002: xiii–xiv). Yet, there is a way for women to break this tendency in relative independence from changes in the structural conditions generating it: they can seek out in themselves the grains of self-love which do exist, and cultivate or 'exercise' this capacity from within. In order to transcend the double-bind of unworthiness, they need to focus their struggle on expanding what they *are*, so that they become less exploitable, rather than seeking to fill their void by *getting* more.

From a metaReal point of view, the capacity to empower ourselves as worthy beings through self-love is based in the fact that at the basic level of our constitution we *are* love. Instead of blocking this natural life force by ego boundaries and its must-haves and must-not-haves, if we just are in this power it works maximally through and for us – and, hence, others. Irigaray highlights that if we are generally used to finding strength and security in a rigid self warded off from the 'relational becoming' that is our true ontological ground, we can find another kind of shelter or dwelling place in the act of corresponding with this becoming, 'that place of ours where life still lives, still palpitates, … where Being still quivers' (2002b: 93). For Irigaray this is not some unworldly heaven disconnected from nature and the body; yet, it is a spiritual endeavour insofar, as I interpret it, as it involves a transcendence of one's instinct to use the other (2002b: 78) as well as of the limits of space and time. In this 'work of becoming human … [a]nother relation to space and time becomes necessary', she states, 'nature being transmuted into a spiritual matter which little by little envelops and protects the subjects on their path while constraining them to pursue it' (2002b: 81).

There is a sense, then, in which this abode where 'Being quivers', which is arguably the same place as Bhaskar's non-dual ground-state, transcends the space–time relations of embodied, relative reality, so that 'in your ground-state you will transcend your circumstances' (Bhaskar, 2002b: 234). Although this view of causality as relatively disconnected from the terms set by material, relative reality

162 *The reality of love and power*

is foreign to our disenchanted culture, many common experiences support it. Take, for instance, the radical transformation that can occur in an 'impossible' child, when someone starts to just pay attention, listen, let the child be. Or consider the fact that the body's constructive life forces – such as breathing and staying upright – do their job best when we refrain from trying to control them. In line with meditative traditions, the method proposed by Bhaskar (2002b) for expanding the zone of non-duality is that of non-judging, attentive witnessing of what is.[5] Instead of trying to remove one's anger, for instance, either by repressing it or changing something outside of oneself, one can just pay attention to it, be with it – let it be, but also let it not be. Paradoxically, then the anger tends to dissolve, since the force of loving attention encourages its deep interiority of love to unfold.

The task for women can be formulated as one of expanding the interiority of their selves *from within*. This involves a struggle to break not only with the structural compulsions of demi-reality, but also with western culture's general outwardness. 'In our culture gathering oneself is not secured in proportion to opening oneself to', Irigaray highlights (2002b: 166), proposing a shift towards an attentiveness to our 'own interiority as a space inside and outside the whole' (2002b: 173). Again, Irigaray mirrors Bhaskar's dialectical view of totality: our self is distinct from the whole and therefore has a volume that we can move inside, but it is also part of the whole, so what we do inwards has repercussions outwards. The ontological hiatus between self and other, as the premise of their relation, underlies Irigaray's advocacy of a more indirect kind of love (expressed in her phrase 'I love *to* you' (1992/1996)) than the one dominating western culture. Instead of reaching outwards without mediation, in this mode of loving energies are focused inwards in a way that creates an open space between self and other, where love can arise on its own terms. Inasmuch as the current ego structure of male and female selves is intrinsically bound up with an appropriatory tradition of loving, which eschews distance and difference, the struggle for feminist transformation must hence involve a radical reconceptualization of love (cf. Medina-Doménech *et al.*, 2014; Toye, 2010).

Conclusion

In this chapter I have sketched a twofold mode of feminist struggle, based on my previous theorization of the ontology of male power and female powerlessness in exploitative sociosexuality. A recurrent theme in my elaborations was that if such a struggle is to succeed it must not defy but accommodate the constraints imposed on it by the natural ontological order, such as the impossibility of demanding love from someone and the fact that the only thing we can directly affect is our own responses to external events, over which we have no immediate control. I proposed that women engage in a dialectic between two modes of struggle, with the common denominator of providing means for female empowerment relatively independently from men: (i) a relative collective withdrawal from men, accompanied by the redirection of women's sociosexual energies from men to one another, and (ii) individual women's relative withdrawal from the external world generally and from men in particular, involving a redirection of their sociosexual

Reality and change 163

energies to their own interiority. These projects have a relative autonomy from one another, meaning that individual women may engage in only one of them. They are also mutually entailing and reinforcing, though, and even if particular women are not immediately involved in both kinds of processes, they are likely to be indirectly affected by the collective knowledge and dispositions generated by other women's experiences.

The dialectic sketched here reconciles positions that tend to appear in dialectical antagonism with one another (see pp. 77–8). At one pole we have the conventional tendency to conceptualize political struggle in collectivist, externalized and antagonistic terms; at the other we have spiritual methods of inner transformation that are often disconnected from politics. Although this dualism is far from all-pervasive, it is salient in the Marxist tradition in which both critical realism and most feminisms have their roots.[6] Although there is a sense in which feminism has partaken, at least indirectly, in the overcoming of this dualism, by its challenge of the traditional gulf between the personal and the political, as witnessed by several commentators (e.g. Fernandes, 2003; Robinson, 2001) spirituality is quite taboo among leading branches of feminism. There are indeed feminists and branches of feminism embracing spirituality (Alexander, 2005; Daly, 1978; Fernandes, 2003; Gross, 1993; hooks, 2000a, 2000b, 2004; Ingram, 2000; King, 1994; Levitt, 1996; Lorde, 1984), but, as Hilary Robinson highlights, 'the predominantly secular movement that is feminism (like the left in general) has tended to regard its spiritual wing … as a bit of an embarrassment' (2001: 588). In my view, this taboo on spirituality reproduces the untenable dualism between the external and the internal and the political and the personal, and this is what led me to devote the main part of this chapter to elaborating the second, depth moment in the dialectic of feminist transformation.

Spiritual depth work with self is largely conceived as a private, apolitical and ahistorical endeavour. However, the acknowledgment that love is a productive power whose organization determines the course of history opens up the notion that new techniques of making use of this power have political significance. This should include new skills, based on collectively accumulated knowledge, of how to empower and liberate oneself – and concomitantly others – by focusing the powers at one's disposal in directions hitherto unexplored on a collective scale. Actualizing the Marxian dialectic between forces and relations of production, I propose that the productive power of love could be unfettered through a different mode of structuring human selves. This would involve a struggle to shed the ego structure that compels us to reach outwards to *get*, so that our energies can be increasingly focused on accessing the power and love that we already *are*. Although I have argued that love power is a given, transhistorical property of human beings, as the Marxian notion of the historical evolution of the human species indicates, the character and scope of fundamental human powers may evolve. If spiritual techniques of turning inwards and letting go would be available on a broader scale, this would, I contend, imply a transformation of the human constitution as such, which might entail at least a partial overcoming of the current contradiction of love.

164 *The reality of love and power*

After some decades of painful sociosexual struggle in the wake of women's partial emancipation, the time is perhaps ripe now for women to accept the impossibility of getting what they need from men by struggling, by means of demands and complaints, on the terrain of demi-reality. I tentatively suggest that if women are not to be torn apart by the contradictions in which they find themselves, it will be *necessary* for them to explore new strategies. A reserve that remains, in our outward culture, a relatively unexplored resource of sociosexual production and transformation is the potentials at the root of our being. Women need to become aware of their objective interest in accessing these potentials, by turning inwards. And insofar as men's existence is linked up with women's, they will have to follow.

While I have not focused on men here, they too can of course engage in the transformative depth practice outlined above. Although, for them, getting to the root of existence will generally imply greater awareness of their dependence and vulnerability, ultimately the ego shedding process that it entails is empowering for men too. This kind of male empowerment is conducive rather than obstructive of feminist change, though, inasmuch as it means that men will no longer have any interest in exploiting others in order to be powerful.

From the viewpoint of the confines of the current organization of selves and love, the task of working inwards and 'downwards' for change may seem, if not impossible, so at least demanding. At present, the spiritual struggle that it requires is generally seen as something in which only a small minority or spiritual elite can and should engage. And indeed, as Irigaray poetically puts it, the gesture of 'gathering oneself' is more difficult for the human subject 'than for certain flowers' (2002b: 166). Yet, human skills have developed before, in ways that were seen as impossible by our foremothers and fathers. In her famous essay on how women can get in touch with the power at the depth of their erotic being, Audre Lorde states that although this power inevitably carries us towards an 'internal requirement toward excellence', this 'must not be misconstrued as demanding the impossible from ourselves nor from others'. Once we have experienced the fullness, power and 'internal sense of satisfaction' at the depth of our selves, she states, 'in honor and self-respect we can require no less of ourselves' (1984: 54).

Notes

1 Arthur argues that the self-identity of capital is 'both true and false'. The reality of its self-imposing totality, he argues, 'is not "really real" ontologically, in that its *actuality* requires it generate its own content which it cannot fully achieve (albeit it resignifies the material given to it)' (2009: 178). Enrique Dussel similarly invokes the term 'real reality', arguing that '[t]he truth of Marx's analysis rests on and departs from the "real Reality" of the Other different from capital, the living labor as activity, as creator of value' (1988/2001: 8–9).

2 Rachel Crowder (2012), who has documented the healing effects of mindfulness (see p. 165, note 5) therapy on female victims of male violence, highlights that if we acknowledge that the personal is political a focus on changing the woman's mode of responding to life does not need to imply that the societal context is ignored.

3 '[E]very human emotion experienced embodies an element of love which is its driving force, even though in the case of negative emotions such as anger, jealousy, hate or

Reality and change 165

pride, that small iota of love which binds and coheres the emotion is outweighed by the presence of states which oppose it' (Bhaskar, 2002b: 57).

4 Irigaray sees sexual difference as the paradigmatic difference underpinning all other differences. Although I agree in the sense that it is the generative mechanism of human – and a lot of non-human – life as such, in my view Irigaray over-emphasizes the particularity and importance of the difference between the sexes (which she sees as stretching far beyond the crudely biological).

5 In the west this method is gaining ground under the label of 'mindfulness', classically defined by Jon Kabat-Zinn as 'paying attention in a particular way: on purpose, in the present moment, and nonjudgmentally' (1994: 4). (See Crowder (2012) for a notion of 'mindfulness based feminist therapy'). As for the relation between meditative techniques and dialectics, there is, interestingly, a therapeutic method termed 'dialectical behaviour therapy', which combines techniques from cognitive behaviour therapy with mindfulness. Its dialectic character refers, among other things, to the recognition that inner and outer reality is in interplay and, implicitly tying in with Bhaskar's idea of holistic causality, that 'change is an aspect of all systems, and is present at all levels of any given system' (Robins *et al.*, 2004: 33).

6 It is in light of this that we should make sense of the strong hostility that many critical realists and Marxists have expressed towards Bhaskar's spiritual turn (see p. 20, note 8). Interestingly, though, as Hartwig (in Bhaskar with Hartwig, 2010) and Jónasdóttir (2014) observe, there is a current of resurgent spirituality among progressive intellectuals.

10 Conclusion
Necessity and the power of love

This book has offered a theorization of why and how, in contemporary societies characterized by formal-legal equality and women's relative economic independence from individual men, women continue to be subordinated to men through sexuality, defined broadly so as to include women and men's practices as both desiring-ecstatic and loving-caring beings. While acknowledging that economic gender inequalities prevail in all societies, it was a point of departure of the book that inasmuch as a growing number of women are today bound to men only through the dependencies of sexuality, there is an unprecedented possibility of analytically laying bare the power mechanisms *internal* to our existence as sexual beings.

In order to theorize these mechanisms, in the first part of the book I examined different feminist ways of understanding how gendered power is constituted through sexuality, with specific focus on the explicit or implicit ontologies of sexuality, power and sex/gender endorsed. Via a comparative assessment of Butler's poststructuralist and Jónasdóttir's realist-materialist ways of dealing with these categories, I embraced Jónasdóttir's ground-breaking understanding of (socio)sexuality as the practical realization of 'love power', a basic human capacity understood as comprised by both caring and erotic-ecstatic elements. In this way, while setting off with a focus on sexuality, by adopting Jónasdóttir's way of understanding what it means to be a sexual being, the focus of the book shifted to love and its relation to gendered power.

A central conclusion of my evaluation of Butler's and Jónasdóttir's theories was that the logical and explanatory superiority of Jónasdóttir's account hinges crucially on the fact that it is anchored in a conceptualization of transhistorical necessities. Butler fails to specify what it is *about* sexuality that makes it such a fertile ground for oppression. By contrast, Jónasdóttir's theorization of the basic human neediness stemming from our sociosexual nature enables her to make specified sense of the vulnerability that makes it possible for power structures to get a hold over people. Unless women had sociosexual needs that must be met if they are to be recreated as persons, they would not be, as they are now, compelled to enter bonds with men on conditions that disempower them. By contrast, despite the fact that, basically, men are as sociosexually needy as women, their collective-structural accumulation of women's love lends to them a male authority that makes their sociosexual needs relatively non-urgent. This gives men the upper hand in determining the conditions of their sociosexual bonds with women, so that they can continue appropriating more erotic empowerment and care from women than they offer in return.

In the second part of the book I shifted focus away from the themes of sexuality and love for a while and engaged with some general meta-theoretical concerns, which are not only pertinent for the specific arguments laid out in this work, but also at the centre of current debates in feminist theory more generally. The general aim was to provide a critical realist critique of some problematic features of poststructuralist reasoning that have come to dominate feminist theory. Lingering on the theme of the relation between the social(ly constructed) and the natural or transhistorical, I challenged the nature-phobia dominating contemporary feminist theory, arguing that acknowledging that social relations are based in natural structures beyond social control need not imply a threat to the possibilities of social transformation. Assessing recent feminist work that does embrace the natural, I did however caution against the reluctance in these writings to acknowledge that nature puts constraints on what societies can be like. If we are to be able to effectively and realistically create a different future, we need to identify both what possibilities and what limits natural conditions pose on our social existence. If, for instance, women neglect the fact that they have sociosexual needs, they may develop unrealistic visions of emancipation based on refraining from engaging sociosexually with others. By contrast, if women recognize the reality of these needs *and* of how they are currently involved in their subordination to men, they can create visions of how to meet them in ways that are not so dependent on men.

I also addressed the taboo on the category 'women', offering a critical realist understanding of this category that is compatible with complexity and social constructionism. The taboo against making positive theoretical claims about the structural tendencies of being a woman or a man is destructive for the feminist project, since it undermines analyses of the systematic power hierarchy which does prevail between women and men, despite intersectional complexity and the processual nature of gendered subjects. Hence, this chapter should be of crucial general importance for feminist theorists and gender scholars who feel restrained by poststructuralist dogmas which prescribe, against most people's intuitions, that the categories of 'women' and 'men' do not represent real groupings in the world.

A feminist dialectical-realist depth ontology of love and power

In the third part of the book I continued drawing on the theme of natural necessity, so as to develop a feminist dialectical-realist depth approach to sociosexual reality, underpinning my dialectical deepening and partial recasting of Jónasdóttir's claims about love and power. At the centre was the question of to what extent, or in which sense, love can properly be thought of as a force possible to organize in ways that benefit some at the cost of others. I argued that, seen from one vantage

168 *Conclusion: Necessity and the power of love*

point, it is a fact that men exploit women of their love, in a relation where men's empowerment is entailed by women's disempowerment. Yet, I relativized the realness of this reality, so to speak, by showing that it is *constituted* by falsity, insofar as it is premised on the suppression of deeper and more invincible realities on which it is in fact founded. The fact that this demi-real level of being depends on the basic necessities that it must deny in order to emerge as real, makes it ridden with internal contradictions which constitute a constant threat of breakdown.

Drawing on Bhaskar's philosophy of metaReality I argued that, fundamentally, love is unexploitable, a self-generating force that is replenished rather than exhausted when used. It becomes exploitable, something that can be won and lost, only within a demi-real context of ego selves disconnected from the truth of essential non-duality between self and other. *As such* ego selves men are empowered in the current sociosexual order, but insofar as the ego is disconnected from the intrinsic connections with others which *really* constitutes it, a powerful ego in fact constitutes a disempowerment of the more encompassing interconnected self on which the ego depends. In this sense, the authority and power of men under patriarchy is premised on a suppression of men's own fundamental reality, and this inevitably gives rise to a set of contradictions that must be held at bay.

One such tension is that between men's patriarchal need for women to be (structurally) controlled on one hand and free on the other. The nature of love is such that it can only be generated from the irreducible subjectivity of its practitioner, if it is to be empowering, if it is to be love. Hence, the freer women are, the stronger their capacity for empowering others, including men. Yet, in exploitative sociosexuality men's empowerment is premised on their structural control of women (at times flipping over into overt control), since the suppression of the dependency and vulnerability on which the patriarchal self relies is put at risk by lack of such control. Whereas, within the ontologically fragile confines of patriarchal sociosexuality, men thus have an interest in reproducing the exploitative structure which secures their structural control of women, they have a deeper interest in breaking with this structure. For it is only if women are maximally free to determine how to make use of their love on conditions equal to men's, that men will gain the possibility of being empowered as the more unlimited and interconnected selves that they really and inescapably are. Only by finding a sense of power that is compatible with this reality, will their power be really real.

Although I have carefully endorsed Jónasdóttir's claim that in contemporary western societies men are empowered by their exploitation of women's love, the above is also a critique or, perhaps better, nuancing of this claim. The crux, in my view, is that Jónasdóttir fails to draw out the full consequences of her acknowledgement that the natural ontology of love puts constraints on how it can be practised and used. She emphasizes that love cannot be extracted by force and that, consequently, men can only receive sociosexual empowerment from women if they offer it voluntarily. Yet, although she does state that the love women give men 'voluntarily' under conditions of structural compulsion is an alienated kind of love, Jónasdóttir does not address what this means for its empowering scope. In my view, a structural control of women's ability to use their sociosexual capacities

Conclusion: Necessity and the power of love 169

freely – that is without the pressure of sociosexual poverty and the quality of urgency that it lends to women's need for love – will also hamper their capacity for empowering others. Jónasdóttir highlights that loving someone means treating her as important in her own right, but fails to attend to the fact that if women are urgently dependent on men, they will in fact relate to them primarily as means rather than ends. Hence, she overlooks the fact that under exploitative conditions women's love of men is in a fundamental sense as poor as men's love of women.

The argument laid out in Part III depends on a particular way of understanding the basic structure of social being, based on Bhaskar's dialectical critical realism and philosophy of metaReality. I pursued the argument that social reality can be seen as differentiated, with a basic and necessary stratum of being that is invincible and thus 'really real', and a superstructure that exists only by virtue of its negation of this basic reality on which it nevertheless depends, making it ontologically false or demi-real. In the final chapter I elaborated on the implications of this dialectical social ontology for how we should conceive of feminist change. I highlighted that just as the empowerment of men in the current structure of love is ontologically fragile, women's disempowerment is real only in a half sense. Stressing the importance for women to de-actualize their powerlessness and dependency on men, by increasingly directing their sociosexual energies towards one another, I also elaborated an emancipatory model in which women turn inwards in a struggle to expand their constitutive reality of power and non-exploitability. As an alternative to fighting on the terrain of demi-reality in a way that is destined to reproduce its destructive dualisms, I offered a new paradigm of spiritual-political struggle, in which one's transformative loving energies are focused inwards in a way that is bound to effectuate change outwards, by virtue of the interconnectedness of being.

A project of reconciliation

I hope to have demonstrated that the dialectical approach endorsed in this book has served not only as a means of better grasping the contradictions constituting current sociosexual reality, but also as a reconciliatory bridge between theoretical perspectives that tend to appear in opposition to one another, although they in fact complement one another. First, the project of this book can be said to serve as a bridge between a critical realist community that is alarmingly male-dominated and marked by a significant feminist deficit, and a feminist community ridden with the contradictions that its antirealist tendencies produce. It has been a project of, in Bhaskar's terminology, absenting problematic absences in both these camps, by moving them dialectically closer to one another. I hope my application of critical realism to feminist concerns generally and to the topic of sexuality and love in particular has not only opened up new understandings of the substantial feminist concerns of the book. Also, this unique cross-fertilization is likely to have contributed to a deeper comprehension of Bhaskar's philosophical system more generally, in particular of its later developments which, as far as I am aware, have never been applied to feminist concerns.

170 *Conclusion: Necessity and the power of love*

Second, the reconciliatory tendency in this work was also manifested in my concern to dialectically transcend tensions in existing approaches to love and sexuality, so as to break the cycle of ceaseless wavering between dualistic positions. I sought to show that the seemingly opposed ideas of love as no-lose situation on one hand and exhaustible resource on the other both have a truth to them, and demonstrated how this theoretical tension is based in contradictions *in reality*. I also aimed at overcoming the opposition between ideas of women as subordinated to men and as equally powerful as men. In the face of the widespread antifeminist conviction that, by lack of judicial and economic inequality, women cannot be said to be structurally subordinated to men, I argued strongly for the case that women are structurally constrained in a way that men are not in sexuality and love. At the same time, in the face of feminist one-sidedness I demonstrated that there is a truth to the fact that women are *really* as strong and free as men, and explained how these both truths may be thought together. I believe this sublatory move to be an important contribution of the book, since it helps undermine antifeminist claims which draw on the truth that women are fundamentally as powerful as men. By acknowledging the reality on which these arguments draw, while demonstrating that such an acknowledgment does not contradict the fact that women are sociosexually subordinated to men, the antifeminist argument is more effectively incapacitated, than if the reality that women have a relative freedom from the structural constraints of patriarchy is *denied*.

Third, and closely tied in with the above, this work constitutes an effort to transcend the current divide between politics and spirituality. By means of my application of Bhaskar's depth ontology to the issue of sociosexual change, I hope to have underscored the necessity of merging feminist politics with spiritual practices, which aim at getting to the root of reality so as to transform it from there.

References

Aarseth, Helene (2007) 'Between labour and love: the re-erotization of home-making in egalitarian couples within a Nordic context', *NORA – Nordic Journal of Feminist and Gender Research* 15(2/3): 133–43.

Alaimo, Stacy (2008) 'Trans-corporeal feminisms and the ethical space of nature', in S. Alaimo and S. Hekman (eds) *Material feminisms*. Bloomington: Indiana University Press.

Alaimo, Stacy and Susan Hekman (2008a) 'Introduction: emerging models of materiality in feminist theory', in S. Alaimo and S. Hekman (eds) *Material feminisms*. Bloomington: Indiana University Press.

Alaimo, Stacy and Susan Hekman (eds) (2008b) *Material feminisms*. Bloomington: Indiana University Press.

Alcoff, Linda Martín (2000/2001) 'Who's afraid of identity politics?', in P.M.L. Moya and M.R. Hames-García (eds) *Reclaiming identity*. Hyderabad: Orient Longman.

Alcoff, Linda Martín (2006) *Visible identities*. London: Oxford University Press.

Alexander, M. Jacqui (2005) *Pedagogies of crossing*. Durham: Duke University Press.

Allen, Louisa (2003) 'Girls want sex, boys want love: resisting dominant discourses of (hetero)sexuality', *Sexualities* 6(2): 215–36.

Anderson, Celia Smyth and Yolanda Estes (1998) 'The myth of the happy hooker: Kantian moral reflections on a phenomenology of prostitution', in S.G. French *et al.* (eds) *Violence against women*. Ithaca/London: Cornell University Press.

Archer, Margaret (2000) *Being human*. Cambridge: Cambridge University Press.

Archer, Margaret, Roy Bhaskar, Andrew Collier, Tony Lawson and Alan Norrie (eds) (1998) *Critical realism: essential readings*. London: Routledge.

Arthur, Christopher (2001) 'Value, labour and negativity', *Capital & Class* 25(1): 15–39.

Arthur, Christopher (2009) 'Contradiction and abstraction: a reply to Finelli', *Historical Materialism* 17(1): 170–82.

Assiter, Alison (1996) *Enlightened women*. London: Routledge.

Atkinson, Ti-Grace (1974) *Amazon odyssey*. New York: Links Books.

Barad, Karen (2003) 'Posthumanist performativity: toward an understanding of how matter comes to matter', *Signs* 28(3): 801–31.

Barad, Karen (2007) *Meeting the universe halfway*. Durham: Duke University Press.

Bartky, Sandra Lee (1990) *Femininity and domination*. London: Routledge.

Bauman, Zygmunt (2003) *Liquid love*. Cambridge: Polity Press.

de Beauvoir, Simone (1949/1989) *The second sex*. New York: Vintage.

Beck, Ulrich and Elisabeth Beck-Gernsheim (1990/1995) *The normal chaos of love*. Cambridge: Polity.

172 References

Bekkengen, Lisbeth (2006) 'Men's parental leave: a manifestation of gender equality or child-orientation?', in L. Gonäs and J.Ch. Karlsson (eds) *Gender segregation*. Aldershot/Burlington: Ashgate.

Benhabib, Seyla (1995) 'Feminism and postmodernism', in S. Benhabib *et al. Feminist contentions*. New York: Routledge.

Benjamin, Jessica (1988) *The bonds of love*. New York: Pantheon Books.

Benjamin, Jessica (1998) *Shadow of the other*. New York: Routledge.

Bericat, Eduardo (2013) 'Matrimonio, desigualdad de género y bienestar socioemocional de los miembros de la pareja', in A. García Andrade and O. Sabido Ramos (eds) *Cuerpo y afectividad en la sociedad contemporánea*. Mexico City: Universidad Autónoma Metropolitana.

Bhaskar, Roy (1975/2008a) *A realist theory of science*. London: Verso.

Bhaskar, Roy (1979/1998) *The possibility of naturalism*. London: Routledge.

Bhaskar, Roy (1986/2009) *Scientific realism and human emancipation*. London: Routledge.

Bhaskar, Roy (1989) *Reclaiming reality*. London: Verso.

Bhaskar, Roy (1993/2008b) *Dialectic*. London: Routledge.

Bhaskar, Roy (1994) *Plato etc*. London: Verso.

Bhaskar, Roy (1997) 'On the ontological status of ideas', *Journal for the Theory of Social Behaviour* 27(2–3): 139–47.

Bhaskar, Roy (2000) *From east to west*. London: Routledge.

Bhaskar, Roy (2002a) *From science to emancipation*. London: Sage.

Bhaskar, Roy (2002b) *Meta-Reality*. London: Sage.

Bhaskar, Roy (2002c) *Reflections on meta-Reality*. London: Sage.

Bhaskar, Roy (2002c/2012) *Reflections on metaReality*. London: Routledge.

Bhaskar, Roy and Alex Callinicos (2003) 'Marxism and critical realism: a debate', *Journal of Critical Realism* 1(2): 89–114.

Bhaskar, Roy with Mervyn Hartwig (2010) *Formations of critical realism*. London: Routledge.

Bordo, Susan (1988/1992) 'Feminist skepticism and the "maleness" of philosophy', in E. Harvey and K. Okruhlik (eds) *Women and reason*. Ann Arbor: University of Michigan Press.

Boucher, Geoff (2008) *The charmed circle of ideology*. Melbourne: re-press.

Bourdieu, Pierre (1998/2001) *Masculine domination*. Cambridge: Polity.

Brown, Wendy (1997) 'The impossibility of women's studies', *differences* 9(3): 79–101.

Bryson, Valerie (2011) 'Sexuality: the contradictions of love and work', in A.G. Jónasdóttir *et al.* (eds) *Sexuality, gender and power*. London: Routledge.

Butler, Judith (1990/1999) *Gender trouble*. London/New York: Routledge.

Butler, Judith (1992) 'Response to Bordo's "Feminist skepticism and the 'maleness' of philosophy"', *Hypatia* 7(3): 162–5.

Butler, Judith (1993) *Bodies that matter*. New York: Routledge.

Butler, Judith (1994) '*Gender as performance: an interview with Judith Butler*, by Peter Osborne and Lynne Segal', *Radical Philosophy*, no. 67: 32–9.

Butler, Judith (1995) 'Contingent foundations', in S. Benhabib *et al. Feminist contentions*. New York: Routledge.

Butler, Judith (1997a) *Excitable speech*. New York: Routledge.

Butler, Judith (1997b) *The psychic life of power*. Stanford: Stanford University Press.

Butler, Judith (1998) 'Merely cultural', *New Left Review* no. 227: 33–44.

Butler, Judith (2004) *Undoing gender*. New York: Routledge.

Butler, Judith, Pheng Cheah, Drucilla Cornell and Elizabeth Grosz (1998) 'The future of sexual difference: an interview with Judith Butler and Drucilla Cornell', *Diacritics* 28(1): 19–42.

References 173

Cahill, Ann (2011) *Overcoming objectification*. New York: Routledge.

Callinicos, Alex (1989) *Against postmodernism*. Cambridge: Polity.

Callinicos, Alex (2006) *The resources of critique*. Cambridge: Polity.

Carleheden, Mikael (2003) 'The emancipation from gender: a critique of the utopias of postmodern gender theory', in S. Ervø and T. Johansson (eds) *Among men*. Aldershot: Ashgate.

Carleheden, Mikael (1997) 'Människan utan egenskaper: om de normative grundvalarna för den postmoderna konstruktivismens genusteori', in *Res Publica* no. 35–36: 50–70.

Cheah, Pheng (1996) 'Mattering,' *Diacritics* 26(1): 108–39.

Chodorow, Nancy (1978) *The reproduction of mothering*. Berkeley: University of California Press.

Collier, Andrew (1994) *Critical realism*. London: Verso.

Collier, Andrew (1999) *Being and worth*. London: Routledge.

Collier, Andrew (2002) 'Dialectic in Marxism and critical realism', in A. Brown *et al.* (eds) *Critical realism and Marxism*. London: Routledge.

Collier, Andrew (2003) *In defence of objectivity and other essays*. London: Routledge.

Collins, Patricia H. (1990) *Black feminist thought*. Boston: Unwin Hyman.

Connell, R.W. (1987) *Gender and power*. Cambridge: Polity.

Connell, R.W. (2002) *Gender*. Cambridge: Polity.

Connell, R.W. and James W. Messerschmidt (2005) 'Hegemonic masculinity? Rethinking the concept', *Gender & Society* 19(6): 829–59.

Coole, Diana and Samantha Frost (eds) (2010) *New materialisms*. Durham: Duke University Press.

Craig, Lyn and Killian Mullan (2011) 'How mothers and fathers share childcare: a cross-national time-use comparison', *American Sociological Review* 76(6): 834–61.

Creaven, Sean (2000) *Marxism and realism*. London: Routledge.

Creaven, Sean (2009) *Against the spiritual turn*. New York: Routledge.

Crenshaw, Kimberlé (1991) 'Mapping the margins: intersectionality, identity politics, and violence against women of color', *Stanford Law Review* 43: 1241–79.

Crowder, Rachael (2012) *Healing the self*. Dissertation. Carleton University.

Daly, Mary (1978) *Gyn/ecology*. Boston: Beacon Press.

Danermark, Berth, Mats Ekström, Liselotte Jacobsen and Jan Ch. Karlsson (1997/2002) *Explaining society*. London: Routledge.

Davis, Kathy (2008) 'Intersectionality as buzzword: a sociology of science perspective on what makes a feminist theory successful', *Feminist Theory* 9(1): 67–85.

Davis, Noela (2009) 'New materialism and feminism's anti-biologism: a response to Sara Ahmed', *European Journal of Women's Studies* 16(1): 67–80.

Dempsey, Ken (2001) 'Women's and men's consciousness of shortcomings in marital relations, and the need for change', *Family Matters* no. 58: 58–63.

Djikic, Maja and Keith Oatley (2004) 'Love and personal relationships: navigating on the border between the ideal and the real', *Journal for the Theory of Social Behaviour* 34(2): 199–209.

Douglas, Carol Anne (1990) *Love and politics*. San Francisco: Ism Press.

Dowd, Nancy (2010) *The man question*. New York: New York University Press.

Dryden, Caroline (1999) *Being married, doing gender*. London: Routledge.

Duncombe, Jean and Dennis Marsden (1993) 'Love and intimacy: the gender division of emotion and "emotion work"', *Sociology* 27(2): 221–41.

Dussel, Enrique (1988/2001) *Towards an unknown Marx*. London: Routledge.

Eagleton, Terry (2003) *After theory*. London: Allen Lane.

174   *References*

Engels, Friedrich (1878/1939) *Anti-Dühring*. New York: International Publishers.

Epstein, Barbara (1995) 'Why poststructuralism is a dead-end for progressive thought', *Socialist Review* 25(2): 89–119.

Evans, Dylan (1996) *An introductory dictionary of Lacanian psychoanalysis*. New York: Routledge.

Farough, Steven (2004) 'The negative consequences of male privilege', in C.P. Harvey and M.J. Allard (eds) *Understanding and managing diversity*. Harlow: Pearson.

Fausto-Sterling, Anne (2000) *Sexing the body*. New York: Basic Books.

Featherstone, Mike (1999) 'Love and eroticism: an introduction', in M. Featherstone (ed.) *Love and eroticism*. London: Sage Publications.

Ferguson, Ann (1989) *Blood at the root*. London: Pandora.

Ferguson, Ann (1991) *Sexual democracy*. Boulder: Westview Press.

Ferguson, Ann (2011) 'How is global gender solidarity possible?', in A.G. Jónasdóttir *et al.* (eds) *Sexuality, gender and power*. London: Routledge.

Ferguson, Ann (2012) Email correspondence, June 11, 2012.

Fernandes, Leela (2003) *Transforming feminist practice*. San Francisco: Aunt Lute Books.

Firestone, Shulasmith (1970/1979) *The dialectic of sex*. London: Women's Press.

Foucault, Michel (1978) *The history of sexuality, volume 1*. New York: Random House.

Fracchia, Joseph (2005) 'Beyond the human-nature debate: human corporeal organisation as the "first fact" of historical materialism', *Historical Materialism* 13(1): 33–62.

Fraser, Nancy (1998) 'Heterosexism, misrecognition and capitalism: a response to Judith Butler', *New Left Review* no. 228: 140–9.

Freud, Sigmund (1901/1938) *Psychopathology of everyday life*. The Excel Centre. Available HTTP: http://www.excelcentre.net/Psychopathology%20of%20Everyday%20 Life.pdf (accessed 6 December 2012).

Fromm, Erich (1947/1990) *Man for himself*. New York: Henry Holt.

Fromm, Erich (1956) *The art of loving*. New York: Harper.

Frye, Marilyn (1983) *The politics of reality*. Trumansburg: Crossing Press.

Geras, Norman (1971) 'Essence and appearance: aspects of fetishism in Marx's *Capital*', *New Left Review* no. 65: 69–85.

Giddens, Anthony (1992) *The transformation of intimacy*. Stanford: Stanford University Press.

Gross, Rita (1993) *Buddhism after patriarchy*. Albany: State University of New York Press.

Grosz, Elizabeth (2004) *The nick of time*. Durham: Duke University Press.

Grosz, Elizabeth (2005) *Time travels*. Durham: Duke University Press.

Grosz, Elizabeth (2011) *Becoming undone*. Durham: Duke University Press.

Gubar, Susan (1998) 'What ails feminist criticism?', *Critical Inquiry* 24(4): 878–902.

Gunnarsson, Lena (2004) 'Heterosexuell och feminist – en (o)möjlig ekvation', Candidate Thesis in Gender Studies, Lund University.

Gunnarsson, Lena (2011a) 'A defence of the category "women"', *Feminist Theory* 12(1): 23–37.

Gunnarsson, Lena (2011b) 'Love – exploitable resource or "no-lose situation"? Reconciling Jónasdóttir's feminist view with Bhaskar's philosophy of meta-reality', *Journal of Critical Realism* 10(4): 419–41.

Gunnarsson, Lena (2013a) 'The naturalistic turn in feminist theory: a Marxist-realist contribution', *Feminist Theory* 14(1): 3–19.

Gunnarsson, Lena (2013b) *On the ontology of love, sexuality and power*. Dissertation. Örebro University.

References   175

Gunnarsson, Lena (2014) 'Loving him for who he is: the microsociology of power', in A.G. Jónasdóttir and A. Ferguson (eds) *Love – a question for feminism in the twenty first century*. London: Routledge.

Haavind, Hanne (1984) 'Love and power in marriage', in H. Holter (ed.) *Patriarchy in a welfare society*. Oslo: Universitetsforlaget.

Haavind, Hanne (1985) 'Förändringar i förhållandet mellan kvinnor och män', *Kvinnovetenskaplig tidskrift* no 3: 17–27.

Halberstam, Judith (1994) 'F2M: the making of female masculinity', in L. Doan (ed.) *The lesbian postmodern*. New York: Columbia University Press.

Harding, Sandra (2003) 'Representing reality: the critical realism project', *Feminist Economics* 9(1): 151–9.

Hardt, Michael and Antonio Negri (2009) *Commonwealth*. Cambridge: Harvard University Press.

Hartwig, Mervyn (1993/2008) 'Introduction', in R. Bhaskar *Dialectic*. London: Routledge.

Hartwig, Mervyn (2007) 'Category', in M. Hartwig (ed.) *Dictionary of critical realism*. London: Routledge.

Hartwig, Mervyn (2012) 'New introduction', in R. Bhaskar *Reflections of metaReality*. Abingdon/New York: Routledge.

Hekman, Susan (2010) *The material of knowledge*. Bloomington: Indiana University Press.

Held, Virginia (1976) 'Marx, sex, and the transformation of society', in C. Gould and M. Wartofsky (eds) *Women and philosophy*. New York: G.P. Putnam and Sons.

Hemmings, Clare (2005a) 'Invoking affect: cultural theory and the ontological turn', *Cultural Studies* 19(5): 548–67.

Hemmings, Clare (2005b) 'Telling feminist stories', *Feminist Theory* 6(2): 115–39.

Hennessy, Rosemary (2000) *Profit and pleasure*. New York: Routledge.

Hird, Myra and Celia Roberts (2011) 'Feminism theorises the nonhuman', *Feminist Theory* 12(2): 109–17.

Hirsch, Elizabeth and Gary Olsen (1995) '"Je-Luce Irigaray": a meeting with Luce Irigaray', *Hypatia* 10(2): 93–114.

Hochschild, Arlie (2003a) *The commercialization of intimate life*. Berkeley: University of California Press.

Hochschild, Arlie (2003b) 'Love and gold', in B. Ehrenreich and A.R. Hochschild (eds) *Global woman*. New York: Metropolitan.

Holland, Janet, Caroline Ramazanoglu, Sue Sharpe and Rachel Thomson (1998/2004) *The male in the head*. London: Tufnell Press.

Holmberg, Carin (1993/1995) *Det kallas kärlek*. Stockholm: Månpocket.

hooks, bell (1981) *Ain't I a woman*. Boston: South End Press.

hooks, bell (2000a) *All about love*. London: Women's Press.

hooks, bell (2000b) *Feminism is for everybody*. Cambridge: South End Press.

hooks, bell (2002) *Communion*. New York: Perennial.

hooks, bell (2004) *The will to change*. New York: Atria Books.

Hull, Carrie (2006) *The ontology of sex*. London: Routledge.

Illouz, Eva (2007) *Cold intimacies*. Cambridge: Polity.

Illouz, Eva (2012) *Why love hurts*. Cambridge: Polity.

Imray, Linda (1984) 'From heterosexual feminist to political lesbian: the painful transition', *Women's Studies International Forum* 7(1): 39–41.

Ingram, Penelope (2000) 'From goddess spirituality to Irigaray's angel: the politics of the divine', *Feminist Review* no. 66: 46–72.

Irigaray, Luce (1977/1985) *This sex which is not one*. Ithaca: Cornell University Press.

176 References

Irigaray, Luce (1992/1996) *I love to you*. London: Routledge.

Irigaray, Luce (1994/2001) *To be two*. New York: Routledge.

Irigaray, Luce (1999/2002a) *Between east and west*. New York: Columbia University Press.

Irigaray, Luce (2002b) *The way of love*. London: Continuum.

Jack, Dana (1991) *Silencing the self*. Cambridge: Harvard University Press.

Jackson, Stevi and Sue Scott (2004) 'Sexual antinomies in late modernity', *Sexualities* 7(2): 233–48.

Jónasdóttir, Anna G. (1991) *Love power and political interests*. Dissertation. Örebro University.

Jónasdóttir, Anna G. (1991/1994) *Why women are oppressed*. Philadelphia: Temple University Press.

Jónasdóttir, Anna G. (1998) 'Kvinnoord-i-Norden: varför använda "genus" när "kön" finns?', *Nytt fra NIKK* no. 2 1998: 8–9.

Jónasdóttir, Anna G. (2009) 'Feminist questions, Marx's method and the theorization of "love power"', in A.G. Jónasdóttir and K.B. Jones (eds) *The political interests of gender revisited*. Manchester: Manchester University Press.

Jónasdóttir, Anna G. (2011) 'What kind of power is "love power"?', in A.G. Jónasdóttir *et al*. (eds) *Sexuality, gender and power*. London: Routledge.

Jónasdóttir, Anna G. (2014) 'Love studies: a (re)new(ed) field of knowledge interests', in A.G. Jónasdóttir and A. Ferguson (eds) *Love – a question for feminism in the twenty first century*. London: Routledge.

Jónasdóttir, Anna G. and Kathleen B. Jones (2009) 'Out of epistemology: feminist theory in the 1980s and beyond', in A.G. Jónasdóttir and K.B. Jones (eds) *The political interests of gender revisited*. Manchester: Manchester University Press.

Jones, Kathleen B. (1994) 'Foreword', in A.G. Jónasdóttir *Why women are oppressed*. Philadelphia: Temple University Press.

Joseph, Lauren and Pamela Black (2012) 'Who's the man? Fragile masculinities, consumer masculinities, and the profiles of sex work clients', *Men and Masculinities* 15(5): 486–506.

Kabat-Zinn, Jon (1994) *Wherever you go, there you are*. New York: Hyperion.

Kaufman-Osborn, Timothy (1997) 'Fashionable subjects: on Judith Butler and the causal idioms of postmodern feminist theory', *Political Research Quarterly* 50(3): 649–74.

King, Ursula (ed.) (1994) *Feminist theology from the third world*. Maryknoll: Orbis.

Kirby, Vicky (2008) 'Natural convers(at)ions: or, what if culture was really nature all along?', in S. Alaimo and S. Hekman (eds) *Material feminisms*. Bloomington: Indiana University Pres.

Kirby, Vicky and Elizabeth A. Wilson (2011) 'Feminist conversations with Vicky Kirby and Elizabeth A. Wilson', *Feminist Theory* 12(2): 227–34.

Kittay, Eva Feder (1999) *Love's labor*. New York: Routledge.

Kitzinger, Celia (1987) *The social construction of lesbianism*. London: Sage.

Klose, Michael and Frank Jacobi (2004) 'Can gender differences in the prevalence of mental disorders be explained by sociodemographic factors?', *Archives of Women's Mental Health* 7(2): 133–48.

Lagarde, Marcela (2001) *Claves feministas para la negociación en el amor*. Managua: Puntos de Encuentro.

Langford, Wendy (1994) 'Gender, power and self-esteem: women's poverty in the economy of love', *Feminist Theology* 3(7): 94–115.

Langford, Wendy (1999) *Revolutions of the heart*. London: Routledge.

References 177

Laplanche, Jean and Jean-Bertrand Pontalis (1988) *The language of psycho-analysis.* London: Karnac.

Lasch, Christopher (1977) *Haven in a heartless world.* New York: Basic Books.

Lawson, Tony (1999) 'Feminism, realism, and universalism', *Feminist Economics* 5(2): 25–59.

Leeds Revolutionary Feminist Group (1979/1981) 'Political lesbianism: the case against heterosexuality', in Onlywomen Press Collective (ed.) *Love your enemy.* London: Onlywomen Press.

Lerner, Harriet Goldhor (1985/2004) *The dance of anger.* London: Element.

Levitt, Laura (1996) 'Feminist spirituality', in P.H. van Ness (ed.) *Spirituality and the secular quest.* New York: Crossroad.

Lewis, Thomas, Fari Amini and Richard Lannon (2000/2001) *A general theory of love.* New York: Vintage Books.

Lindberg, Helen (2009) *Only women bleed?* Dissertation. Örebro University.

Longino, Helen (2010) 'Feminist epistemology at *Hypatia's* 25th anniversary', *Hypatia* 25(4): 733–41.

Lorde, Audre (1984) *Sister outsider.* Trumansburg: Crossing Press.

Lovell, Terry (2007) 'Introduction', in T. Lovell (ed.) *(Mis)recognition, social inequality and social justice.* London: Taylor & Francis.

Lykke, Nina (2007) 'Intersektionalitet på svenska', in B. Axelsson and J. Fornäs (eds) *Kulturstudier i Sverige.* Lund: Studentlitteratur.

Lynch, Kathleen (2007) 'Love labour as a distinct and non-commodifiable form of care labour', *Sociological Review* 55(3): 550–70.

MacKinnon, Catharine (1989) *Toward a feminist theory of the state.* Cambridge: Harvard University Press.

Marcuse, Herbert (1955/1962) *Eros and civilization.* New York: Vintage.

Marecek, Jeanne (2003) 'Mad housewives, double shifts, mommy tracks and other invented realities', *Feminism & Psychology* 13(2): 259–64.

Marx, Karl (1844/2007) *Economic and philosophical manuscripts of 1844.* Mineola: Dover Publications.

Marx, Karl (1845/2011) '"Preface" to *A contribution to a critique of political economy*', in I. Szeman and T. Kaposy (eds) *Cultural theory.* Oxford: Wiley-Blackwell.

Marx, Karl (1939/1993) *Grundrisse.* London: Penguin.

Marx, Karl and Friedrich Engels (1845/1970) *The German ideology, part I.* New York: International Publishers.

Marx, Karl and Friedrich Engels (1848/2010) 'The communist manifesto', in D. McLellan (ed.) *Karl Marx: selected writings.* New York: Classic Books International.

McCall, Leslie (2005) 'The complexity of intersectionality', *Signs* 30(3): 1771–800.

Medina-Doménech, Rosa Mari Luz Esteban-Galarza and Ana Távora-Rivero (2010) '"Moved by love": how love research can change our deep-rooted emotional understandings and affective consciousness'. Paper presented at the conference *Love in our time – a question for feminism*, 2–4 December 2010, Örebro University.

Medina-Doménech, Rosa Mari Luz Esteban-Galarza and Ana Távora-Rivero (2014) '*Moved by love*: how love research can change our deep-rooted emotional understandings and affective consciousness', in A.G. Jónasdóttir and A. Ferguson (eds) *Love – a question for feminism in the twenty first century.* London: Routledge.

Messner, Michael (1997) *Politics of masculinities.* Thousand Oaks: Sage.

Merriam-Webster (2013) 'Compromise formation'. Available http://www.merriam-webster.com/dictionary/compromise%20formation (accessed 19 January 2013).

178 References

Milnes, Kate (2004) 'What lies between romance and sexual equality? A narrative study of young women's sexual experiences', *Sexualities, Evolution & Gender* 6(2–3): 151–70.

Mitchell, Juliet (1974/2000) *Psychoanalysis and feminism*. New York: Basic Books.

Mohanty, Chandra Talpade (1988) 'Under western eyes: feminist scholarship and colonial discourses', *Feminist Review* no. 30: 61–88.

Mohanty, Chandra Talpade (2003) *Feminism without borders*. Durham: Duke University Press.

Moi, Toril (1999) *What is a woman?* Oxford: Oxford University Press.

Morgan, Jamie (2003) 'What is metaReality? Alternative interpretations of the argument', *Journal of Critical realism* 1(2): 115–46.

Moye, Andy (1985) 'Pornography', in A. Metcalf and M. Humphries (eds) *The sexuality of men*. London/Sydney: Pluto Press.

New, Caroline (1998) 'Realism, deconstruction and the feminist standpoint', *Journal for the Theory of Social Behaviour* 28(4): 349–72.

New, Caroline (2001) 'Oppressed and oppressors? The systematic mistreatment of men', *Sociology* 35(3): 729–48.

New, Caroline (2003) 'Feminism, critical realism, and the linguistic turn', in J. Cruickshank (ed.) *Critical realism: the difference it makes*. London/New York: Routledge.

New, Caroline (2004) 'Sex and gender: a critical realist approach', paper presented at the Annual Conference of IACR, University of Cambridge, 17–19 August, 2004. Available http://www.csog.group.cam.ac.uk/iacr/papers/New.pdf (accessed 30 April 2011).

New, Caroline (2005) 'Sex and gender: a critical realist approach', *New Formations* no. 56: 54–70.

Noddings, Nel (1984/2003) *Caring*. Berkeley: University of California Press.

Norrie, Alan (2010) *Dialectic and difference*. London: Routledge.

Nussbaum, Martha (1999) 'The professor of parody: the hip defeatism of Judith Butler', *New Republic* no. 220(8): 37–45.

Ollman, Bertell (1971/1976) *Alienation*. Cambridge: Cambridge University Press.

Ollman, Bertell (2001) 'Critical realism in light of Marx's process of abstraction', in J. Lopez and G. Potter (eds) *After postmodernism*. New York/London: Athlone press.

Ortner, Sherry (1974) 'Is female to male as nature is to culture?', in M.Z. Rosaldo and L. Lamphere (eds) *Woman, culture, and society*. Stanford: Stanford University Press.

Paz, Octavio (1993/1995) *The double flame*. New York: Harcourt Brace.

Pease, Bob (2010) *Undoing privilege*. London: Zed.

Porpora, Douglas (1998) 'Four concepts of social structure,' in M. Archer *et al.* (eds) *Critical realism*. London: Routledge.

Radden, Jennifer (1996) 'Relational individualism and feminist therapy', *Hypatia* 11(3): 71–96.

Rich, Adrienne (1980/1983) 'Compulsory heterosexuality and lesbian existence', in C. Stansell *et al.* (eds) *Powers of desire*. New York: Monthly Review Press.

Robins, Clive J., Henry Schmidt III and Marsha M. Linehan (2004) 'Dialectical behaviour therapy: synthesizing radical acceptance with skillful means', in S.C. Hayes *et al.* (eds) *Mindfulness and acceptance*. New York: Guilford Press.

Robinson, Hilary (2001) 'The realm of the spirit: introduction', in H. Robinson (ed.) *Feminism, art, theory*. Malden: Blackwell.

Rogers, Anna (2005) 'Chaos to control: men's magazines and the mastering of intimacy', *Men and Masculinities* 8(2): 175–94.

Rubin, Gayle (1975) 'The traffic in women: notes on the "political economy" of sex', in R.R. Reiter (ed.) *Toward an anthropology of women*. New York: Monthly Review Press.

References 179

Rubin, Lillian (1983) *Intimate strangers*. New York: Harper & Row.

Rudman, Laurie and Peter Glick (2008/2010) *The social psychology of gender*. New York: Guilford.

Sanders, Teela (2006) 'Female sex workers as health educators with men who buy sex: utilising narratives of rationalisations', *Social Science & Medicine* 62(10): 2434–44.

Sayer, Andrew (1984/1992) *Method in social science*. London: Routledge.

Sayer, Andrew (1997) 'Essentialism, social constructionism, and beyond', *The Sociological Review* 45(3): 453–87.

Sayer, Andrew (2000a) *Realism and social science*. London: Sage.

Sayer, Andrew (2000b) 'System, lifeworld and gender: associational versus counterfactual thinking', *Sociology* 34(4): 707–25.

Sayer, Andrew (2006) 'Language and significance – or the importance of import: implications for critical discourse analysis', *Journal of Language and Politics* 5(3): 449–71.

Sayer, Andrew (2011) *Why things matter to people*. Cambridge: Cambridge University Press.

Schwalbe, Michael (1992) 'Male supremacy and the narrowing of the moral self', *Berkeley Journal of Sociology* 37: 29–54.

Scott, Joan Wallach (1996) *Only paradoxes to offer*. Cambridge: Harvard University Press.

Sedgwick, Eve Kosofsky (1985) *Between men*. New York: Columbia University Press.

Sedgwick, Eve Kosofsky (2003) *Touching feeling*. Durham: Duke University Press.

Segal, Lynne (1990) *Slow motion*. London: Virago Press.

Sichtermann, Barbara (1983/1986) *Femininity*. Cambridge: Polity.

Smith, Christian (2010) *What is a person?* Chicago/London: The University of Chicago Press.

Soper, Kate (1979) 'Marxism, materialism and biology', in J. Mepham and D-H. Ruben (eds) *Issues in Marxist philosophy, vol. II*. Atlantic Highlands: Humanities Press.

Soper, Kate (1995) *What is nature?* Oxford/Cambridge: Blackwell.

Spelman, Elizabeth (1990) *Inessential woman*. London: Women's Press.

Spitz, René (1946) 'Anaclitic depression: an inquiry into the genesis of psychiatric conditions in early childhood II', *Psychoanalytic study of the child, vol 2*. New York: International Universities Press.

Spivak, Gayatri (1987/2006) *In other worlds*. London: Routledge.

Stainton Rogers, Wendy and Rex Stainton Rogers (2001) *The psychology of gender and sexuality*. Buckingham: Open University Press.

Stoller, Silvia (2010) 'Sex and/or love?' Paper presented at the conference *Love in our time – a question for feminism*, 2–4 December 2010, Örebro University.

Stone, Alison (2004) 'From political to realist essentialism: rereading Luce Irigaray', *Feminist Theory* 5(1): 5–23.

Strazdins, Lyndall and Dorothy H. Broom (2004) 'Acts of love (and work): gender imbalance in emotional work and women's psychological distress', *Journal of Family Issues* 25(3): 356–78.

Thagaard, Tove (1997) 'Gender, power, and love: a study of interaction between spouses', *Acta Sociologica* 40(4): 357–76.

Thompson, Linda (1993) 'Conceptualising gender in marriage: the case of marital care', *Journal of Marriage and the Family* 55(3): 557–69.

Tormey, Judith Farr (1976) 'Exploitation, oppression and self-sacrifice', in C.C. Gould and M.W. Wartofsky (eds) *Women and philosophy*. New York: Capricorn Books.

Toye, Margaret (2010) 'Towards a poethics of love', *Feminist Theory* 11(1): 39–55.

Tuana, Nancy (2008) 'Viscous porosity: witnessing Katrina', in S. Alaimo and S. Hekman (eds) *Material feminisms*. Bloomington: Indiana University Press.

180 References

Young, Iris Marion (1994) 'Gender as seriality: thinking about women as a social collective,' *Signs* 19(3): 713–38.

Yuval-Davis, Nira (2006) 'Intersectionality and feminist politics,' *European Journal of Women's Studies* 13(3): 193–209.

Walby, Sylvia, Jo Armstrong and Sofia Strid (2012) 'Intersectionality: multiple inequalities in social theory', *Sociology* 46(2): 224–40.

Walker, Alice (1979/1998) 'did this happen to your mother? did your sister throw up a lot?', in W. Mulford *et al.* (eds) *The Virago book of love poetry*. London: Virago.

Weeks, Jeffrey (2007) *The world we have won*. London: Routledge.

Weitman, Sasha (1999) 'On the elementary forms of the socioerotic life', in M. Featherstone (ed.) *Love and eroticism*. London: Sage.

Wiederman, Michael (1997) 'Pretending orgasm during sexual intercourse: correlates in a sample of young adult women', *Journal of Sex and Marital Therapy* 23(2): 131–39.

Williams, Raymond (1978) 'Problems of materialism', *New Left Review* no. 109: 3–17.

Wilton, Tamsin (2004) *Sexual (dis)orientation*. New York: Palgrave Macmillan.

Zack, Naomi (2005) *Inclusive feminism*. Lanham: Rowman & Littlefield.

Index

abstractions and abstract concepts 90–2
actualism (Bhaskar) 12–13
agency 30, 38
Alaimo, Stacy 65, 70
Alcoff, Linda Martín 36, 89–90
Allen, Louisa 8
Anderson, Celia Smyth 138
anger 109, 154–6, 162
antifeminist arguments 170
antinomy 77–8
Archer, Margaret 31
Aristophanes 125
Arthur, Christopher 133–4, 148–9
Assiter, Alison 80
autonomous relationality 157
Avineri, Schlomo 113, 141

Bachelard, Gaston 10
Barad, Karen 10, 77
Bartky, Sandra Lee 123
de Beauvoir, Simone 4, 113
Beck, Ulrich 5
Beck-Gernsheim, Elisabeth 5
Bekkengen, Lisbeth 8
Benjamin, Jessica 121, 133–41, 145
Bergson, Henri 64, 66, 69–70
Bhaskar, Roy 9–16, 19, 34, 43, 57, 72–7, 85, 88, 114–29, 132, 139, 148–62, 168–70
biological determinism 64–6, 143
biological reductionism 67
biological sex 12, 28–9, 41, 45; rejection of 85–8
Birke, Lynda 70
Black, Pamela 138
Bohr, Niels 10
Bordo, Susan 32
Boucher, Geoff 27, 36, 38
Bourdieu, Pierre 112
Brooks, Gwendolyn 90

Brown, Wendy 83–4, 92
Bryson, Valerie 135–6
Butler, Judith 3–4, 12, 17–18, 25–41, 44–8, 52, 57–8, 63–72, 77, 79, 83–90, 147–9, 166

Cahill, Ann 136
Callinicos, Alex 72
capitalism 43, 53–8, 117–19, 124, 131–8, 150
care as a channel for sociosexuality 56–7, 140–2
care of the self 158
Carleheden, Mikael 93
causality, holistic 153; linear view of 13; mechanical 86–7; metonymic 153
change: depth mode of 153; men's interest in 143–5
Cheah, Pheng 71
childcare 8
climate change 76
collective action by women 150
Collier, Andrew 16, 69, 75–7, 118, 144
Combahee River Collective 82
compulsory heterosexuality 3, 33
concrete identity 91–2
conflict, necessity of 125–7
conformist strategy 107–9
Connell, R.W. 39, 87
consciousness-raising 151–2
constellational totalities 16
contradiction, definition of 132; *see also* dialectical contradictions
control over women 137–40, 168
Creaven, Sean 55, 74
Crenshaw, Kimberlé 81–2
critical realism 10–16, 19, 31, 87, 92, 114–16, 128, 132, 148, 152–3, 163, 167, 169
Cutrufelli, Maria Rosa 82

Index

Danermark, Berth 91
Darwin, Charles 10, 64–70, 75
Davis, Kathy 81–2
Davis, Noela 73, 76
deconstructionism 28, 32–3
Deleuze, Gilles 64, 66
demi-reality 117–28, 131, 135–6, 144, 148, 151–4, 158, 162, 164, 168–9
dependency 135, 149–50, 166–8
derivitization 136
Derrida, Jacques 158
dialectical contradictions 131–4, 139–41, 144
dialectics 15–17, 38
discourse 37–8
division of labour, sexual 3, 34
divorce 9
domination 137, 147
double standard, sexual 8, 141
Duncombe, Jean 103, 109

Eagleton, Terry 36
economic independence of women 44
ecstasy as a channel for sociosexuality 56–7, 140–2
ego, male and female 157, 162, 168
ego empowerment 123
ego wants and needs 126
ego weakness 125–6
Eichler, Margrit 46
emancipation 154, 158, 169
embedding of love practices 127–8
emergence, concept of 31, 75–7, 89
empiricism 148
empowerment 161, 164, 168–9; sociosexual 138–9
Engels, Friedrich 51, 63, 125
epistemic fallacy 12, 15, 85
epistemology 10, 15–16
Epstein, Barbara 26
essentialism 14; strategic 32, 90
Esteban-Galarza, Mari Luz 157–8
Estes, Yolanda 138
exploitative relationships and practices 47–8, 53–7, 113, 123, 131–40, 149, 168–9
exploiter's burden 133–5
exploiter's privilege 145

Featherstone, Mike 135
female masculinity (Halberstam) 86
femininity 106–10, 126, 144
feminism: compatibility with heterosexuality 7; radical 3, 43, 48, 81, 113, 137–8; second-wave 2–4, 64, 151; socialist 48; third-wave 7
feminist theory 2–5, 9–10, 13, 63–4, 77–8, 80–2, 85–6, 89, 112–14, 128, 143–5, 150–1, 154, 157, 163, 167, 170
Ferguson, Ann 50, 85
Firestone, Shulamith 1, 123
Foucault, Michel 26, 33–7, 89
Fracchia, Joseph 71
Fraser, Nancy 34
Freud, Sigmund 4, 14, 139

gender, concepts of 45–6
gender equality and inequality 6–9, 99–100
gender identity 106, 109
Geras, Norman 117, 150
Giddens, Anthony 5, 99
Glick, Peter 8
Godelier, Maurice 150
Grosz, Elizabeth 10, 64–70, 75–6
Gubar, Susan 80

Haavind, Hanne 100, 106–7
Halberstam, Judith 86
Hartwig, Mervyn 116–17
Hegel, Friedrich 15, 63, 74, 116
Hekman, Susan 10, 65
Held, Virginia 129, 141, 160
Hemmings, Clare 10, 80, 82
Hennessy, Rosemary 17, 25, 35, 48
heteronormativity 33
heterosexual imperative 35; see also compulsory heterosexuality
Hird, Myra 73
historical materialism 43–4, 48, 57–8, 74
Hochschild, Arlie 106, 109, 126–7, 150–1
Holland, Janet 8
Holmberg, Carin 100–6, 109
hooks, bell 4, 52, 72, 143, 161
household work 3, 8–9, 49
Hull, Carrie 27, 85–8
human nature 40, 69–72
human needs 49

identity 115; see also gender identity, concrete identity
Illouz, Eva 5–6
indeterminacy, principle of 67–70
intersectionality 80–5, 93; anti-categorical 82–4
Irigaray, Luce 4–5, 66, 116, 121, 154, 158–64

Index 183

Jackson, Stevi 8
Jónasdóttir, Anna G. 4–6, 11, 17–19, 35, 43–59, 63, 72, 82–3, 88–9, 93–4, 99, 103, 106–14, 122, 128–9, 134–42, 149, 161, 166–9
Jones, Kathleen B. 35, 43, 82–3, 88
Joseph, Lauren 138

Kaufman-Osborn, Timothy 29
Kessler, Suzanne 88
Kirby, Vicky 73–4

Lacan, Jacques 32–5, 158
Langford, Wendy 100, 103–4, 108, 126
Lasch, Christopher 113
Lawson, Tony 11
Lerner, Harriet 155–6
lesbianism 3; political 151
Lévi-Strauss, Claude 32
Lewontin, Richard 86
liberal individualism 154
linguistic fallacy 27
Lorde, Audre 164
love: definition of 100, 126; energizing quality of 127; feminist theorization of 4–5, 72–3; nature of 50–2; objective and subjective dimensions of 107, 109; as a renewable resource 127; sense of self-worth provided by 6; social significance of 5–6
love crisis 6
love power 17, 44, 48–50, 53, 134, 166
Lykke, Nina 85
Lysistrata 125, 152

McCall, Leslie 82
McKenna, Wendy 88
MacKinnon, Catharine 32–3, 123–4, 147–8, 151–2
McLennan, Gregor 44
Madonna/Whore syndrome 141
male authority 54–6, 123–4, 136, 149
'male-in-the-head' 8
malestream theory 5, 10, 113, 128
marriage 9, 55, 99, 104
Marsden, Dennis 103, 109
Marx, Karl 13, 15, 43, 45, 51–2, 74, 91, 113, 117–19, 124–5, 131–2, 150
Marxian scholarship 3, 34–5, 45, 48, 53, 58, 75, 116, 144, 163
masculinist self 141–2
materiality 28–9
Mayeroff, Milton 126
Medina-Doménech, Rosa 157–60

Messerschmidt, James 39
metaReality 15–16, 19, 114–23, 129, 153–4, 161, 168–9
Milnes, Kate 8
Mitchell, Juliet 4
Mohanty, Chandra Talpade 82–5, 93–4
Moi, Toril 37, 65, 79
Moye, Andy 133
mutual satisfaction of men and women 142–3
mystification and demystification 117, 149–50

natural selection 70
nature: conceptualizations of 66–70; constraining force of 70–3
nature-phobia in feminism 64, 66, 149, 167
necessity, concept of 14
New, Caroline 10–11, 85–6, 88, 143–4
new materialism 10, 64, 68–9
Nietzsche, Friedrich 30, 64, 66, 69
Norrie, Alan 15, 77–8, 132, 139–40
Nussbaum, Martha 25, 30

Ollman, Bertell 90–1
ontology 9–16, 34, 152
oppression of men 143
orgasm, faking of 141–2

patriarchal dividend 144–5
patriarchal reality, illusoriness of 122–5
patriarchy 3, 7, 13, 43–7, 56–8, 122–6, 131–44, 149–52, 168
Paz, Octavio 135
performativity 26
'The personal is political' 2
'pomo flip' 77, 87, 89
pornography 8, 141
Porpora, Douglas 92
positivist science 10–11
postmodernism 36, 75, 158
poststructuralism 4, 10, 13–14, 18, 64–5, 69, 77, 79, 82, 87–9, 93, 143, 167
poverty, sociosexual 54
power, theory of 35–7
prostitution 138
psychoanalytic theory 4, 29

queer theory 3–4, 32–4, 40

realism 10–11; *ad hoc* 39–40; *see also* critical realism
reality criteria and the 'really real' 148–50, 169

184   *Index*

reality principle 14, 139, 158
reductionism 41
resisting strategy 108–9
Rich, Adrienne 3, 151
Roberts, Celia 73
Robinson, Hilary 163
role-taking: analytical and receptive 105; asymmetrical 100–6
role theory 40
Rubin, Gayle 64
Rubin, Lillian 9
Rudman, Laurie 8

Sanders, Teela 138
Sayer, Andrew 27, 36, 38, 52, 63, 65, 71, 74, 77, 82, 84, 87, 90–3
Schwalbe, Michael 105–7, 136, 141–2
science, natural and social 12; *see also* positivist science
Scott, Sue 8
Sedgwick, Eve Kosofsky 38–9
Segal, Lynne 131
self-love 161
self-referentiality and self-change 153
Sex and the City (television series) 7
sex/gender categories in Jónasdóttir 46
sex workers 138
sexual difference 12, 28–9, 41, 45, 86
sexual freedom and the sexual revolution 7–8
sexual relations and sexual stimulation 113, 137
sexuality: Butler's understanding of 35; concepts of 63, 72; definition of 17; as distinct from gender 32–3; and feminist theory 2–4; Jónasdóttir's view of 40, 43–4, 48–9
Sichtermann, Barbara 7, 140
social circumstances and social norms 45, 55

social construction of gender and sexuality 66–7, 89, 147–8, 167
sociosexuality: concept of 47–59; essential quality of 134
Soper, Kate 63–4, 69, 74–5
Spelman, Elizabeth 83–4, 90, 92
Spinoza, Baruch 118
spirituality 163, 170
Stone, Alison 28
strategic essentialism 90
subjectivity, women's 142–3
subordination of women 6–7
Sweden 2

Távora-Rivero, Ana 157–8
Thagaard, Tove 106
TINA necessities and TINA compromise formations 139–41
Toye, Margaret 5
transformation of women 153–6, 162–4
Tuana, Nancy 12

unworthiness, circle of 160–2

violence 137–9

Walker, Alice 99
Wilton, Tamsin 9
withdrawal, female 150–6
'women' as a category for analysis 79–94, 150–6, 167

Young, Iris Marion 79–80
Yuval-Davis, Nina 92

Zack, Naomi 84
zero-sum accounts of human interaction 112–13, 145